Music Theory

JONATHAN E. PETERS

Copyright © 2014 Jonathan E. Peters

All rights reserved.

ISBN-10: 1499113374
ISBN-13: 978-1499113372

To Jennifer

- my wife, best friend, and soul mate -

CONTENTS

1	Defining Music	Pg. 1
2	Relative Durations of Sound	Pg. 7
3	Assigning Values to Note Durations	Pg. 16
4	Meter	Pg. 24
5	Rests	Pg. 32
6	Dotted Notes	Pg. 36
7	The Tie	Pg. 41
8	Redesignating the Unit	Pg. 45
9	Cut Time	Pg. 51
10	Classifying Meters	Pg. 56
11	Triplets	Pg. 64
12	Duplets	Pg. 71
13	Pitch	Pg. 76
14	Introduction to the Staff	Pg. 82
15	Letter Names of the Staff	Pg. 92
16	Introduction to the Keyboard	Pg. 99
17	Sharps & Flats on the Keyboard	Pg. 107
18	Sharps & Flats on the Staff	Pg. 112
19	Introduction to Intervals	Pg. 119
20	Introduction to the Scale	Pg. 130
21	Major Keys	Pg. 139
22	Major, Minor & Perfect Intervals	Pg. 152

23	Augmented & Diminished Intervals	Pg. 160
24	Complementary & Compound Intervals	Pg. 172
25	Introduction to Chords	Pg. 183
26	Augmented & Diminished Chords	Pg. 190
27	The Mathematical Proportions of Triads	Pg. 196
28	Chords of the Major Scale	Pg. 205
29	The Natural Minor Scale	Pg. 210
30	Harmonic & Melodic Minor Scales	Pg. 214
31	Minor Keys	Pg. 220
32	Chords of the Minor Scale	Pg. 227
33	Degrees of the Scale	Pg. 231
34	Primary Chords	Pg. 235
35	Chord Inversions	Pg. 240
36	Voice Leading	Pg. 247
37	Functions	Pg. 252
38	The Dominant Seventh Chord	Pg. 258
39	Other Forms of Seventh Chords	Pg. 264
40	Cadences	Pg. 269
41	Other Forms of Scales	Pg. 276
42	Polytonal & Atonal	Pg. 282
43	Modes	Pg. 286
44	The Harmonic Series - Part 1	Pg. 298

45	The Harmonic Series - Part 2	Pg. 305
46	Tuning Systems	Pg. 313
47	The Periods of Classical Music	Pg. 322

1. DEFINING MUSIC

BEFORE WE BEGIN

To get free life-time access to all of the audio samples for the diagrams in this book and also quizzes for each lesson please go to:

https://www.udemy.com/music-theory-companion

Click on "Enter Password" and enter: **1c56sg2**

Click on, "Start Learning Now".

The next window will ask you to sign up for a Udemy account. Enter your name, e-mail address, and create a password for your account.

That's it!

SO WHAT IS MUSIC ANYWAY?

Asking someone to define music is like asking the average person to define what gravity is. Like gravity, music is so closely connected to all of us and has such an effect on all of us that trying to understand what it is can be quite difficult. Over the centuries many definitions for music have been put forth by musicians and composers. Although many of these definitions are decent definitions, most have fallen short of a precise and complete definition. Let's begin our study of music by looking at some of these definitions and observing how they fall short. By doing so, this will help us to discover a more complete definition of the subject we wish to study.

One such definition that falls short is to define music by its "material substance" (i.e., what it's made out of). Simply calling music "sound" or "vibrations of air" is not really saying what music "is". For example, if we define a chair as "a thing made of wood" we have not really said what a chair "is". Just as not all things made of wood are chairs, so too not all things made from vibrations of air are music. Take for example a rock slide. A rockslide produces a large number of vibrations in the air but one would not call the sound that a rock slide makes "music".

Another definition that falls short is one that defines music by its parts. As you will learn later in this course, the parts of music are rhythm and pitch. If we were to define music as "rhythm and pitch" we would simply be listing its parts and would still not have said anything about what music "is". Let's take our example of a chair again. If we define a chair as "a thing with four legs" we haven't really stated what a chair "is". Just as not everything with four legs is a chair, so too not everything that has rhythm and pitch is music. Take for example a cooking timer that has just gone off. Its beeping sound may have a pitch and it may have a rhythm and yet one does not consider the sound it produces to be "music".

A very common definition of music that falls short of a complete definition is "organized sound". Although we are getting closer to a complete definition with this one, it still only states what the material substance of music is. Morse code, for example is "organized sound" but no one would consider Morse code to be music. So what is a more precise and complete definition of music?

For any definition to be complete it must contain a statement about the "end" or "purpose" of the thing being defined. Let's take a final look at the definition of a chair. If we define a chair as "a thing made of wood that has four legs and is used for sitting on", we have included a statement about a chairs' "end" or "purpose". The "end" or "purpose" of a chair is to be sat on. We can conclude from the above that if we want to have a precise and complete definition of music we must first discern what music's purpose is.

MUSIC'S PURPOSE

Since man's existence he has used music for many different purposes. The one unifying factor in all of these purposes is that they involve the moving of the emotions. Let's briefly go over some of the main purposes music has been used for throughout the history of man.

Probably the most basic of these is the purpose of entertainment. Music entertains us by giving pleasure to those who hear it. Whether it's music on the radio or TV, in a play or in a movie, in each of these instances we receive pleasure from listening to music because it moves our emotions and changes how we feel. A cheerful tune, for example, can brighten our mood when we are feeling down. Calm music can sooth one's anger or stress. Certain music can frighten us or even make us cry. Man by his nature derives pleasure from having his emotions affected.

Music has also been used in time of war. Its purpose was to rally the troops and to plant fear into the minds and hearts of the enemy. This happens once again through the moving of man's emotions.

Then of course we have the role music plays during social events. For example, the purpose of music during a Fourth of July celebration, college graduation, or a parade, is to create a shared emotional experience or atmosphere which unites the people who are partaking in the event.

And finally, there is the use of music in religion. Throughout history we find that religion and music are common to all cultures and peoples. Furthermore, all cultures have used music as a tool in their religious ceremonies. They all recognized the same fact: music has the ability to move human emotions. Sometimes religions have used music to excite the emotions, and at other times to calm them. An example of music used to calm the emotions would be the Gregorian chant of the Roman Catholic Church

The above are just a few of the uses music has had throughout history. Although music can be seen to have many different purposes, the main thing to take note of is that all of these purposes share one thing in common – the moving of the emotions. For our definition of music to be complete it must therefore include a statement about its ability to move human emotions.

UNIQUE TO MANKIND

Since music seems to be all about moving the emotions, and because emotions are unique to mankind, it follows that music must therefore also be unique to mankind. A horse for example, can hear the vibrations of air but they cannot be moved to tears like a human would when listening to the exact same piece of music.

What's even more astounding than music being unique to mankind is the fact that it affects all people in the same manner. A sad piece of music, for example, is considered sad by any person, from any culture, from any time period. In other words, no one can hear a piece of sad music and think it sounds happy. Because of this truly amazing fact, music is able to be communicated from person to person with an understanding. Music is therefore in essence a kind of language. It is a universal language that we all speak – the language of emotions.

At this point, we have ascertained a sufficient amount of knowledge of what music is to be able to give a more complete definition. The definition of music used in this course will be as follows: **music is the universal language of emotions communicated through intelligently ordered sounds consisting of rhythm and pitch**. (The first half of this definition was arrived at through common sense and reasoning in this lesson. The second half of the definition will become clear over the period of this course.)

Important: At the end of most lessons in this course you will find memory questions and a quiz (some also contain exercises). Memory questions aid in summarizing and reinforcing the key concepts learned in the lesson. Study them well in order to pass the on-line lesson quiz. The quizzes for each lesson can be found by logging in to your course at www.udemy.com

Memory Questions

What is music?
Music is the universal language of emotions communicated through intelligently ordered sounds consisting of rhythm and pitch.

How is music a universal language?
Music is a universal language because all peoples, cultures, and times have understood it in the same way.

What are four uses music has had throughout history?
Four uses music has had throughout history are: use in entertaining, use in battle, use in social events, and use in religious ceremonies.

What is common to all uses of music?
The moving of man's emotions is common to all uses of music.

Why is music unique to mankind?
Music is unique to mankind since music is the universal language of emotions and emotions are unique to mankind.

Lesson 1 Quiz

Log in to your course at www.udemy.com and take the quiz for this lesson.

2. RELATIVE DURATIONS OF SOUND

MUSIC'S ELEMENTS

Music is made up of two basic elements – **rhythm** and **pitch**. The study of rhythm is concerned with the relative duration of sound (how short or long one sound is relative to another). The study of pitch is concerned with the relative frequency of sound (how low or high one sound is relative to another).

We will begin our study of music with the study of rhythm, since rhythm is more fundamental than pitch. Why is rhythm more fundamental than pitch? First of all, rhythm can exist without pitch, whereas pitch cannot exist without rhythm.

Here is an example of a rhythm without pitch. Try and identify what song the rhythm is from. (To hear any of the audio examples in this book, log into your course at www.udemy.com. Navigate to the section (lesson) you are currently on and click on the lecture titled "Lesson 2 Audio Files". You will find all the audio under the "Downloadable Materials" tab.)

(Lesson 2 - Audio 1)

Hopefully you recognized that this was the rhythm to "Happy Birthday". Here is "Happy Birthday" with both rhythm and pitch.

(Lesson 2 - Audio 2)

It is impossible to sing "Happy Birthday" (or any song for that matter) using only pitch. This is because every pitch, whether high or low, must have a duration or length of time that it is heard for. If it did not have duration, then we would not be able to hear it.

The second reason that rhythm is more fundamental than pitch is because it is more natural to people. Let's explain what is meant by this.

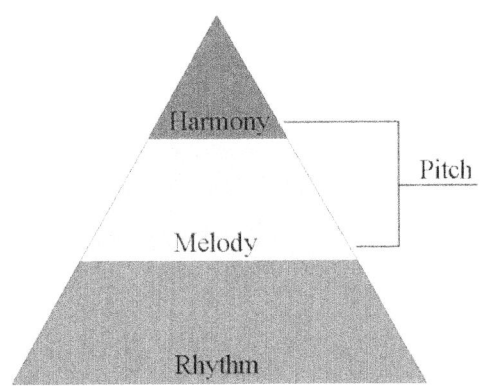

Find the elements of rhythm and pitch in the preceding diagram. Notice that pitch is divided into two categories: melody and harmony. (Melody is an ordered sequence of pitches; harmony is when two or more pitches are heard simultaneously.) Rhythm is placed on the bottom of the pyramid because it is the foundation for the rest of music. Pitch is placed above rhythm because it cannot exist without rhythm.

Now look at the size of each section of the pyramid. Rhythm is the biggest section because it comes naturally to more people. For example, without any previous study of music, the "average Joe" is able to hear a rhythm once and then repeat it from memory. Fewer people are able to do this with a melody and even fewer people with harmonies.

NOTATING DURATION

In music, we communicate the duration of sound through written symbols called "notes". There are three basic parts to a note: the note head, the stem, and the flag. We are able to alter the duration of a note by changing any of its three parts.

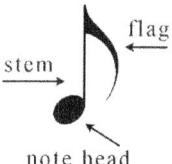

In this lesson we are going to look at five different types of note durations. The first is called the **whole note**. It has no flag and no stem.

○

The whole note is the note of longest duration. The exact amount of time a whole note is played for is determined by various factors which we will learn about in the coming lessons. In this lesson, we are only concerned with the "relative" duration (i.e., the duration of one note compared to the duration of another note).

The next four notes derive their names from their relation to the whole note.

MUSIC THEORY

The note above is called a **half note**. It has a note head and a stem. It is called a half note because it is half the duration of a whole note. Because of this fact, the duration of 2 half notes is equal to the duration of 1 whole note. (The lines represent time)

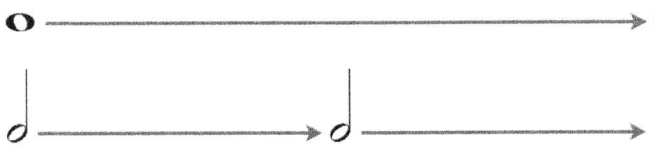

The next note we are going to look at is called the **quarter note**.

A quarter note has a note head which is colored in and a stem. It is called a quarter note because it is one quarter the duration of a whole note. Because of this fact, the duration of 4 quarter notes is equal to the duration of 1 whole note.

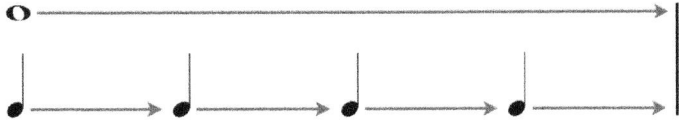

RELATIVE DURATIONS OF SOUND

The following note is called an **eighth note**.

An eighth note has a note head which is colored in, a stem, and a flag. It is called an eighth note because it is one eighth the duration of a whole note. Because of this fact, the duration of 8 eighth notes is equal to the duration of 1 whole note.

The final note we are going to look at in this lesson is called the **sixteenth note**.

A sixteenth note has a note head which is colored in, a stem, and two flags. It is called a sixteenth note because it is one sixteenth the duration of a whole note. Because of this fact, the duration of 16 sixteenth notes is equal to the duration of 1 whole note.

As you have probably noticed that each time a flag is added the duration of the note is shortened by one half. (Eighth notes have one flag, sixteenth notes have two flags, thirty-second notes would have three flags, and so on and so forth.)

Very often in music, notes with flags are grouped together. When this happens, the flags are replaced with beams. For example, two eighth notes that are grouped together would be joined with a beam like this.

Four sixteenth notes that are grouped together would be joined with two beams like this.

Below you will find a chart of the note durations learned in this lesson. It is very important that you recognize the mathematical proportions between the notes. Notice how each type of note is half the duration of the note above it. For example, a sixteenth note is half of an eighth note; an eighth note is half of a quarter note; a quarter note is half of a half note; etc. Be sure to study the chart thoroughly before taking the lesson quiz. A good idea would be to take one duration at a time and observe how many notes of that duration it takes to equal each of the other durations.

RELATIVE DURATIONS OF SOUND

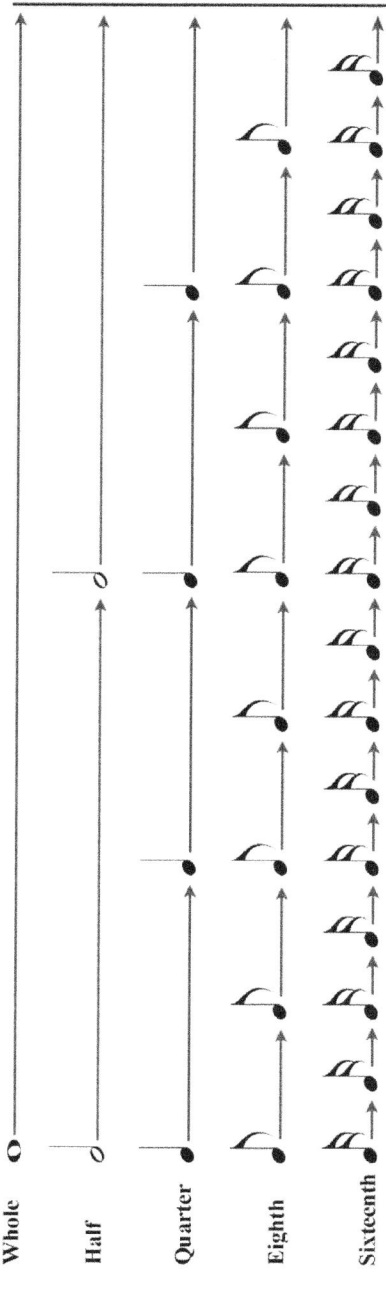

– MUSIC THEORY –

Memory Questions

What two basic elements is music made up of?
Music is made up of the elements of rhythm and pitch.

What is the study of rhythm concerned with?
The study of rhythm is concerned with the relative duration of sound (how short or long one sound is relative to another).

What is the study of pitch concerned with?
The study of pitch is concerned with the relative frequency of sound (how low or high one sound is relative to another).

What are the two ways in which pitch can be classified?
Pitch can be classified as melody or harmony.

What is melody?
Melody is an ordered sequence of pitches.

What is harmony?
Harmony is pitches heard simultaneously.

What are the two reasons why rhythm is more fundamental than pitch?
Rhythm is more fundamental than pitch because rhythm can exist without pitch, and because rhythm comes more naturally to people than pitch does.

What are the three parts of a note called?
The three parts of a note are called the note head, the stem, and the flag.

How can we alter the duration of a note?
We can alter the duration of a note by changing any of its three parts.

What is the relative duration of a half note?
A half note is half of a whole note.

What is the relative duration of a quarter note?
A quarter note is a quarter of a whole note.

What is the relative duration of an eighth note?
An eighth note is an eighth of a whole note.

What is the relative duration of a sixteenth note?
A sixteenth note is a sixteenth of a whole note.

Why are some notes connected with beams?
When notes with flags are grouped together the flags are replaced by beams.

Lesson 2 Quiz

Log in to your course at www.udemy.com and take the quiz for this lesson.

3. ASSIGNING VALUES TO NOTE DURATIONS

THE DEFINITION OF BEAT

In the last lesson we learned some basic note names and their relative durations. In this lesson we are going to assign numerical values to the note durations. But before we can proceed, we first need to define what **beat** is. People often comment that a song has a nice beat, when what they are actually referring to is the song's rhythm. Although beat and rhythm are often used interchangeably, they are not the same thing. Rhythm deals with the relative duration of sound, whereas beat is a **unit of measurement**. Let's explain what is meant by this.

When we measure the physical length of a thing we may do so using different units of measurement, such as inches, feet, yards, miles, etc. Let's say that we want to measure something using inches. When we do so, we are designating the inch as our unit of measurement by assigning to it a value of "1". We can apply this same concept of measurement to musical notes; but instead of measuring physical length we will be measuring duration of time.

ASSIGNING VALUES TO NOTE DURATIONS

Any type of note may be chosen as a unit of measurement if we assign to it a value of "1". In this lesson we will be studying what happens when we assign a value of "1" to the quarter note. By assigning a value of "1" to the quarter note we are designating the quarter note as the "beat" or the "unit of measurement" by which we will measure the duration of all other notes. Let's look at some examples.

In the last lesson we learned that the duration of a quarter note is one quarter the duration of a whole note. If we assign a value of "1" to the quarter note, the whole note will therefore be equal to a value of "4". In musical terms, when a quarter note equals 1 beat, the whole note equals 4 beats.

Note: in the next four audio clips, the clicking sound represents the quarter note (value of "1"); the piano represents all other notes.

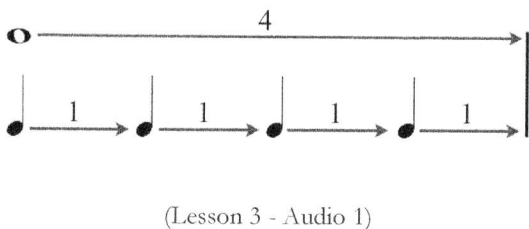

(Lesson 3 - Audio 1)

We also learned in the last lesson that the duration of a quarter note is one half the duration of a half note. If we assign a value of "1" to the quarter note, the half note will therefore be equal to a value of "2". In musical terms, when a quarter note equals 1 beat, the half note equals 2 beats.

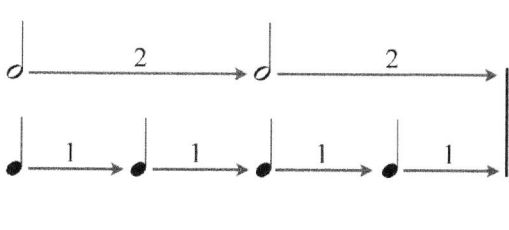

(Lesson 3 - Audio 2)

MUSIC THEORY

Remember: a half note is _not_ half of a beat. Its name comes from its relation to the whole note.

We also know from the previous lesson that the duration of a quarter note is twice the duration of an eighth note. If we assign a value of "1" to the quarter note, the eighth note will therefore be equal to a value of "1/2". In musical terms, when a quarter note equals 1 beat, the eighth note equals 1/2 of a beat.

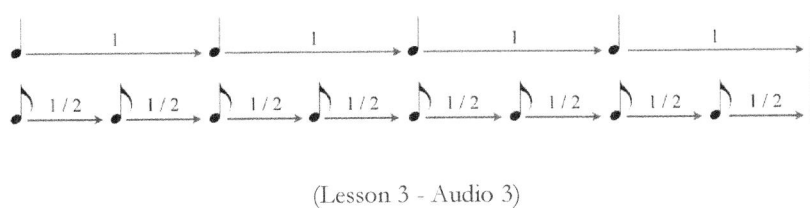

(Lesson 3 - Audio 3)

Remember: an eighth note is _not_ an eighth of a beat. Its name comes from its relation to the whole note.

And finally, we know that the duration of a quarter note is four times the duration of a sixteenth note. If we assign a value of "1" to the quarter note, the sixteenth note will therefore be equal to a value of "1/4". In musical terms, when a quarter note equals 1 beat, the sixteenth note equals 1/4 of a beat.

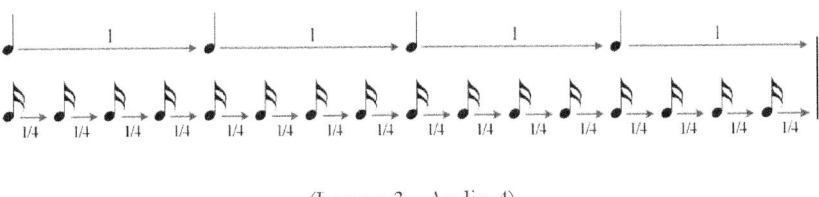

(Lesson 3 - Audio 4)

Remember: a sixteenth note is _not_ a sixteenth of a beat. Its name comes from its relation to the whole note.

ASSIGNING VALUES TO NOTE DURATIONS

Here is a helpful chart that shows the quarter note as the unit of measurement and its relation to all the other notes we have learned thus far. Half notes and whole notes are called "multiples" of the unit since they are doubles and quadruples of the unit. Eighth notes and sixteenth notes are called "subdivisions" of the unit since they are halves and fourths of the unit.

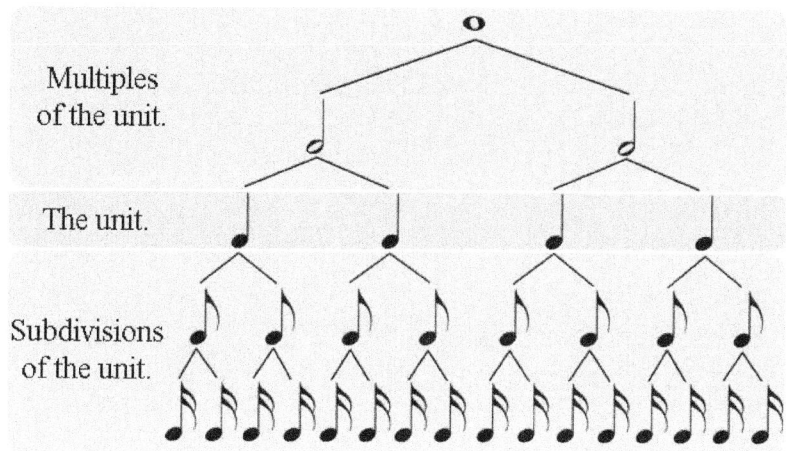

BEAT VS. TEMPO

It is a common mistake for beginning music students to associate "1 beat" with "1 second" of time. When we assign numerical values to notes we are not designating that they be played for any specific amount of time. The actual time it takes to play a note is determined by something called **tempo**. Tempo is Italian for "rate of speed". When the tempo of a song is quick, the beats will be occurring at a much faster rate and therefore the durations of the notes in actual time will be shorter. When the tempo of a song is slow, the beats will be occurring at a much slower rate and therefore the durations of the notes in actual time will be longer.

Let's demonstrate this using a whole note. Although a whole note has a numerical value of 4 beats, its duration may be longer or shorter depending on how quickly or slowly the beats occur in actual time. When beats occur at a faster rate, the whole note will be played for a shorter period of time.

(Lesson 3 - Audio 5)

When the beats occur at a slower rate, the whole note will be played for a longer period of time.

(Lesson 3 - Audio 6)

The tempo is always indicated above the first measure of music in a song, usually with a metronome marking. (A metronome is a mechanical device that keeps track of musical time.) Here is an example of a metronome marking.

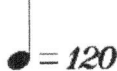

This marking indicates to the performer that they are to play at a rate of 120 "beats per minute" or "BPM". In other words, quarter notes will occur at a rate of two per second.

Up until the early 19th century, tempo was indicated with Italian words above the first notes of a song. For example, the word "Allegro" placed at the beginning of a song would indicate to the performer that they are to play quickly. As you can see, this method is not as precise as metronome markings, since the word only gives us a rough idea of the tempo and does not indicate an exact measurable speed. Here is a list of some common tempo markings.

ASSIGNING VALUES TO NOTE DURATIONS

Largo = very slow (LAR-go)
Adagio = slow (uh-DAH-jee-oh)
Andante = literally "walking", a medium slow tempo (on-DON-tay)
Moderato = moderate, or medium (MOD-er-AH-toe)
Allegretto = Not as fast as allegro (AL-luh-GRET-oh)
Allegro = fast (uh-LAY-grow)
Presto = very fast (PRESS-toe)
Prestissimo = very, very fast (press-TEE-see-moe)

Here is another list with modern day metronome (beats per minute) equivalents.

Largo (40-60 bpm)
Adagio (66-76 bpm)
Andante (76-108 bpm)
Moderato (101-110 bpm)
Allegro (120-139 bpm)
Presto (168-200 bpm)
Prestissimo (over 200 bpm)

Memory Questions

What is beat?
Beat is the unit of measurement.

Can we designate any note as the unit of measurement?
Yes, we can designate any note as the unit of measurement by assigning to it a value of 1.

If the quarter note is assigned a value of 1, what will the numerical value of a whole note be?
If the quarter note is assigned a value of 1, the numerical value of a whole note will be 4.

If the quarter note is assigned a value of 1, what will the numerical value of a half note be?
If the quarter note is assigned a value of 1, the numerical value of a half note will be 2.

If the quarter note is assigned a value of 1, what will the numerical value of an eighth note be?
If the quarter note is assigned a value of 1, the numerical value of an eighth note will be 1/2.

If the quarter note is assigned a value of 1, what will the numerical value of a sixteenth note be?
If the quarter note is assigned a value of 1, the numerical value of a sixteenth note will be 1/4.

What are multiples of the unit?
Multiples of the unit are whole notes and half notes.

What are subdivisions of the unit?
Subdivisions of the unit are eighth notes and sixteenth notes.

What is tempo?
Tempo is the rate at which the beats occur in actual time.

How is tempo indicated?
Tempo is indicated with an Italian word or metronome marking above the first measure of music in a song.

What does "BPM" stand for?
"BPM" stands for "beats per minute".

Lesson 3 Quiz

Log in to your course at www.udemy.com and take the quiz for this lesson.

4. METER

THE DEFINITION OF METER

In the previous lessons we learned that the study of rhythm is concerned with relative duration of sound. In this lesson we will begin our study of **meter**. Rhythm is connected with meter but they are not the same thing. Meter is the natural division of rhythms into equal sized groups. Let's explain what is meant by this.

The six quarter notes above can be grouped in various ways using what we call "bar lines". By placing a bar line every two notes, these six notes can be grouped into three sets of two.

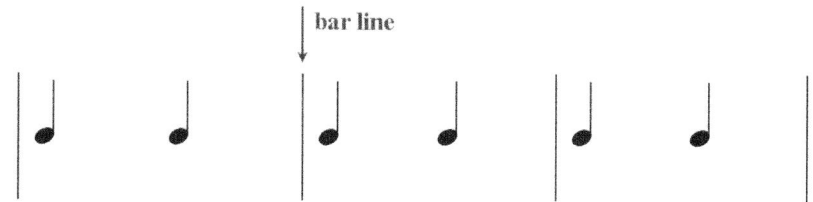

By placing a bar line every three notes, the six notes can be grouped into two sets of three.

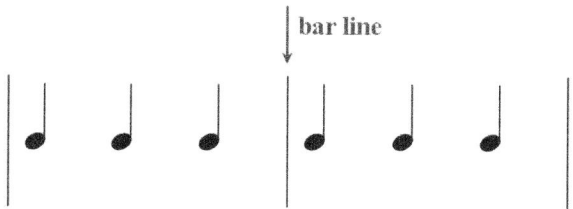

We call the space from one bar line to the next a **measure**. In the first example there are 3 measures. In the second example there are only 2 measures. What are we measuring? We are measuring time through beats.

Have you ever heard someone say that a piece of music is "in 3"? What they mean by this is that there are 3 beats between each bar line (i.e., 3 beats in each measure). The preceding example is "in 3" because there are 3 beats in each measure. The example before that is "in 2" because there are 2 beats in each measure. (Remember, the quarter note has been designated as the "unit" or "beat".) Let's look at another example.

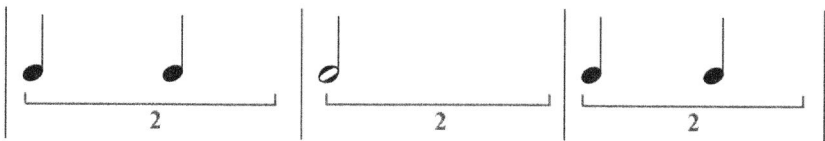

It is very important to understand that 2 "beats" per measure does not necessarily mean 2 "notes" per measure. For example, although there is only one note in the second measure above (the half note), it is equal to 2 beats. Therefore every measure above contains the same number of beats (2) but not the same number of notes.

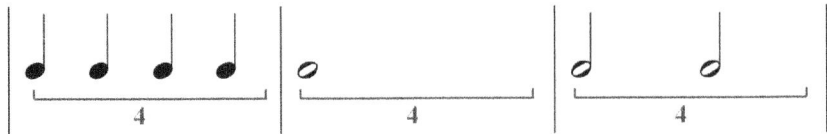

In the preceding example there are 4 notes in the first measure, 1 note in the second measure, and 2 notes in the last measure. But when adding up the total number of beats in each measure, it can be seen that there are 4 beats in each. This is an example of music "in 4".

TIME SIGNATURES

Meter is always indicated at the start of a song by two numbers. We call these two numbers a **time signature**.

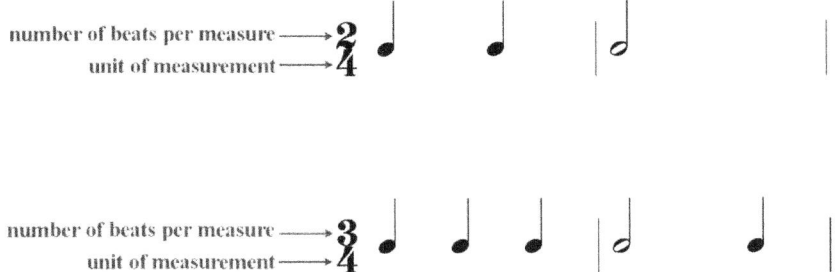

METER

As you can see from the preceding diagrams, the top number indicates the number of beats in each measure. The bottom number indicates which note has been designated as the unit of measurement. In each of the time signatures above, the number 4 appears on the bottom. 4 stands for "quarter". It is indicating that the quarter note has been designated as the unit of measurement (i.e., assigned a value of 1). In the previous lesson we learned that any note can be designated as the unit, but for now we are only dealing with the quarter note as the unit. We will learn about other notes being designated as the unit in subsequent lessons.

The time signature "4/4" can also be written using the letter "C".

The use of the letter "C" originated in the 15th and 16th centuries. It actually stems from a circle that had been cut in half. The half circle signified "imperfect time". (The number 4 was considered imperfect, while 3 was considered perfect.) Today the "C" has come to stand for "common" time. This is due to the fact that so much music has been written in "4/4" time.

OCUURENCE OF STRONG BEATS

Let's delve deeper into our definition of meter. Meter was defined above as "the natural division of rhythms into equal sized groups". It was previously demonstrated that through placement of bar lines, music can be divided into equal sized groups which contain the same number of beats. We will now explain what is meant by "natural" division using our example of six quarter notes.

As we saw previously, these six notes can be grouped into sets of 2 or into sets of 3 using bar lines. But what determines where the bar lines are placed? Bar lines are placed based on where the strongest pulses in the music "naturally" occur. If you have ever seen people clapping along to music, they are usually clapping along with the strongest beats. This is because music is natural to man. Even someone who knows nothing about music can instinctively recognize the strongest pulses of the music.

When the strongest pulse occurs every two beats, then the six quarter notes above will be grouped into sets of 2. (Strong beats are marked with arrows.)

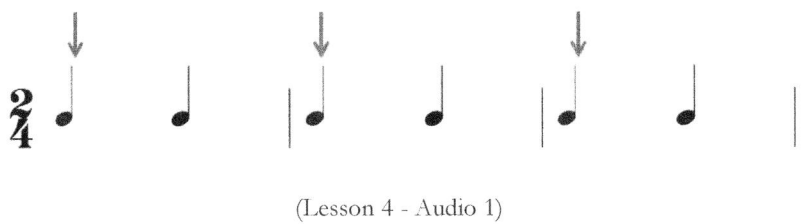

(Lesson 4 - Audio 1)

When the strongest pulse occurs every three beats, then the six quarter notes will be grouped into sets of three.

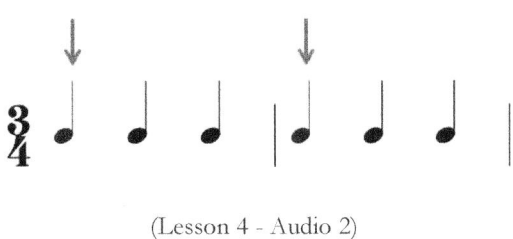

(Lesson 4 - Audio 2)

METER

Music that has a strong pulse every four beats will be written in 4/4 meter. Note: musicians will often times place a strong pulse on the first beat of each measure and a slightly less strong pulse on the third beat of each measure.

(Lesson 4 - Audio 3)

Sometimes it is easier to understand strong pulses by singing the words to a song. What meter do you think the song "Mary Had a Little Lamb" is in? Sing the song in your head and try to determine where the strong pulses naturally occur. Now listen to the audio below and decide which meter is correct.

Mary Had a Little Lamb in 4/4

(Lesson 4 - Audio 4)

Mary Had a Little Lamb in 3/4

(Lesson 4 - Audio 5)

Could you tell that 4/4 was the correct meter? The strongest pulses in the 3/4 version did not match up with where the strongest pulses occur in the words.

Memory Questions

What is meter?
Meter is the natural division of rhythms into equal sized groups.

What is a bar line?
A bar line is the vertical line that divides the music into equal groups of beats.

What is a measure?
A measure is the distance from one bar line to the next.

What is a time signature?
A time signature indicates the meter of a piece of music and is signified by two numbers placed at the start.

What does the top number of a time signature indicate?
The top number of a time signature indicates the amount of beats per measure.

What does the bottom number of a time signature indicate?
The bottom number of a time signature indicates which note has been designated as the unit of measurement.

What does the number 4 as the bottom number of a time signature represent?
The number 4 as the bottom number of a time signature represents the quarter note. It indicates that a quarter note has been designated as the unit of measurement (i.e., assigned a value of 1).

What other way can the time signature 4/4 be written?
The time signature 4/4 can also be written using the letter "C".

What does the letter "C" as a time signature stand for?
The letter "C" as a time signature stands for "common time".

What determines the meter of a piece?
The meter of a piece is determined by where the strongest pulses naturally occur in the music.

What is the meter if the strongest pulses occur every 2 beats?
If the strongest pulses occur every 2 beats, the meter is 2/4.

What is the meter if the strongest pulses occur every 3 beats?
If the strongest pulses occur every 3 beats, the meter is 3/4.

What is the meter if the strongest pulses occur every 4 beats?
If the strongest pulses occur every 4 beats, the meter is 4/4.

Lesson 4 Quiz

Log in to your course at www.udemy.com and take the quiz for this lesson

5. RESTS

RELATIVE DURATION OF SILENCE

During a piece of music there are not always notes being played. Sometimes there are periods of silence. Just as there are relative durations of sound, so too there are relative durations of silence. We call the symbols for these durations of silence **rests**.

Take a look at the chart below. On the left side of the chart are all of the notes you have learned up to this point in the course. On the right side of the chart are the corresponding rests of equal duration. Because they are of equal duration they share the same names with their counterparts. For example, a half "rest" is half the duration of a whole "rest", just as a half "note" is half the duration of a whole "note". Make sure that you commit this chart to memory before taking the lesson quiz.

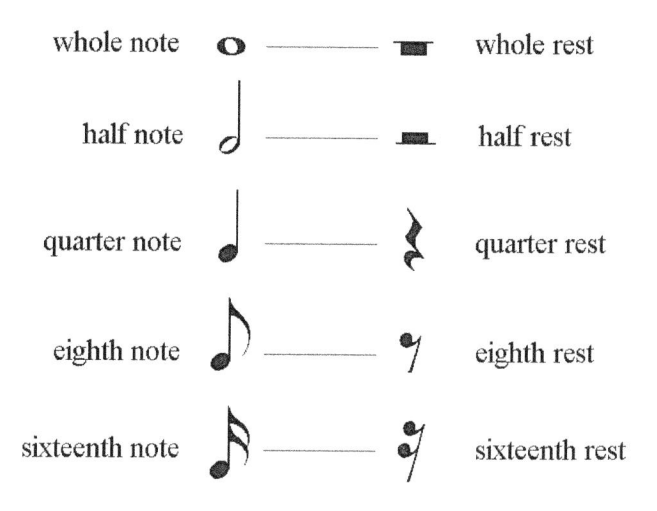

RESTS

whole note	𝅝	𝄻	whole rest
half note	𝅗𝅥	𝄼	half rest
quarter note	♩	𝄽	quarter rest
eighth note	♪	𝄾	eighth rest
sixteenth note	𝅘𝅥𝅯	𝄿	sixteenth rest

Everything we studied about rhythm and meter in the previous lessons applies to rests as well. There is one important exception. The whole rest fills an entire measure with silence no matter what the meter. This means that the whole rest will be equal to 2 beats in a measure of 2/4 meter.

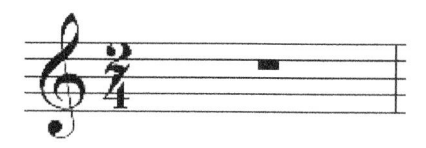

A whole rest will be equal to 3 beats in a measure of 3/4 meter.

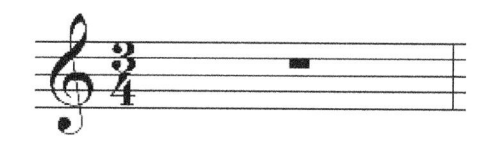

A whole rest will be equal to 4 beats in a measure of 4/4 meter.

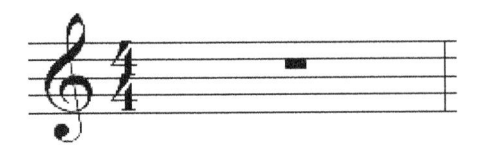

Memory Questions

What is a rest?
A rest is a symbol that indicates a relative duration of silence.

Assuming 4/4 meter, what is the relative duration of a whole rest?
The relative duration of a whole rest is 4 beats.

Assuming the quarter note has been assigned a value of 1, what is the relative duration of a half rest?
The relative duration of a half rest is 2 beats.

Assuming the quarter note has been assigned a value of 1, what is the relative duration of a quarter rest?
The relative duration of a quarter rest is 1 beat.

Assuming the quarter note has been assigned a value of 1, what is the relative duration of an eighth rest?
The relative duration of an eighth rest is 1/2 of a beat.

Assuming the quarter note has been assigned a value of 1, what is the relative duration of a sixteenth rest?
The relative duration of a sixteenth rest is 1/4 of a beat.

Does a whole rest always equal 4 beats of silence?
No, the number of beats a whole rest is equal to is dependent on the meter.

Lesson 5 Quiz

Log in to your course at www.udemy.com and take the quiz for this lesson.

6. DOTTED NOTES

ADDING ON DURATION

In this lesson we will be learning about some new note durations. These notes have a dot directly to the right of the note head. When a dot is placed to the right of the note head, the duration of the note is increased by one half of the note's value. Let's demonstrate this with some examples.

$$\d.$$

The note above is called a dotted half note. As we know, a half note is 2 beats in duration. By placing a dot to the right of the note head, the note's duration is increased by one half. Half of 2 = 1; therefore the half note is 2 beats in duration, the dot is 1 beat in duration, and together they are 3 beats in duration. This can be seen more clearly in the following diagram.

DOTTED NOTES

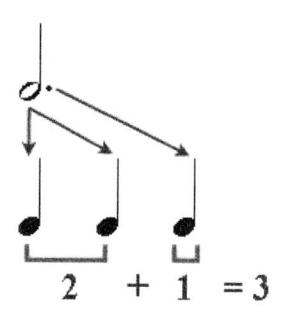

$$2 + 1 = 3$$

Let's take a look at the dotted whole note. As we know, a whole note is 4 beats in duration. By placing a dot to the right of the note head, the note's duration is increased by one half. Half of 4 = 2; therefore the whole note is 4 beats in duration, the dot is 2 beats in duration, and together they are 6 beats in duration.

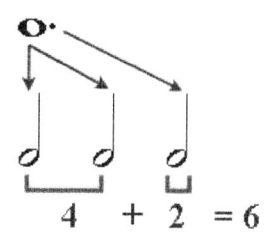

$$4 + 2 = 6$$

Let's see what happens when we add a dot to a quarter note. As we know, a quarter note is 1 beat in duration. By placing a dot to the right of the note head, the note's duration is increased by one half. Half of 1 = 1/2; therefore the quarter note is 1 beat in duration, the dot is 1/2 of a beat in duration, and together they are 1 & 1/2 beats in duration.

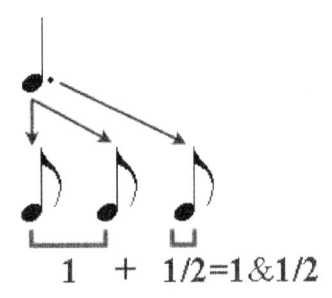

And finally, let's take a look at the dotted eighth note. As we know, an eighth note is 1/2 of a beat in duration. By placing a dot to the right of the note head, the note's duration is increased by one half. Half of 1/2 = 1/4; therefore the eighth note is 1/2 of a beat in duration, the dot is 1/4 of a beat in duration, and together they are 3/4 of a beat in duration.

Adding dots to notes originated in medieval times. Previous to this, the duration of notes was determined by musical context. Franco Cologne, a mid-13th century German music theorist, was very influential in developing a system of notation in which duration would be determined by the actual note itself and not by the musical context. The idea of the dot was called "puntus perfectionis" (the dot of perfection). To musicians of the time, the dot meant that the note was divisible by three and therefore perfect. Medieval thinkers and writers thought that the number three represented perfection. This was due to their belief in a triune God (three persons in one God). Because of this, all notes divisible by three were called "perfect" and all notes divisible by two were called "imperfect".

Recognizing that non-dotted notes are divisible by two and that dotted notes are divisible by three is very important to understanding rhythm. Before moving on, go back and look at each of the preceding diagrams and notice how every dotted note can be divided into three shorter notes.

Memory Questions

What does placing a dot to the right of a note head do?
Placing a dot to the right of a note head increases the note's duration by 1/2 of the note's value.

Assuming the quarter note is 1 beat in duration, what is the duration of a dotted whole note?
The duration of a dotted whole note is 6 beats.

Assuming the quarter note is 1 beat in duration, what is the duration of a dotted half note?
The duration of a dotted half note is 3 beats.

Assuming the quarter note is 1 beat in duration, what is the duration of a dotted quarter note?
The duration of a dotted quarter note is 1 & 1/2 beats.

Assuming the quarter note is 1 beat in duration, what is the duration of a dotted eighth note?
The duration of a dotted eighth note is 3/4 of a beat.

Lesson 6 Quiz

Log in to your course at www.udemy.com and take the quiz for this lesson.

7. THE TIE

ADDING NOTES TOGETHER

The note of longest duration we have learned thus far is 6 beats in duration (the dotted whole note). To create notes of longer duration we must add two or more notes together. For example, to create a note that is 12 beats in duration we could add together three whole notes. This is done using something called a "tie". A tie is a curved line strung between two notes, indicating that the durations are to be added together.

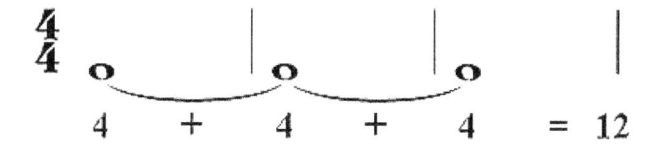

In the preceding example, the first whole note is played and then held for a duration of 12 beats. (The second and third notes are not "replayed" but are continued to be held.) The use of the tie also allows for note durations that last longer than a single measure.

Notice that the notes are tied across the bar lines in the preceding example.

Notes that are tied together do not necessarily need to be of the same length. Any two note durations may be tied together. For example, a whole note can be tied to a quarter note (4+1=5); a whole note can be tied to a dotted half note (4+3=7); etc.

TIES VS DOTS

Sometimes, rather than adding a dot to a note, notes are tied together to create a duration equal in length to that of a dotted note. For example, a half note tied to a quarter note is 3 beats.

This is the same as adding a dot to a half note.

A quarter note tied to an eighth note is 1 & 1/2 beats.

42

THE TIE

This is the same as adding a dot to a quarter note.

In fact, the same piece of music written using dotted notes can also be written using ties. Here is a diagram that shows the advantages and disadvantages of both methods.

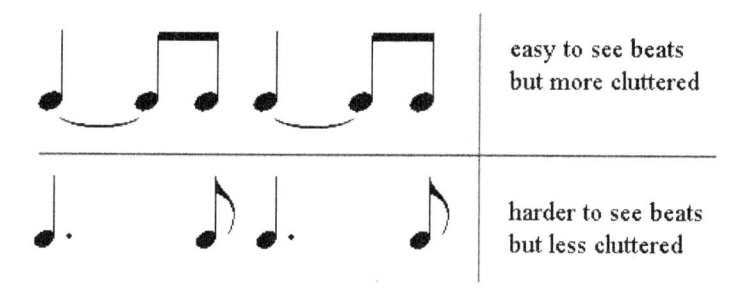

easy to see beats but more cluttered

harder to see beats but less cluttered

(Lesson 7 - Audio 1)

Did you notice that both lines sounded exactly the same? That's because the rhythm in the first line is the same as the rhythm in the second line. They are two ways of writing the same thing. Note: the dotted version is more common.

Memory Questions

What is a tie?
A tie is a curved line strung between two notes, indicating that the durations are to be added together.

How many notes may be tied together?
Two or more notes may be tied together.

Can notes be tied across bar lines?
Yes, notes can be tied across bar lines.

Do the notes tied together need to be of the same duration?
No, any note durations may be tied together.

Lesson 7 Quiz

Log in to your course at www.udemy.com and take the quiz for this lesson.

8. REDESIGNATING THE UNIT

3/8 and 6/8 METER

In lesson 3 we learned that any note can be designated as the unit of measurement if we assign to it a value of "1". Thus far we have only studied meters in which the quarter note was designated as the unit of measurement. In this lesson we are going to look at meters in which the eighth note is designated as the unit of measurement. Let's begin with 3/8 meter.

$$
\begin{aligned}
\text{beats per measure} &\longrightarrow 3 \\
\text{note designated as the unit} &\longrightarrow 8
\end{aligned}
$$

As we have previously learned, the top number of a time signature always indicates how many beats there are in each measure. In 3/8 meter there are 3 beats per measure. The bottom number in a time signature always indicates which note has been designated as the unit of measurement. In this case, the number 8 represents the eighth note. (Just as the number 4 in 3/4 represented the quarter note.)

This means that the eighth note has been designated as the unit of measurement (i.e., the eighth note has been assigned a value of 1).

Now let's take a look at 6/8 meter.

$$\begin{array}{r} \text{beats per measure} \longrightarrow 6 \\ \text{note designated as the unit} \longrightarrow 8 \end{array}$$

Once again, the top number indicates how many beats there are in each measure. In the case of 6/8 meter there are 6 beats in each measure. The bottom number indicates that the eighth note has been designated as the unit of measurement and assigned a value of 1.

What are the ramifications of changing our unit of measurement? By making the eighth note equal to 1 beat, we are also changing the numerical values of all the other notes. It is very important to understand that although each note's numerical value will be changed, their durations relative to one another will remain the same (i.e., a half note will still be half the duration of a whole note). The following chart will illustrate this.

REDESIGNATING THE UNIT

Quarter Note as Unit	Eighth Note as Unit
♫ = 1/4	♫ = 1/2
♪ = 1/2	♪ = 1
♩ = 1	♩ = 2
♩. = 1&1/2	♩. = 3
𝅗𝅥 = 2	𝅗𝅥 = 4
𝅗𝅥. = 3	𝅗𝅥. = 6
𝅝 = 4	𝅝 = 8

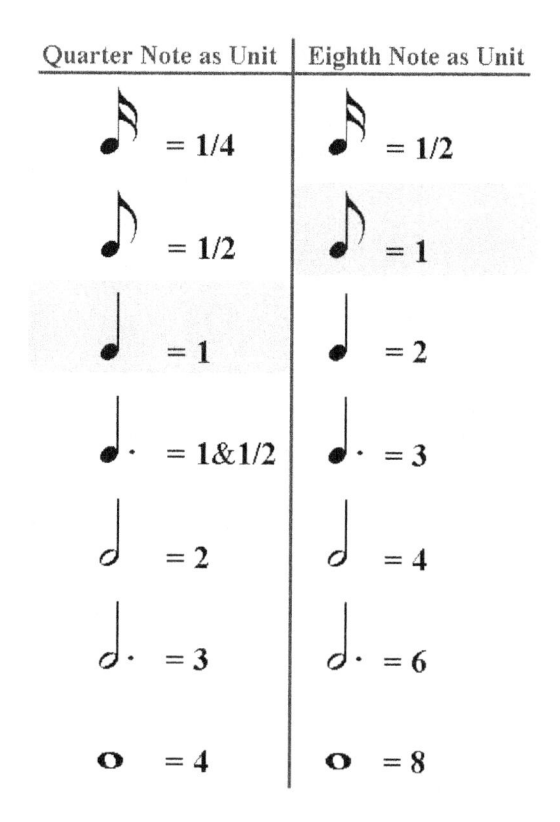

If you study the chart above, you will find that the values on the right side are double those on the left. When we made the eighth note equal to 1 beat, we doubled its duration (from 1/2 to 1). We must therefore double all the other notes so that their durations relative to one another remain the same (i.e., they maintain the same proportions to one another). Memorize this chart before taking the lesson quiz.

STRONGEST PULSES

When we studied 2/4, 3/4, and 4/4 meter, we learned where the strong pulses occurred. In 3/8 meter the pulse strength of the beats is "strong - weak - weak". (The arrow indicates the strong pulse.)

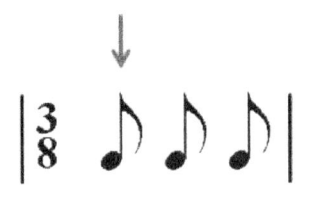

(Lesson 8 - Audio 1)

In 6/8 meter the pulse strength of the beats is "very strong - weak - weak - less strong - weak - weak".

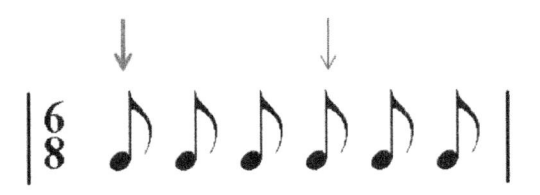

(Lesson 8 - Audio 2)

Memory Questions

What does the 3 in 3/8 meter indicate?
The 3 in 3/8 meter indicates that there are 3 beats in each measure.

What does the 6 in 6/8 meter indicate?
The 6 in 6/8 meter indicates that there are 6 beats in each measure.

What does the 8 in 3/8 meter and 6/8 meter indicate?
The 8 in 3/8 meter and 6/8 meter indicates that the eighth note has been designated as the unit of measurement and assigned a value of 1.

Assuming the eighth note equals 1 beat, what is the numerical value of the sixteenth note?
When the eighth note equals 1 beat, the sixteenth note equals 1/2 of a beat.

Assuming the eighth note equals 1 beat, what is the numerical value of the quarter note?
When the eighth note equals 1 beat, the quarter note equals 2 beats.

Assuming the eighth note equals 1 beat, what is the numerical value of the dotted quarter note?
When the eighth note equals 1 beat, the dotted quarter note equals 3 beats.

Assuming the eighth note equals 1 beat, what is the numerical value of the half note?
When the eighth note equals 1 beat, the half note equals 4 beats.

Assuming the eighth note equals 1 beat, what is the numerical value of the dotted half note?
When the eighth note equals 1 beat, the dotted half note equals 6 beats.

Assuming the eighth note equals 1 beat, what is the numerical value of the whole note?
When the eighth note equals 1 beat, the whole note equals 8 beats.

What is the pulse strength of the beats in 3/8 meter?
The pulse strength of the beats in 3/8 meter is "strong - weak - weak".

What is the pulse strength of the beats in 6/8 meter?
The pulse strength of the beats in 6/8 meter is "very strong - weak - weak - less strong - weak - weak".

Lesson 8 Quiz

Log in to your course at www.udemy.com and take the quiz for this lesson.

9. CUT TIME

THE HALF NOTE AS UNIT

Thus far we have seen the quarter note designated as the beat in 2/4, 3/4, and 4/4 meters, and the eighth note designated as the beat in 3/8, and 6/8 meters. In this lesson we are going to learn about a meter which designates the half note as the beat. It is known as "cut time" or 2/2 meter. It can be notated as 2 over 2 or as the letter "C" with a vertical line through it.

As you know by now, the top number in a time signature always indicates how many beats per measure. In 2/2 meter there are 2 beats in each measure. The bottom number in a time signature always indicates which note has been designated as the unit of measurement. In this case, the number 2 represents the half note. (Just as the number 4 in 3/4 represented the quarter note, and the number 8 in 3/8 represented the eighth note.) This means that the half note has been designated as the unit of measurement (i.e., the half note has been assigned a value of 1).

By making the half note equal to 1 beat, we are also changing the numerical values of all the other notes. It is very important to understand that although each note's numerical value will be changed, their durations relative to one another will remain the same (i.e., a half note will still be half the duration of a whole note). The following diagram will illustrate this.

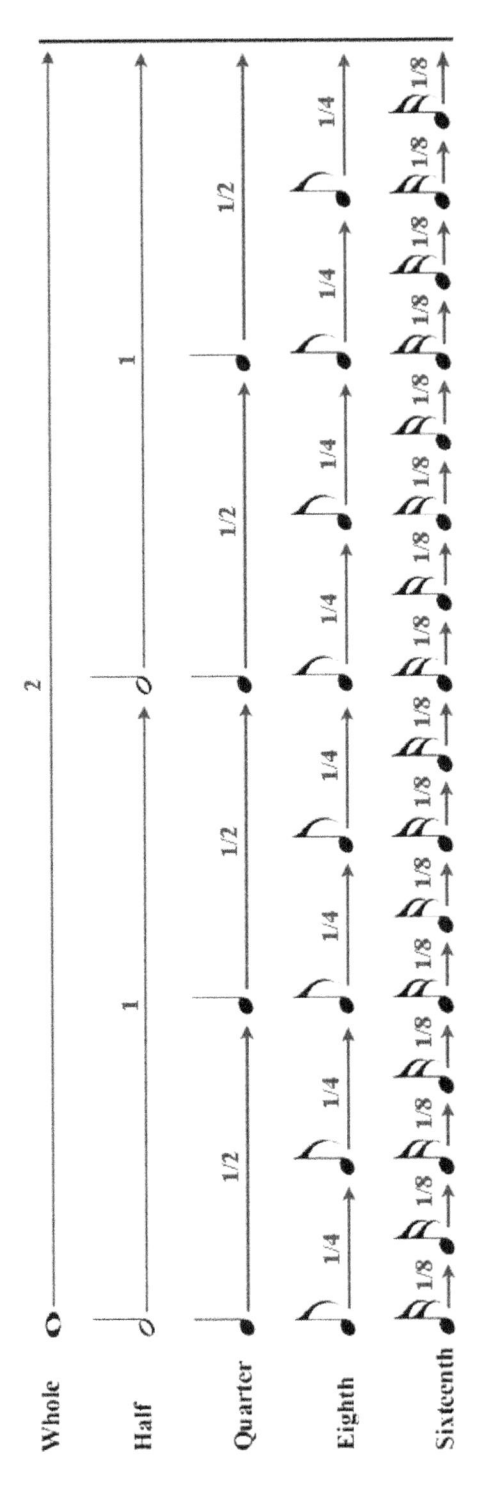

CUT TIME

Here is another chart which shows the numerical values of each note when the quarter note is designated as the unit (left column) and when the half note is designated as the unit (right column). It includes a few of the more common dotted notes as well.

Quarter Note as Unit	Half Note as Unit
♬ = 1/4	♬ = 1/8
♪ = 1/2	♪ = 1/4
♩ = 1	♩ = 1/2
♩. = 1&1/2	♩. = 3/4
𝅗𝅥 = 2	𝅗𝅥 = 1
𝅗𝅥. = 3	𝅗𝅥. = 1&1/2
𝅝 = 4	𝅝 = 2

An easy way to remember the note values in cut time is to picture each of the note values in 4/4 as having been "cut" in half. Note: all the values on the right of the chart are half of the values on the left.

Meters such as 2/2 are actually very helpful when reading music at fast tempos. Here is an example of the same rhythm written first in common time and then in cut time.

Even though each line has the same number of notes, the second line is much easier to read when playing at faster tempos. This is because there are fewer beams, thus making the music much cleaner (less cluttered looking).

Note: The strong beat in cut time occurs on beat 1 of each measure.

Memorize and understand the right side of the chart above before continuing on to the lesson quiz.

Memory Questions

What is cut time?
Cut time is the meter in which there are 2 beats per measure and the half note is equal to 1 beat.

How is cut time notated?
Cut time is notated either as the letter "C" with a vertical line through it or as 2 over 2.

What does the top number in 2/2 meter indicate?
The top number in 2/2 meter indicates that there are two beats per measure.

What does the bottom number in 2/2 meter indicate?
The bottom number in 2/2 meter indicates that the half note has been designated as the beat and assigned a value of 1.

Where does the strong beat occur in cut time?
The strong beat in cut time occurs on beat 1 of each measure.

Why is cut time useful?
Cut time is useful for reading music that is meant to be played at fast tempos.

Lesson 9 Quiz

Log in to your course at www.udemy.com and take the quiz for this lesson.

10. CLASSIFYING METERS

SIMPLE METER

By now you are familiar with a few different time signatures. In this lesson we are going to learn how to classify them, and at the same time learn a few new meters.

When a meter has two pulses per measure it is called **duple meter**. An example would be 2/4 time. (The reason we are using the word "pulse" instead of beat will become clear as we move forward.)

When a meter has three pulses per measure it is called **triple meter**. An example would be 3/4 time.

When a meter has four pulses per measure it is called **quadruple meter**. An example would be 4/4 time.

All of these meters are called **simple** because each pulse can be divided by "two". Here are some examples.

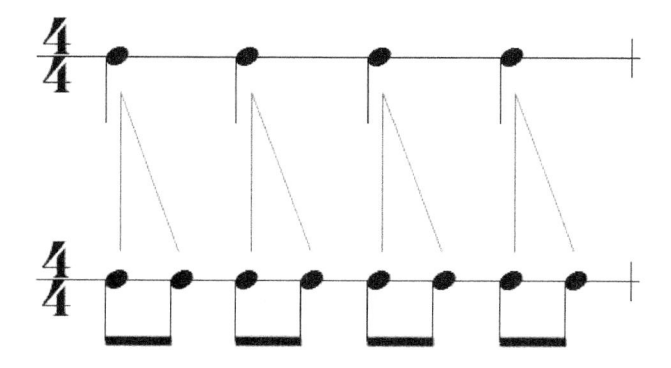

CLASSIFYING METERS

Because each pulse (quarter note) in the preceding diagram can be divided by two, the meter is classified as simple. Because there are 4 pulses in each measure, the meter is classified as quadruple. 4/4 time is therefore called **simple quadruple** meter.

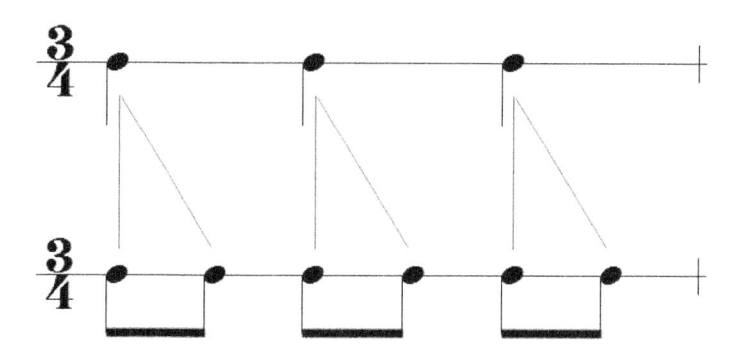

Because each pulse (quarter note) in the preceding diagram can be divided by two, the meter is classified as simple. Because there are 3 pulses in each measure, the meter is classified as triple. 3/4 time is therefore called **simple triple** meter.

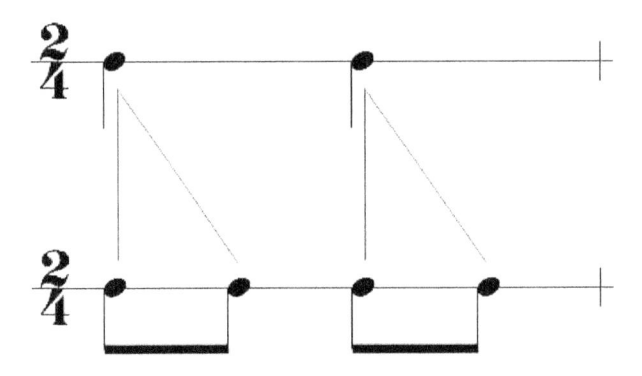

Because each pulse (quarter note) in the preceding diagram can be divided by two, the meter is classified as simple. Because there are 2 pulses in each measure, the meter is classified as duple. 2/4 time is therefore called **simple duple** meter.

COMPOUND METER

In compound meter each pulse can be divided by "three". Let's look at an example of 6/8 meter to explain what this means.

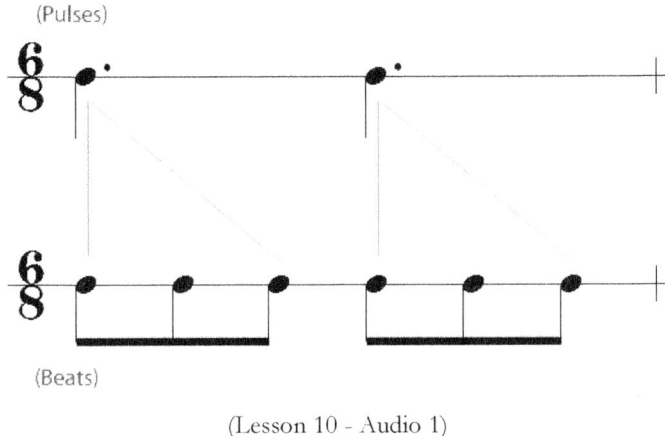

(Lesson 10 - Audio 1)

CLASSIFYING METERS

In the preceding example, even though there are 6 beats in each measure (each eighth note is one beat) the rhythmic pulse falls every 3 beats. The strong pulse is on beat 1 and the second strongest pulse is on beat 4. This gives it the feel that there are 2 "beats" in each measure rather than 6. Play the audio clip above and try tapping your foot along with the music. Do you see how the feel is 2 beats per measure rather than 6?

This may be very confusing to you since you have previously learned that the bottom number of a time signature always indicates which note has been designated as the beat. In order to avoid confusion we use the term "pulse". **In simple meter, "beat" and "pulse" mean the same thing; in compound meter, "beat" refers to the note with a value of 1, whereas "pulse" refers to what is perceived as the beat.** It is very important that you understand this distinction before moving forward.

Because each pulse (dotted quarter note) in the preceding diagram can be divided by three, the meter is classified as compound. Because there are 2 pulses in each measure, the meter is classified as duple. 6/8 time is therefore called **compound duple** meter.

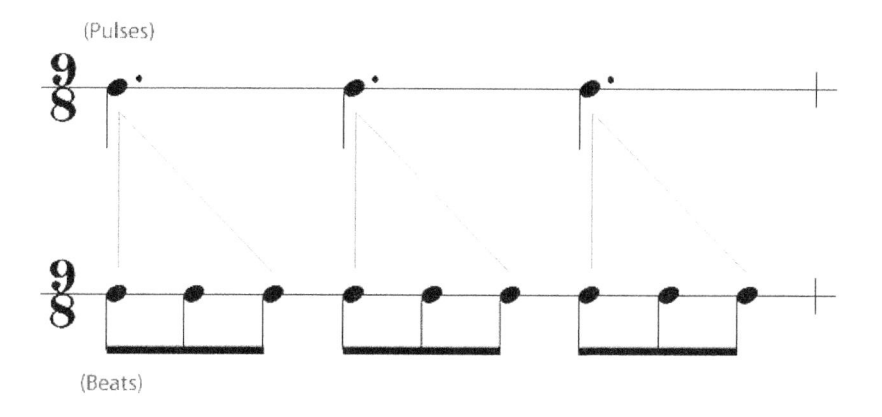

(Pulses)

(Beats)

Because each pulse (dotted quarter note) in the preceding diagram can be divided by three, the meter is classified as compound. Because there are 3 pulses in each measure, the meter is classified as triple.

9/8 time is therefore called **compound triple** meter. (There are 9 eighth note beats in each measure, but we feel 3 pulses per measure.)

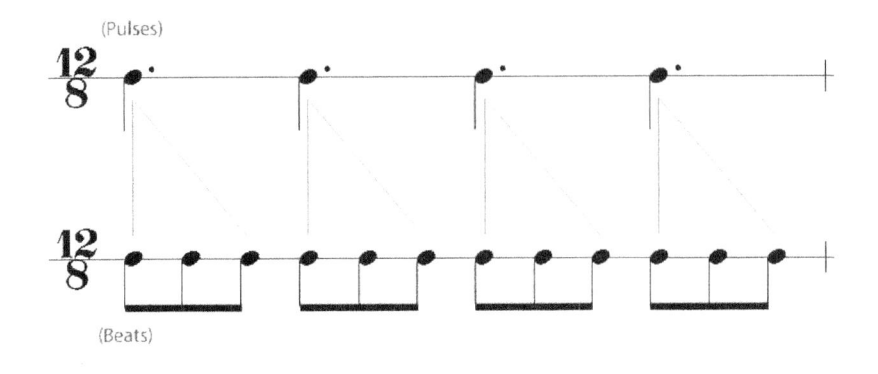

Because each pulse (dotted quarter note) in the preceding diagram can be divided by three, the meter is classified as compound. Because there are 4 pulses in each measure, the meter is classified as quadruple. 12/8 time is therefore called **compound quadruple** meter. (There are 12 eighth note beats in each measure, but we feel 4 pulses per measure.)

Memorize and understand the chart below before taking the lesson quiz. Note: no matter what the meter type, you can only have 2, 4, 8, 16, or 32 for the bottom number of the time signature. That is, either the half, quarter, eighth, sixteenth, or thirty-second note has been designated as the beat. The simple meters are 2, 3, and 4. The compound meters are 6, 9, and 12.

	Simple Meter	Compound Meter
Duple	2/2 2/4 2/8 2/16 2/32	6/2 6/4 6/8 6/16 6/32
Triple	3/2 3/4 3/8 3/16 3/32	9/2 9/4 9/8 9/16 9/32
Quadruple	4/2 4/4 4/8 4/16 4/32	12/2 12/4 12/8 12/16 12/32

COMPLEX METER

Complex meters are meters that are a combination of duple, triple, or quadruple. They are not as common in music and so we will just mention a few of them here in passing.

Probably the most used of the complex meters is 5/4 time. The top number tells us there are 5 beats in each measure and the bottom number tells us that the quarter note has been designated as the beat. It is called complex meter since it is a combination of duple and triple meter. (2+3=5)

Another example of a complex meter would be 7/8. The top number tells us there are 7 beats in each measure and the bottom number tells us that the eighth note has been designated as the beat. It is called complex meter since it is a combination of triple and quadruple meter. (3+4=7)

It is important to note that with simple and compound meters, measures can always be divided into halves or thirds. The measures in complex meters cannot be divided into halves or thirds. This makes the music much harder to play (and also much harder to listen to) since our brains like things that are divisible into halves or thirds and can't make as much sense of numbers like 5 or 7.

Memory Questions

What is duple meter?
Duple meter is any meter in which there are 2 pulses per measure.

What is triple meter?
Triple meter is any meter in which there are 3 pulses per measure.

What is quadruple meter?
Quadruple meter is any meter in which there are 4 pulses per measure.

What is simple meter?
Simple meter is any meter in which the pulse can be divided by two.

What does "pulse" refer to in simple meter?
In simple meter "pulse" refers to the beat.

What is compound meter?
Compound meter is any meter in which the pulse can be divided by three.

What does "pulse" refer to in compound meter?
In compound meter "pulse" refers to the perceived beat.

What is complex meter?
Complex meter is any meter that is a combination of duple, triple, or quadruple meters.

Lesson 10 Quiz

Log in to your course at www.udemy.com and take the quiz for this lesson.

11. TRIPLETS

ARTIFICIAL DIVISIONS

In a previous lesson we learned that beats can be subdivided into equal parts by halving them. (1 quarter note can be divided into 2 eighth notes; 2 eighth notes can be divided into 4 sixteenth notes; 4 sixteenth notes can be divided into 8 thirty-second notes, etc.) In this lesson we are going to learn how beats and other note durations can be subdivided into thirds. Let's begin by looking at the quarter note.

When we subdivide a quarter note into two equal parts it results in two eighth notes. (1/2 + 1/2 =1) If we subdivided a quarter note into three equal parts (1/3 + 1/3 + 1/3 = 1) what type of note would result?

Rather than creating a whole new note symbol to signify the duration of 1/3 of a beat, these notes are also written as eighth notes. To distinguish between eighth notes that are worth 1/2 of a beat and eighth notes that are worth 1/3 of a beat, the number 3 is placed over the notes indicating that these three eighth notes are to be played in the same amount of time it takes to play two eighth notes.

TRIPLETS

In the preceding diagram, the 2 eighth notes on the left hand side of the equation are each equal to 1/2 of a beat. The 3 eighth notes on the right hand side of the equation are each equal to 1/3 of a beat. Each side is equal to 1 beat. But since the 3 eighth notes on the right have to fit into the same duration of time as the 2 eighth notes on the left, they will have to be played at a faster rate. We call this a **triplet**. A triplet is 3 of one type of note played in the same amount of time as 2 of the same type of note.

A diagram might be helpful when trying to understand triplets. The entire pie represents 1 quarter note (1 beat). Each section of the pie represents a triplet eighth note.

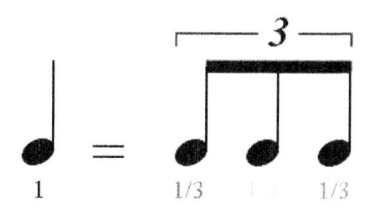

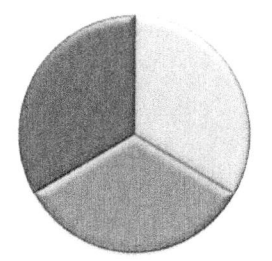

Triplets may be indicated a variety of ways. Probably the most common way is with a single number 3 placed over or under the notes. (Whether it is placed over or under depends on if the note stems are pointing up or down. We will learn more about stem direction when we study pitch.)

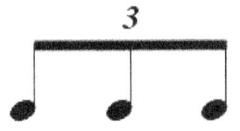

Another method uses a bracket and number 3.

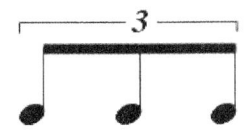

The triplet can also be written with a curved line and number 3.

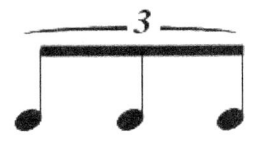

Or the triplet can be written as a ratio.

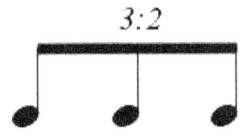

The ratio simply means to play 3 eighth notes in the same amount of time that it would normally take to play 2 eighth notes. Although

TRIPLETS

writing it as a ratio is the least commonly used method, it is the most clear and understandable.

Triplets fall under the category of **tuplets**. A tuplet is an artificial division of the beat, multiples of the beat, or subdivisions of the beat, that does not exist within the meter. This may sound complex, but it's not. In "simple" meter, 1 beat is divisible into 2 parts, 4 parts, 8 parts, etc. But we can "artificially" divide the beat into as many parts as we wish. For example, 1 beat could be divided into 5 parts (Quintuplet), 6 parts (Sextuplet), 7 parts (Septuplet), 9 parts (Nonuplet), etc. These types of divisions do not normally exist in "simple" meter and that is why they are called "artificial".

Not only can we artificially divide beats, the definition also states that we can artificially divide "multiples of the beat" and "subdivisions of the beat". An example of artificially dividing multiples of the beat would be to divide 1 whole note into 3 equal parts. An example of artificially dividing subdivisions of the beat would be to divide 1 eighth note into 3 equal parts. Let's look at a few examples.

The following diagram shows a group of sixteenth note triplets. An eighth note (1/2 of a beat) is normally divided into 2 sixteenth notes (1/4 + 1/4). If we artificially divide a sixteenth note into 3 equal parts, each part will be equal to 1/6 of a beat. (1/6 + 1/6 + 1/6 = 1/2) Remember, the entire pie represents 1 quarter note; half the pie represents 1 eighth note.

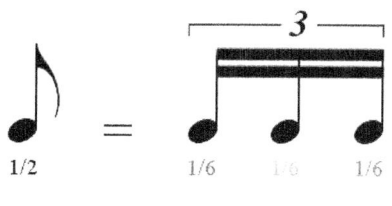

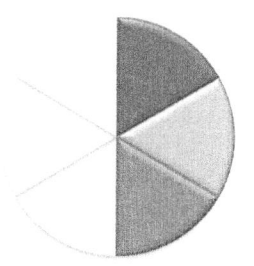

MUSIC THEORY

Next, let's try artificially dividing a multiple of the beat. We'll start with the half note. A half note is 2 beats. If we divide 2 beats into 3 equal parts, what is the duration of each part? We can find the answer with a simple math equation using fractions.

$$\frac{2}{1} \div \frac{3}{1} \quad \text{is the same as} \quad \frac{2}{1} \times \frac{1}{3} = \frac{2}{3}$$

If we write the whole numbers 2 and 3 as fractions (2 over 1, and 3 over 1) and divide, it is the same as multiplying by the inverse. The answer results in 2/3. Therefore each part will equal 2/3 of a beat. You can see this more clearly illustrated in the following diagram. A half note (2 beats) is normally divided into 2 quarter notes (1 + 1). If we artificially divide a half note into 3 equal parts, each part will be equal to 2/3 of a beat. (2/3 + 2/3 + 2/3 = 6/3 = 2) Here each pie represents 1 quarter note; both pies together represent 1 half note.

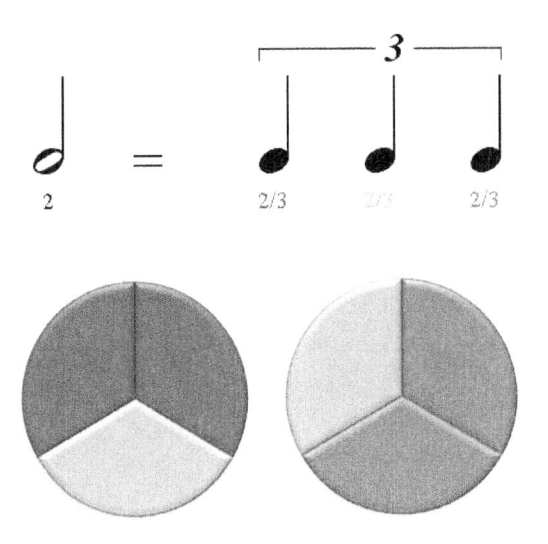

And finally, let's try artificially dividing the whole note into 3 equal parts. A whole note is 4 beats. If we divide 4 beats into 3 equal parts,

TRIPLETS

what is the duration of each part? Once again, we can find the answer with a simple math equation.

$$\frac{4}{1} \div \frac{3}{1} \quad \text{is the same as} \quad \frac{4}{1} \times \frac{1}{3} = \frac{4}{3}$$

Therefore each part will equal 4/3 of a beat. You can see this more clearly illustrated in the following diagram. A whole note (4 beats) is normally divided into 2 half notes (2 + 2). If we artificially divide the whole note into 3 equal parts, each part will be equal to 4/3. (4/3 + 4/3 + 4/3 = 12/3 = 4) Here each pie represents 1 quarter note; the 4 pies together represent 1 whole note.

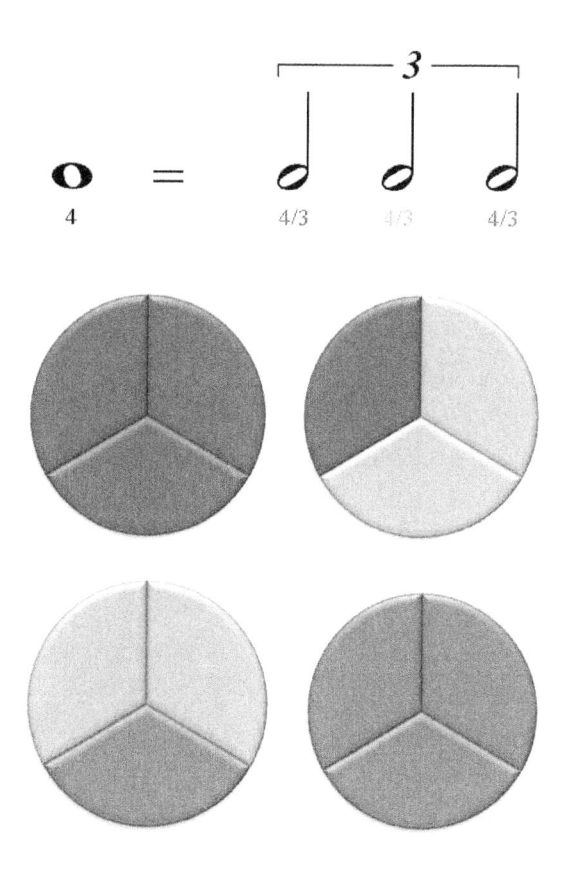

Memory Questions

What is a tuplet?
A tuplet is an artificial division of the beat, multiples of the beat, or subdivisions of the beat, that does not exist within the meter.

What are some types of tuplets?
Some types of tuplets include duplets, triplets, quintuplets, sextuplets, septuplets, and nonuplets.

What is the most common type of tuplet?
The most common type of tuplet is the triplet.

What is a triplet?
A triplet is 3 of one type of note played in the same amount of time as 2 of the same type of note.

What is the ratio of a triplet?
A triplet has a ratio of 3 to 2.

Lesson 11 Quiz

Log in to your course at www.udemy.com and take the quiz for this lesson.

12. DUPLETS

MORE ABOUT TUPLETS

In the previous lesson we learned about a type of tuplet called a triplet. In this lesson we are going to learn about another type of tuplet called a **duplet**. Before we begin, let's review the definition of a tuplet and the definition of a triplet.

A tuplet is an artificial division of the beat, multiples of the beat, or subdivisions of the beat, that does not exist within the meter. The most common type of tuplet is the triplet. A triplet is 3 of one type of note played in the same amount of time as 2 of the same type of note.

Duplets are in sense the opposite of a triplet. With a duplet, 2 of one type of note are played in the same amount of time that it would normally take to play 3 of the same type of note.

Duplets may be indicated a variety of ways. Probably the most common way is with a single number 2 placed over or under the notes. (Whether it is placed over or under depends on if the note stems are pointing up or down. We will learn more about stem direction when we study pitch.)

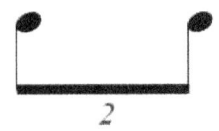

Another method uses a bracket and number 2.

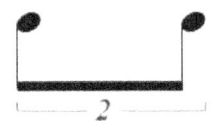

The duplet can also be written with a curved line and number 2.

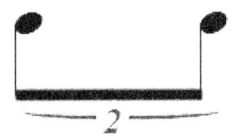

Or the duplet can be written as a ratio.

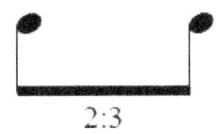

The ratio simply means to play 2 eighth notes in the same amount of time that it would normally take to play 3 eighth notes. Although writing it as a ratio is the least commonly used method, it is the most clear and understandable. Let's look at an example to understand how a duplet is 2 played in the same time as 3.

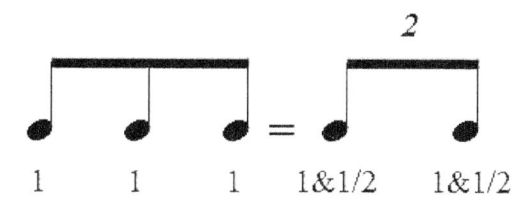

$$\underbrace{\flat\ \flat\ \flat}_{1\ \ \ 1\ \ \ 1} = \underbrace{\flat\ \flat}_{1\&1/2\ \ 1\&1/2}^{2}$$

In the preceding example, the eighth note has been assigned a value of 1. Therefore, 3 eighth notes equal a total of 3 beats. For 2 eighth notes to be played in the same amount of time as 3 eighth notes, each eighth note must be slightly longer in duration. As you can see, both sides of the equation above equal 3 beats. The normal eighth notes are each 1 beat in duration, but the duplet eighth notes are each 1 & 1/2 beats in duration.

ARTIFICIAL DIVISIONS & METER TYPE

Both triplets and duplets are artificial divisions of the beat, multiples of the beat, or subdivisions of the beat, that do not exist within the meter. But there is a distinction to be made here that has to do with "simple" and "compound" meters.

The reason triplets are artificial divisions is because they appear in simple meters where the pulse is normally divisible by 2; the reason duplets are artificial divisions is because they appear in compound meters where the pulse is normally divisible by 3. Let's explain what we mean by this.

Here is an example of a rhythm written in simple duple meter (2/4 time). Since it is simple meter, each pulse should normally be divisible by 2. (The number 2 above each pulse represents the normal division of a pulse into 2 equal parts) When a triplet appears in simple meter (as in the first measure below) it does not fit this division by 2. It is for this reason that it is called an artificial division.

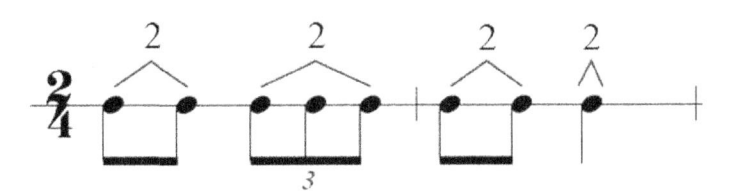

Here is an example of a rhythm written in compound duple meter (6/8 time). Since it is compound meter, each pulse should normally be divisible by 3. (The number 3 above each pulse represents the normal division of a pulse into 3 equal parts) When a duplet appears in compound meter (as in the first measure below) it does not fit this division by 3. It is for this reason that it is called an artificial division.

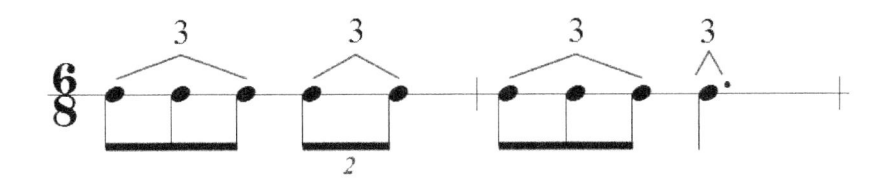

Memory Questions

What is a tuplet?
A tuplet is an artificial division of the beat, multiples of the beat, or subdivisions of the beat, that does not exist within the meter.

What is a triplet?
A triplet is 3 of one type of note played in the same amount of time as 2 of the same type of note.

Why are triplets artificial divisions of the beat?
Triplets are artificial divisions of the beat because they appear in simple meters where the pulse is normally divisible by 2.

What is a duplet?
A duplet is 2 of one type of note played in the same amount of time as 3 of the same type of note.

Why are duplets artificial divisions of the beat?
Duplets are artificial divisions of the beat because they appear in compound meters where the pulse is normally divisible by 3.

Lesson 12 Quiz

Log in to your course at www.udemy.com and take the quiz for this lesson.

13. PITCH

SOUND WAVES

In the beginning of this course we learned that there are two basic elements that make up music: rhythm and pitch. The study of rhythm is concerned with the relative duration of sound (how short or long one sound is relative to another). The study of pitch is concerned with the relative frequency of sound (how low or high one sound is relative to another). Up until this point in the course we have only looked at rhythm. We will now turn our attention to pitch.

When we speak of the "high" and "low" of a sound, what exactly are we referring to? When we say that the drinking glasses are on a higher shelf than the dinner plates, we are referring to "physical" space. In music, high and low refers to "tonal" space. To understand this we must take a brief look at sound waves.

Whenever air is moved, sound is produced. This moving air travels in waves similar to ripples in water.

There are two types of pitch - **indefinite pitch** and **definite pitch**. The sounds produced by random waves of air are called indefinite pitches. Examples include: snapping your fingers, a door slamming shut, or thunder.

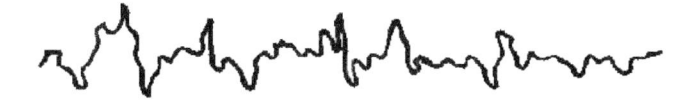

(Sound wave of an indefinite pitch)

The sounds produced by uniform waves of air are called definite pitches. Examples include: speaking, singing, and any sound made by musical instruments. (Whenever we refer to pitch in this course, we will be referring to definite pitch.)

(Sound wave of a definite pitch)

Before the advent of modern technology, the only way to measure pitch was by comparing one pitch to another pitch. The ancient Greek philosopher and mathematician, Pythagoras (570-495 BC), is considered to be the first to discover that particular mathematical divisions of a vibrating string produced different pitches. Because of mathematics he was able to definitively state that a certain pitch was "twice as high" as another pitch. We will learn more of Pythagoras' discoveries when we study intervals in a subsequent lesson.

Today we measure pitch by its frequency. Frequency is the rate at which the waves of air reach our ear. This can be measured in cycles per second. A cycle is from one wave crest to the next wave crest.

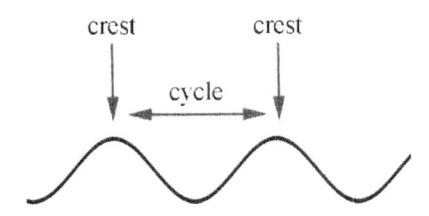

All sound travels at the same speed (when temperature is constant). The speed of sound is about one mile every five seconds. Because of this fact, all of the sound waves in the following diagram will reach the ear at the same moment in time.

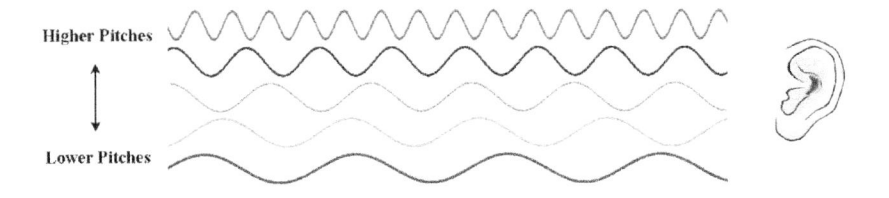

Although the sound is traveling at the same speed, the waves at the top of the diagram are hitting the ear more frequently (more cycles per second), and are thus higher in pitch. The waves at the bottom of the diagram are hitting the ear less frequently (fewer cycles per second), and are thus lower in pitch.

When we speak of the "frequency of a pitch", we are referring to how frequently the waves reach our ears, i.e., how high or low the pitch sounds to us.

Experiment

The following experiments will demonstrate the three things that affect pitch.

Experiment 1:

1. Make a single cut in a medium sized rubber band.
2. Have another person stretch the length until tight.
3. With your ear close to the band, pluck it in the center and listen to the pitch it produces.
4. Keeping the band the same tautness, pinch the middle and drop the other end to make it half the original length.
5. Pluck again, and listen to the pitch it produces.

Were the two pitches the same or different? Was one higher or lower than the other? If so, which pitch was higher and which was lower?

(Conclusion: shorter band = higher pitch)

Experiment 2:

1. Stretch the band from experiment 1 as far as it will go without breaking.
2. Pluck the band and listen to the pitch it produces.
3. Loosen the tautness of the band so that it is now around half the fully stretched length.
4. Pluck again, and listen to the pitch it produces.

Were the two pitches the same or different? Was one higher or lower than the other? If so, which pitch was higher and which was lower?

(Conclusion: tighter band = higher pitch)

Experiment 3:
1. Find a rubber band which is much thicker than the one used above and cut it to the same length.
2. Stretch the thin band tight; pluck and listen to the pitch.
3. Stretch the thick band to the same length; pluck and listen to the pitch.

Were the pitches the same or different? Was one higher or lower than the other? If so, which pitch was higher and which was lower?

(Conclusion: thinner band = higher pitch)

Memory Questions

How is sound produced?
Sound is produced by moving air.

How does sound travel?
Sound travels in waves.

How quickly does sound travel?
Sound travels about one mile in five seconds.

What two basic elements is music made up of?
Music is made up of the elements of rhythm and pitch.

What is the study of pitch concerned with?
The study of pitch is concerned with the relative frequency of sound (how low or high one sound is relative to another).

What are the two types of pitch?
The two types of pitch are indefinite pitch and definite pitch.

How is indefinite pitch made?
Indefinite pitch is made when air travels in random waves.

How is definite pitch made?
Definite pitch is made when air travels in uniform waves.

What does frequency refer to?
Frequency refers to the rate at which the waves of air reach our ear.

How is frequency measured?
Frequency is measured in cycles per second.

What is a cycle?
A cycle is from one wave crest to the next wave crest.

What does the frequency of a sound wave determine?
The frequency of a sound wave determines the pitch (how high or low a sound is).

When the rate at which sound waves reach the ear is more frequent, what is the result?
When the rate at which sound waves reach the ear is more frequent, the result is a higher sounding pitch.

When the rate at which sound waves reach the ear is less frequent, what is the result?
When the rate at which sound waves reach the ear is less frequent, the result is a lower sounding pitch.

Lesson 13 Quiz

Log in to your course at www.udemy.com and take the quiz for this lesson.

14. INTRODUCTION TO THE STAFF

STAFF LINES

A staff is the device by which we indicate pitch. The modern day staff consists of 5 lines called **staff lines**.

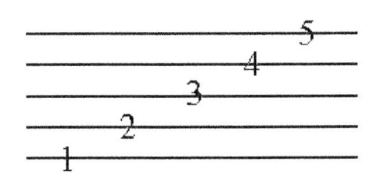

In between the lines are 4 spaces.

INTRODUCTION TO THE STAFF

Notes may be placed on either the staff lines or in the spaces.

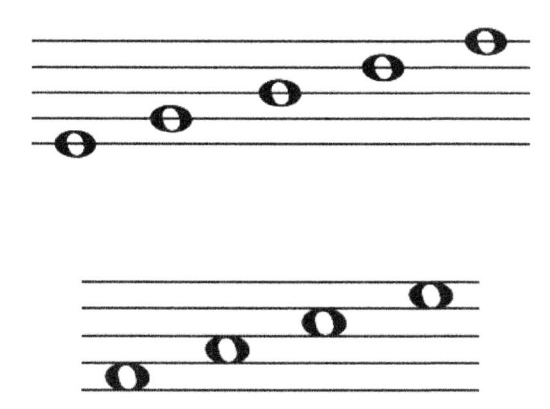

The notes that are placed higher on the staff represent higher pitches. The notes that are placed lower on the staff represent lower pitches. For example, the first note in the following diagram will sound higher than the second note. (It is helpful to think of the 5 staff lines as rungs on a ladder.)

LEDGER LINES

We wouldn't be able to play or sing very high or very low (and very little music could be written) using only 5 lines and 4 spaces. So, to indicate even higher pitches, we add additional lines above the 5 staff lines. To indicate even lower pitches, we add additional lines below the 5 staff lines. These additional lines are called **ledger lines**.

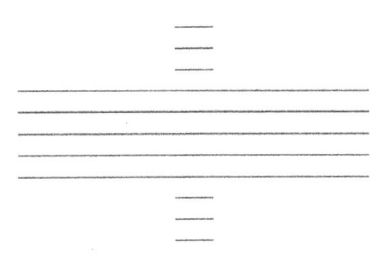

Notes may be placed on the ledger lines, just as they were placed on the staff lines.

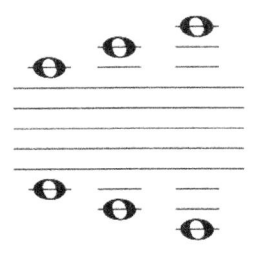

They can also be placed in the spaces.

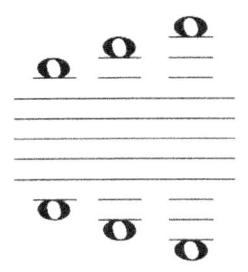

Although the addition of ledger lines allows us to notate a greater number of pitches, it also creates a problem. Extremely high and

INTRODUCTION TO THE STAFF

extremely low pitches would need so many ledger lines, that even the best musicians would have a difficult time reading the music.

To determine the pitches in the preceding example, a musician would have to count every single line and space. This would take a very long time and would not be conducive to the actual reading of music, which needs to be almost instantaneous.

Let's do a little experiment. Glance quickly at the lines below and see if you can tell how many there are.

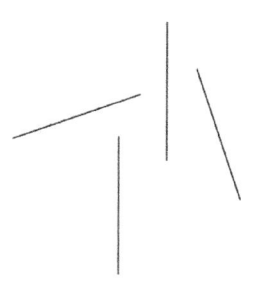

Notice that you did not have to count the lines one at a time. That's because the human brain and eyes are able to take in a small number of objects at a glance (typically 4-5) and recognize how many object there are.

Without counting them, quickly glance at the lines below and see if you can tell how many there are.

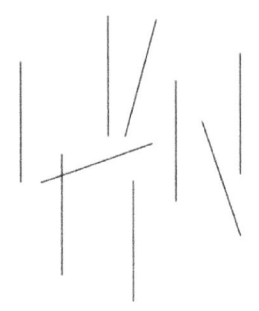

Like the majority of people, you probably had to either count the lines one at a time, or make an educated guess. Because there were more than 4 or 5 lines, your brain and eyes could not take in the objects at a glance and recognize the number without counting them one at a time. This is why the staff is made up of only 5 lines and why ledger lines are usually limited to 4 or 5 above and below the staff.

CLEFS

If we are limited to 4 or 5 ledger lines above and below the staff, how do we indicate pitches which are extremely high or extremely low? This is where the use of clefs comes in. A clef is a symbol placed at the beginning of a staff, which indicates the "exact" pitches the staff lines and spaces will represent. Without a clef we would not know which pitches the lines and spaces represent. This will become clearer as we move through this lesson and the next.

The following symbol is called a **treble clef**. When a treble clef is placed on the staff, it indicates that the 5 staff lines and 4 spaces will represent specific higher pitches. (This will be explained momentarily.) The staff itself is now referred to as a "treble" staff.

INTRODUCTION TO THE STAFF

The following symbol is called a **bass clef**. (pronounced "base") When a bass clef is placed on the staff, it indicates that the 5 staff lines and 4 spaces will represent specific lower pitches. The staff itself is now referred to as a "bass" staff.

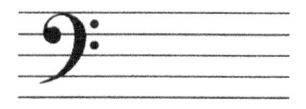

Listen to and compare the following two pitches.

(Lesson 14 - Audio 1)

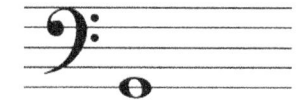

(Lesson 14 - Audio 2)

As you can see from the preceding example, the very same staff lines can represent completely different pitches depending on what clef is used. (We will learn to identify each staff line and space in the next lesson.)

Higher voices and instruments read music written in treble clef. Lower voices and instruments read music written in bass clef. There are many other types of clefs for all ranges of voices and instruments, but in this course we will only be studying the treble and bass clefs (since they are the most commonly used clefs).

TYPES OF MOVEMENT ON THE STAFF

There are three basic movements that notes can make on the staff: stepping, skipping, and repeating. Let's look at examples of each. Note: We read from left to right in music just as we do when reading words.

When a note is on a line and the next note is on the same line, it is called a **repeat**. The following notes are the same pitch.

When a note is in a space and the next note is in the same space, it is also called a **repeat**. Once again, the following notes are the same pitch.

INTRODUCTION TO THE STAFF

When a note is on a line and the next note is in the space above (or below), it is called a **step**. The following notes are stepping higher in pitch.

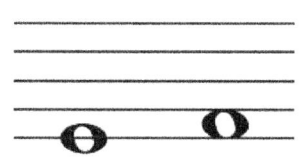

When a note is in a space and the next note is on the line above (or below), it is also called a **step**. Once again, the following notes are stepping higher in pitch.

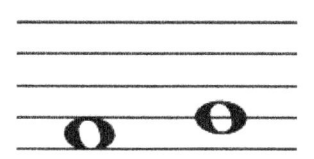

When a note is on a line and the next note is on the line above (or below), it is called a **skip**. The following notes are skipping higher in pitch.

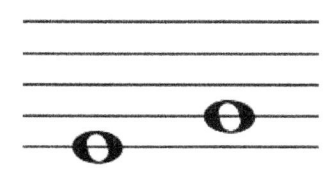

When a note is in a space and the next note is in the space above (or below), it is also called a **skip**. Once again, the following notes are skipping higher in pitch.

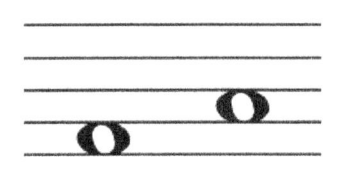

Memory Questions

What is a staff?
A staff is the device by which we indicate pitch.

How many lines does the modern day staff consist of?
The modern day staff consists of 5 lines.

How many spaces does the modern day staff consist of?
The modern day staff consists of 4 spaces.

What does a note's position on the staff determine?
A note's position on the staff determines its pitch.

Which notes placed on the staff have a higher pitch and which have a lower pitch?
Notes placed higher on the staff have a higher pitch; notes placed lower on the staff have a lower pitch.

What are ledger lines?
Ledger lines are the additional lines placed above or below the staff lines.

When are ledger lines necessary?
Ledger lines are necessary when the pitch of a note lies beyond the range of the staff lines.

What is a clef?
A clef is a symbol placed at the beginning of a staff, which indicates the "exact" pitches the staff lines and spaces will represent.

What is treble clef used for?
Treble clef is used when we want the 5 staff lines and 4 staff spaces to represent specific higher pitches.

What is bass clef used for?
Bass clef is used when we want the 5 staff lines and 4 staff spaces to represent specific lower pitches.

What are the three basic movements that notes can make on the staff?
The three basic movements that notes can make on the staff are steps, skips and repeats.

Lesson 14 Quiz

Log in to your course at www.udemy.com and take the quiz for this lesson.

15. LETTER NAMES OF THE STAFF

THE MUSICAL ALPHABET

In the last lesson we learned that a notes' position on the staff determines its pitch. In this lesson we are going to learn the specific names of each pitch. The notes placed on the staff lines and spaces are named with letters of the alphabet. Unlike the 26 letter English alphabet, the musical alphabet uses only 7 letters - A, B, C, D, E, F, and G. Once we reach the letter G, we begin the alphabet all over again. Here are the letter names of the notes on the treble staff and bass staff.

LETTER NAMES OF THE STAFF

If you look carefully you will notice that the pitches of the bass staff are just two letter names apart from those on the treble staff. Recognizing this fact will help you in your memorization of the staff names for the lesson quiz. For example, "G" in the bass staff is two letter names from "E" in the treble staff.

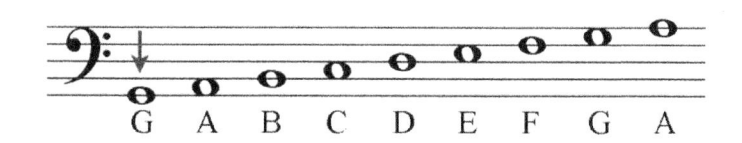

"C" in the bass staff is two letter names from "A" in the treble staff.

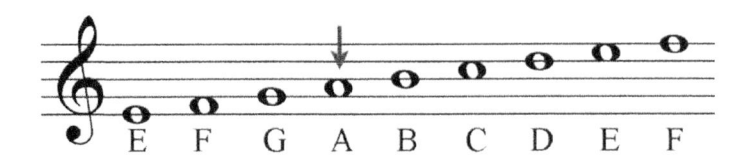

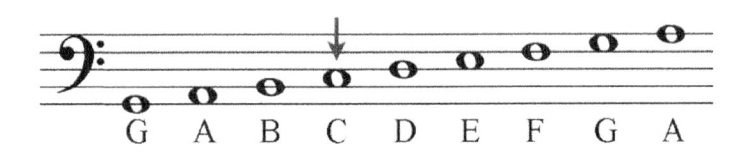

THE GRAND STAFF

The majority of voices and instruments use only one staff. As mentioned previously, the higher voices and instruments use a treble staff, while the lower voices and instruments use a bass staff. Certain instruments, such as the piano, have such a large range of pitches (from extremely high to extremely low) that both a treble and a bass staff is necessary. We call this the **grand staff**. (The brace on the left shows that the clefs have been joined together)

LETTER NAMES OF THE STAFF

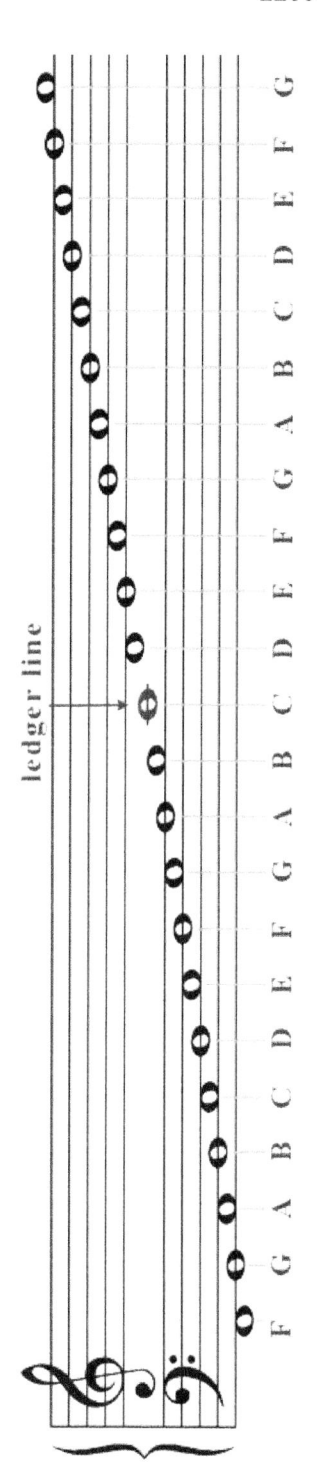

As you can see in the following diagram, by joining the treble and bass staves we can accommodate many more pitches. And with the addition of a single ledger line between the treble staff and the bass staff, the pitches can move from bass to treble without break. The note on this ledger line is called **middle C**.

Note: the letter names continue in either direction with the addition of ledger lines above and below the grand staff.

DIRECTION OF NOTE STEMS

The last thing we need to cover in this lesson is the note stem rule. As mentioned in the lesson on tuplets, we saw that note stems may point up or down. Note stems that point up are placed on the right of the note head.

Note stems that point down are placed on the left of the note head.

The note stem rule is as follows: If a note is **on or above** the middle line, the stem points down; if a note is **below** the middle line, the stem points up.

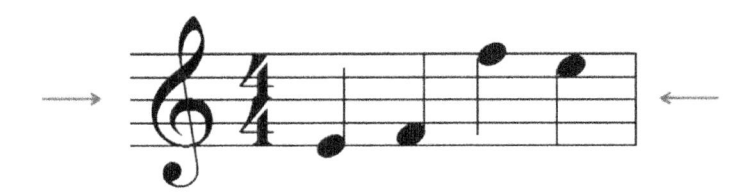

There are two reasons for this rule. First, by following this rule, most stems will stay within the staff, allowing room for text and other musical symbols to be placed below or above the staff lines. Second, by following this rule we also keep note stems in the treble staff from colliding with those in the bass staff. This makes reading the music on the page much easier for the musician. Let's demonstrate with some examples. The following diagram shows what would happen if we didn't have a note stem rule. Notice how the stems in this example nearly collide with one another. It's messy and hard to read.

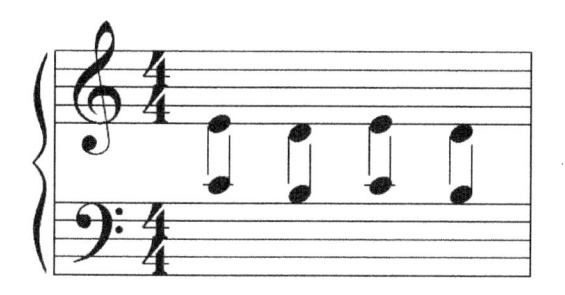

Here is the exact same example with the stem rule being observed. It's much neater and easier to read.

Memory Questions

How are the pitches on the staff lines and spaces named?
The pitches on the staff lines and spaces are named with letters of the alphabet.

How many letters are in the musical alphabet?
There are seven letters in the musical alphabet.

What are the seven letters of the musical alphabet?
The seven letters of the musical alphabet are A, B, C, D, E, F and G.

What comes after G in the musical alphabet?
After G, the musical alphabet begins all over again with A.

What is the grand staff?
The grand staff is the joining of the treble and bass staves.

Where is middle C located on the grand staff?
Middle C is located on the single ledger line between the treble and bass staves.

Lesson 15 Exercises

Log in to your course at www.udemy.com and practice the exercises for this lesson.

Lesson 15 Quiz

Log in to your course at www.udemy.com and take the quiz for this lesson.

16. INTRODUCTION TO THE KEYBOARD

LETTER NAMES OF THE KEYS

Although this is not a course on how to play the piano, understanding the piano keyboard is vital to understanding music theory. This is because most music theory concepts can be easily understood and demonstrated very clearly on the piano. Going forward in this course, you should always use a piano when trying to understand the theory concepts. If you do not own a piano or digital keyboard, you can find many virtual pianos online. Bookmark the following virtual piano for future use:

www.onlinepianist.com/virtual_piano

Let's begin by looking at the black keys. The black keys are arranged into alternating groups of 3's and 2's.

MUSIC THEORY

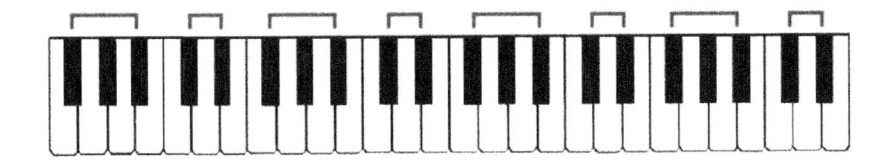

Locate the white key directly to the left of the group of 2 black keys. We call this note "C".

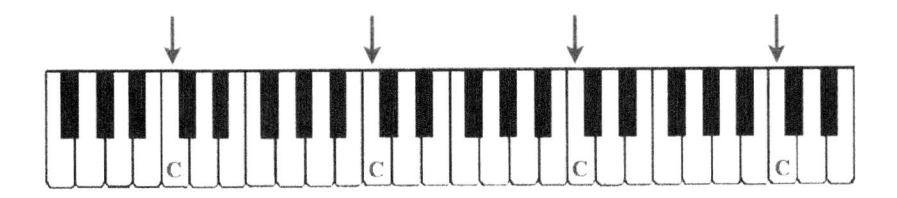

Locate the white key directly to the left of the group of 3 black keys. We call this note "F".

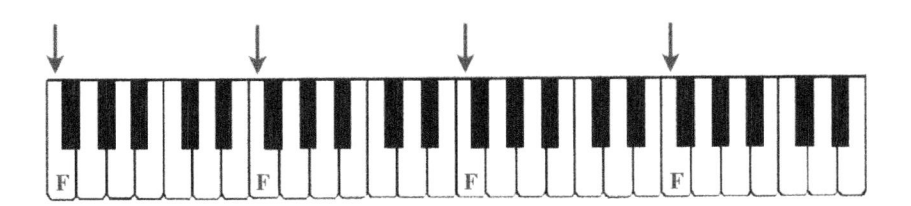

One purpose of the black keys is to serve as points of reference. Without them we would not be able to locate any particular pitch. To illustrate this, try and find the piano key "C" on the following diagram.

Since all of the keys in the preceding example look exactly the same, we are not able to locate "C" (or any other pitch for that matter). We need the black keys as reference points.

Now that we know where "C" and "F" are located on the keyboard, let's learn the names of the other white keys. (We will learn the names of the black keys in another lesson.)

Just as the musical alphabet is repeated on the staff lines, it is also repeated on the keyboard (once "G" is reached we begin again at "A").

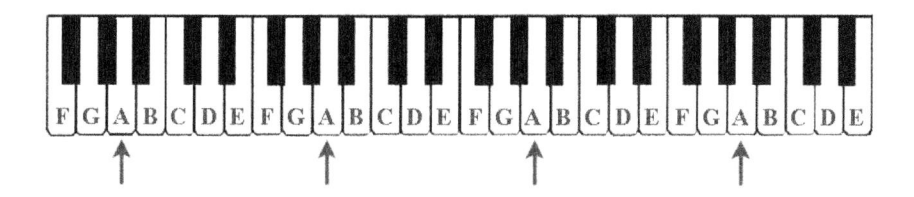

Be sure to memorize the key names before taking the lesson quiz.

RELATION TO THE STAFF

Next, let's take a look at the piano keyboard's relation to the staff. Each of the staff lines we learned in the previous lesson corresponds to a particular piano key.

MUSIC THEORY

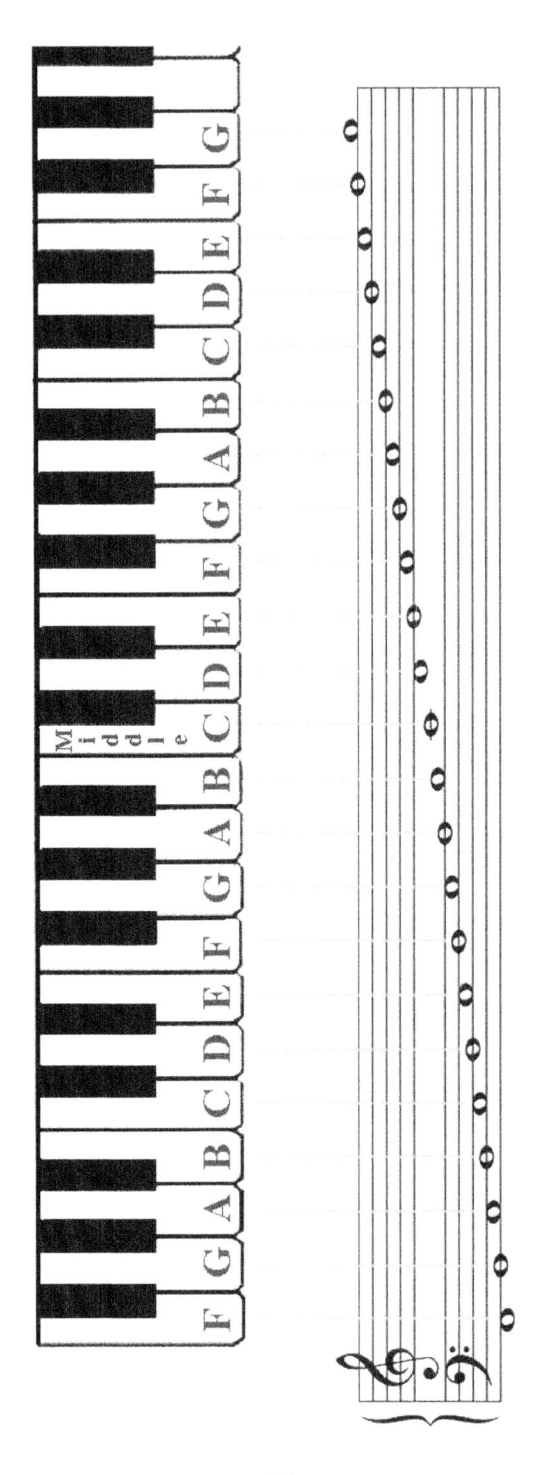

The single ledger line between the treble and bass staves corresponds with the "C" nearest to the middle of the keyboard (middle "C"). Be sure to memorize the diagram before taking the lesson quiz.

There is one important distinction to be made between pitches on the staff and pitches on the piano keyboard. In the previous lesson we saw that pitches on the staff get higher as they are placed higher up on the staff. On the piano keyboard, higher and lower refer to right and left, not up and down. The following diagram will help to illustrate this.

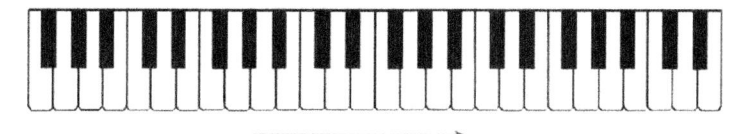

On the keyboard, pitches get higher as you move horizontally (from left to right).

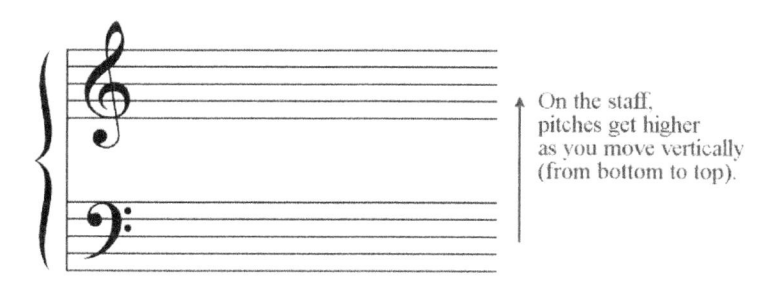

On the staff, pitches get higher as you move vertically (from bottom to top).

HALF STEPS AND WHOLE STEPS

To understand the piano keyboard we also need to understand how distance on the keyboard is measured. We measure distance on the keyboard either in **half steps** or **whole steps**. A half step is the distance from one key to the very next key. This can be the key directly to the right or directly to the left. (It does not matter if the keys are black or white.) Here are a few examples of half steps.

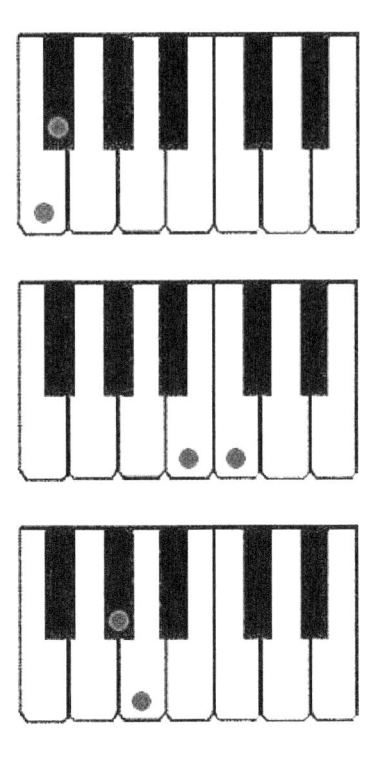

A whole step is equal to the distance of two half steps. This means that there will be a space of one key in between the two keys. Here are a few examples of whole steps.

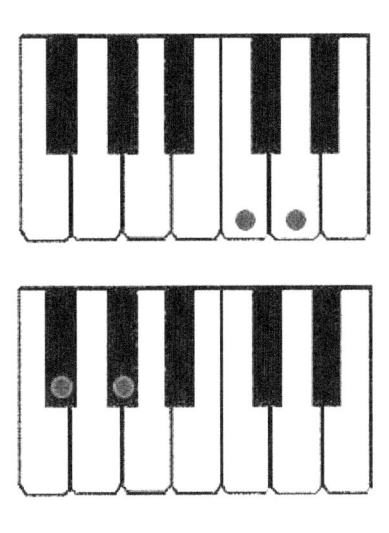

INTRODUCTION TO THE KEYBOARD

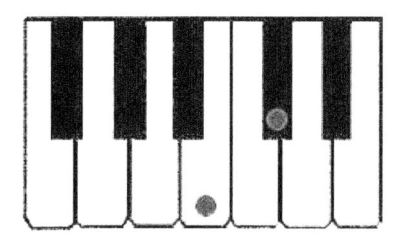

Memory Questions

How are the black keys on the piano keyboard arranged?
The black keys on the piano keyboard are arranged into groups of 3's and 2's.

What is the letter name of the white key directly to the left of the group of two black keys?
The letter name of the white key directly to the left of the group of two black keys is "C".

What is the letter name of the white key directly to the left of the group of three black keys?
The letter name of the white key directly to the left of the group of three black keys is "F".

What is one purpose of the black keys?
One purpose of the black keys is to serve as reference points.

What is the result of playing keys further and further to the right on the piano?
The result of playing keys further and further to the right on the piano is higher pitches.

What is the result of playing keys further and further to the left on the piano?
The result of playing keys further and further to the left on the piano is lower pitches.

What letter comes after "G" on the keyboard?
The letter "A" comes after "G" on the keyboard.

Where is middle "C" located on the keyboard?
Middle "C" is the "C" nearest to the middle of the keyboard.

What is a half step?
A half step is the distance from one key to the very next key. This can be the key directly to the right or directly to the left. (black or white)

What is a whole step?
A whole step is equal to the distance of two half steps.

Lesson 16 Quiz

Log in to your course at www.udemy.com and take the quiz for this lesson.

17. SHARPS & FLATS ON THE KEYBOARD

SHARPS

At the end of the last lesson we learned that distance on the piano keyboard is measured in half steps and whole steps. If you remember, a half step was defined as the distance from one key to the very next key. This will be important for understanding sharps and flats.

A sharp sign is a symbol which indicates that we are to play a particular pitch one half step higher. The sharp sign looks like this...

♯

The letter "F" with a sharp sign after it indicates that we are to play the pitch one half step higher than "F" (the next key to the right). We call this key "F sharp".

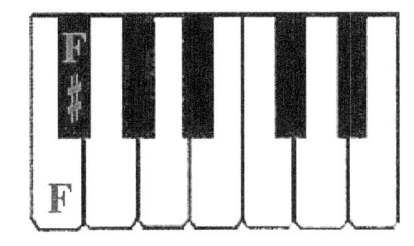

It is a common misconception that sharps are the black keys. While it is true that some sharps are black keys, not all of them are. Here is an example of a sharp that is a white key.

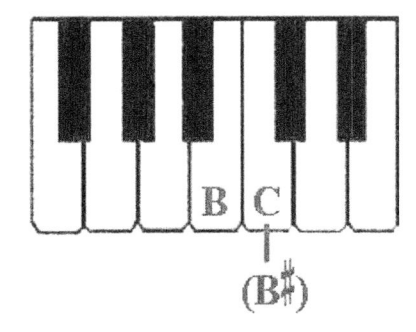

As you can see, the key one half step to the right of "B" is a white key. Since this key is already named "C" it will therefore have two different names. "C" and "B sharp" are two different names for the same key.

When two notes sound the same but are spelled differently, they are called **enharmonic equivalents**. An example of something analogous to this in language would be the words "beet" and "beat". Both words have the same sound when spoken, but they look differently on the page. (They also have different meanings and are therefore used differently in a sentence.) "B sharp" is the enharmonic equivalent of "C". This probably seems a little silly, but there is a reason for certain piano keys having two different names. We will learn why in later lessons.

FLATS

A flat sign is a symbol which indicates that we are to play a particular pitch one half step lower. The flat sign looks like this:

$$\flat$$

The letter "B" with a flat sign after it indicates that we are to play the pitch one half step lower than "B" (the next key to the left). We call this key "B flat".

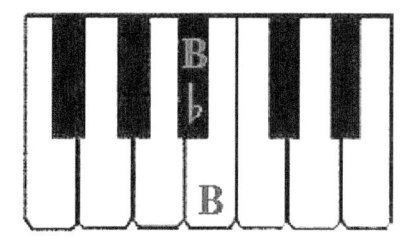

It is a common misconception that flats are the black keys. While it is true that some flats are black keys, not all of them are. Here is an example of a flat that is a white key.

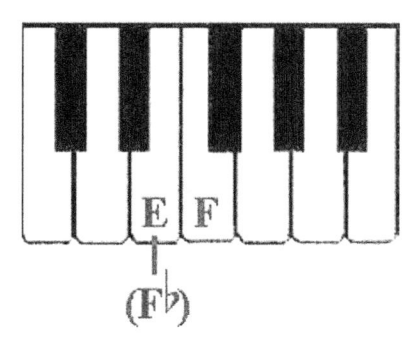

As you can see, the key one half step to the left of "F" is a white key. Since this key is already named "E", it will therefore have two different names. This key can be called "F", or in certain circumstances (which we will learn about later) it can be called by the enharmonic equivalent name "F flat".

White keys are not the only keys that can have two names. Every black key also has two names. Here is an example.

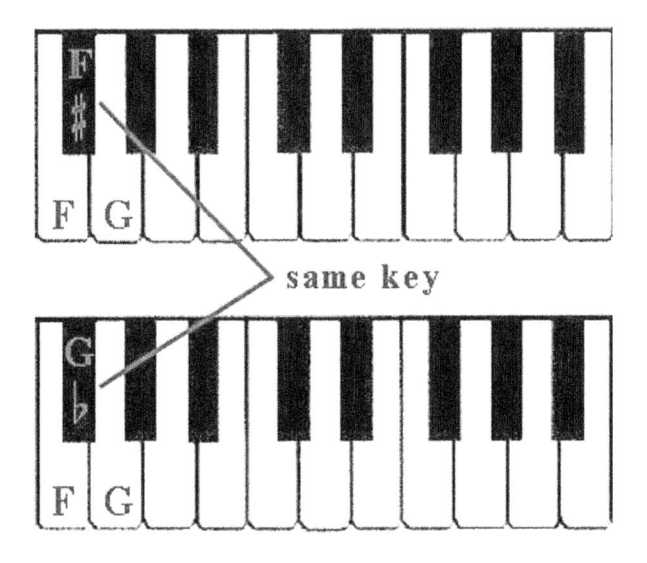

Since the key to the right of "F" and the key to the left of "G" is the exact same key, it will therefore have two names (one half step higher than "F" is "F sharp", one half step lower than "G" is "G flat"). "F sharp" and "G flat" are therefore enharmonic equivalents.

The following diagram lists all the possible letter names for each key. Be sure to memorize it before taking the lesson quiz.

SHARPS & FLATS ON THE KEYBOARD

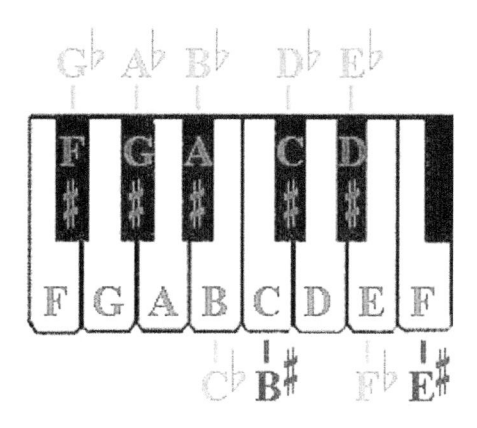

Memory Questions

What is a sharp sign?
A sharp sign is a symbol which indicates that we are to play a particular pitch one half step higher.

What is a flat sign?
A flat sign is a symbol which indicates that we are to play a particular pitch one half step lower.

What are enharmonic equivalents?
Enharmonic equivalents are notes that sound the same but are spelled differently.

Can piano keys have multiple names?
Yes, piano keys can have multiple names.

Lesson 17 Quiz

Log in to your course at www.udemy.com and take the quiz for this lesson.

18. SHARPS & FLATS ON THE STAFF

READING SHARPS ON THE STAFF

In the last lesson we learned about sharps and flats on the piano keyboard. In this lesson we will learn how to read sharps and flats when they are placed next to notes on the staff. Let's begin with sharps.

For this example we will use the note on the bottom space of the treble staff, or "F". When we see a sharp sign in front of an "F" it indicates that we are to play an "F sharp" instead of an "F". In the following diagram, you will see the note on the staff as well as its location on the keyboard.

(Important: all sharps are placed to the left of the note on the same line or space as the note.)

SHARPS & FLATS ON THE STAFF

To determine which line or space the sharp is on, locate the two thick horizontal bars of the sharp sign. If the line passes between these two bars, the sharp is on the line.

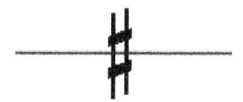

If the two thick horizontal bars of the sharp sign fall between the staff lines, the sharp is in a space.

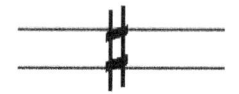

The most important thing to remember about sharps is the following rule: all notes on the same line or space that occur after the sharp are also played as sharped notes until the end of the measure. In the next measure, the sharp has no affect and all sharped notes return to non-sharped notes. This is illustrated in the following diagram.

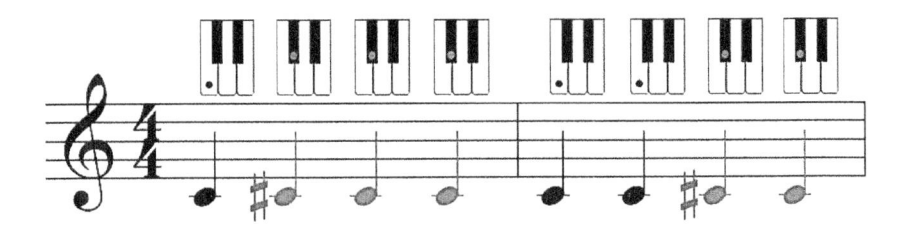

(Lesson 18 - Audio 1)

As you can see, the first note is played as a non-sharped note; the next three notes are played as sharped notes because the sharp sign affects all the subsequent notes on the same line for the remainder of the measure. In the second measure, the first two notes are played as non-sharped notes; the last two notes are played as sharped notes because the sharp sign affects all the subsequent notes on the same line for the remainder of the measure.

READING FLATS ON THE STAFF

For our next example we will use the note on the middle line of the treble staff, or "B". When we see a flat sign in front of a "B" it indicates that we are to play a "B flat" instead of a "B". In the following diagram, you will see the note on the staff as well as its location on the keyboard.

(Important: all flats are placed to the left of the note on the same line or space as the note.)

SHARPS & FLATS ON THE STAFF

To determine which line or space the flat is on, locate the belly of the flat sign. If the line passes through the belly, the flat is on the line.

If the belly of the flat sign falls between the staff lines, the flat is in a space.

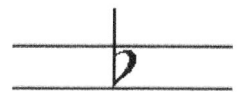

As with sharps, the most important thing to remember about flats is the following rule: all notes on the same line or space that occur after the flat are also played as flatted notes until the end of the measure. In the next measure, the flat has no affect and all flatted notes return to non-flatted notes. This is illustrated in the following diagram.

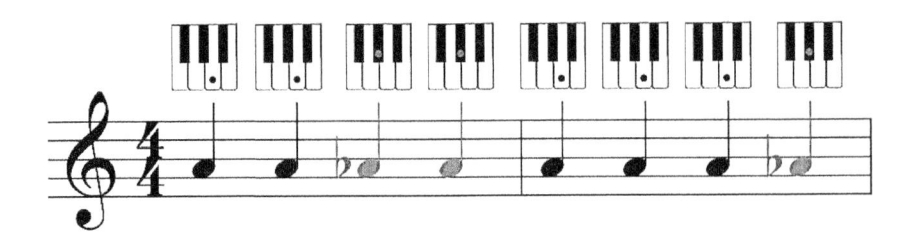

(Lesson 18 - Audio 2)

As you can see, the first two notes are played as non-flatted notes; the next two notes are played as flatted notes because the flat sign affects all the subsequent notes on the same space for the remainder of the measure. In the second measure, the first three notes are played as non-flatted notes; the last note is played as a flatted note because of the new flat sign.

THE NATURAL SIGN

As we learned above, sharps and flats apply to all subsequent notes on the same line or space until the end of measure. To eliminate a sharp or flat from any of the subsequent notes in the measure, a natural sign is used.

A natural sign is a symbol to the left of a note head that eliminates the effects of any preceding sharp or flat for the remainder of the measure (or until another sharp or flat is seen). This is illustrated in the following diagram.

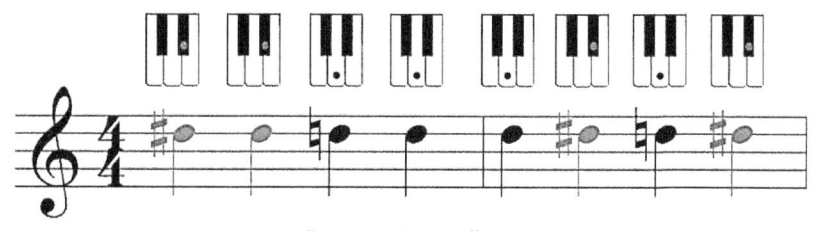

(Lesson 18 - Audio 3)

As you can see, the first two notes are played as sharped notes; the next two notes are played as non-sharped notes because the natural sign eliminated the effects of the previous sharp. In the second measure, the first note is played as a non-sharped note; the second note is played as a sharped note; the third note is played as a non-sharped note because the natural sign eliminated the effects of the previous sharp; the last note is played as a sharped note again since another sharp sign has been placed subsequent to the natural sign.

Memory Questions

Where are sharps and flats placed?
Sharps and flats are placed to the left of the note head on the same line or space.

What does the sharp rule state?
The sharp rule states: all notes on the same line or space that occur after the sharp are also played as sharped notes until the end of the measure.

What affect does the sharp have in the next measure?
In the next measure the sharp has no affect and all sharped notes return to non-sharped notes.

What does the flat rule state?
The flat rule states: all notes on the same line or space that occur after the flat are also played as flatted notes until the end of the measure.

What affect does the flat have in the next measure?
In the next measure, the flat has no affect and all flatted notes return to non-flatted notes.

What is a natural sign?
A natural sign is a symbol to the left of a note head that eliminates the effects of any preceding sharp or flat for the remainder of the measure (or until another sharp or flat is seen).

Lesson 18 Quiz

Log in to your course at www.udemy.com and take the quiz for this lesson.

19. INTRODUCTION TO INTERVALS

MEASURING MUSICAL DISTANCE

In this lesson we are going to learn how distance in music is measured. The distance from one pitch to another is called an **interval**. (From the Latin, "Intervallum", meaning "the space between two walls"; *inter* = between, *vallum* = wall)

Distance between pitches can be measured on the piano keyboard or on the staff. Measuring an interval on the keyboard is simply counting keys. We call the interval below a 5th since it encompasses 5 keys. (Always remember to count the starting and ending keys!)

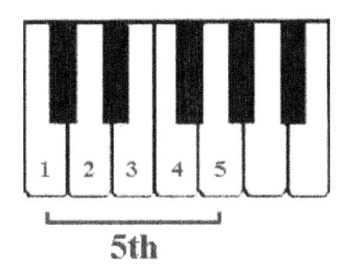

Measuring an interval on the staff is simply counting lines and spaces. We call the interval below a 5th, since it encompasses 5 lines and spaces. (Always remember to count the starting and ending lines or spaces!)

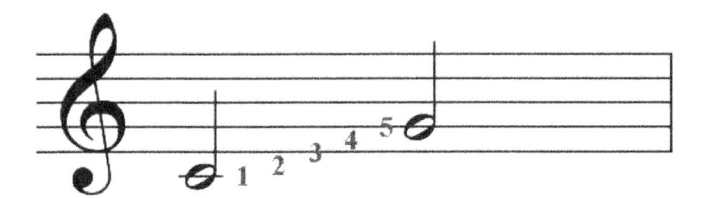

There are 7 basic intervals. Here are examples of each (both on the staff and the keyboard).

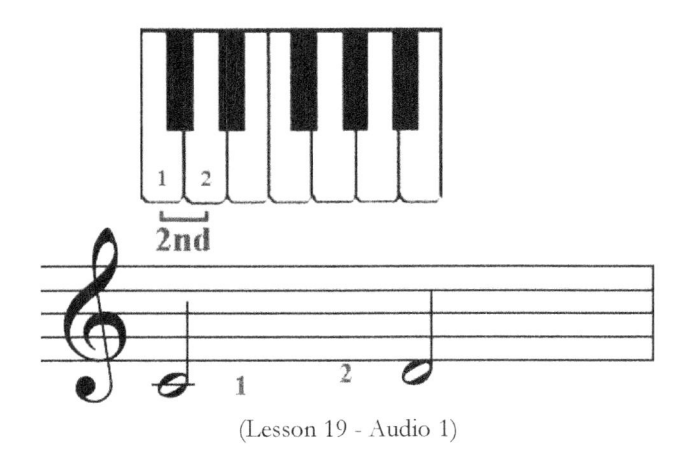

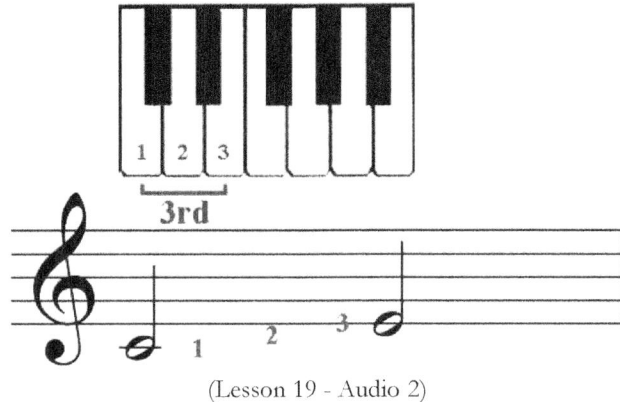

(Lesson 19 - Audio 1)

(Lesson 19 - Audio 2)

INTRODUCTION TO INTERVALS

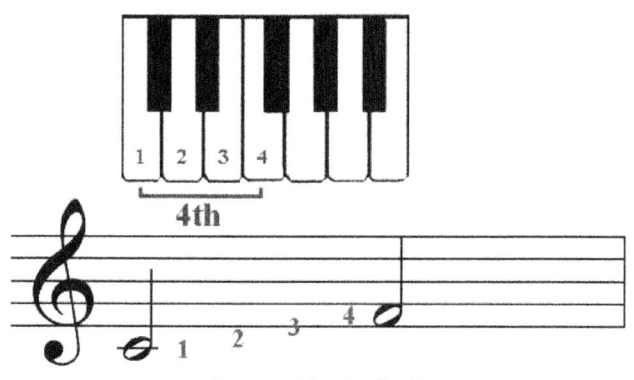

4th

(Lesson 19 - Audio 3)

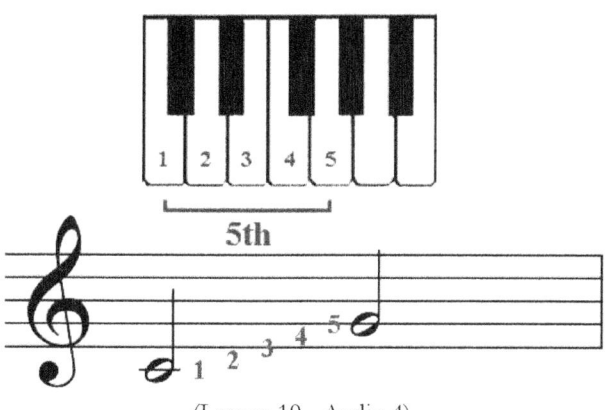

5th

(Lesson 19 - Audio 4)

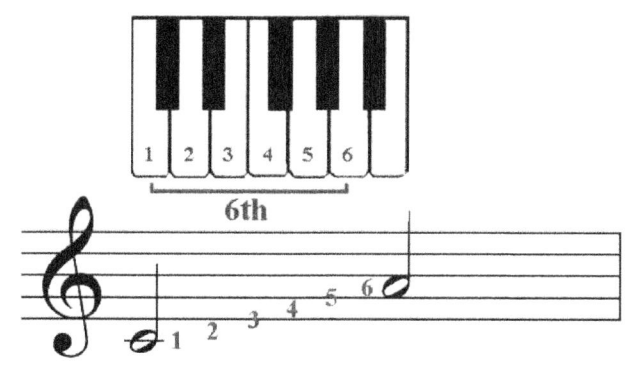

6th

(Lesson 19 - Audio 5)

MUSIC THEORY

(Lesson 19 - Audio 6)

(Lesson 19 - Audio 7)

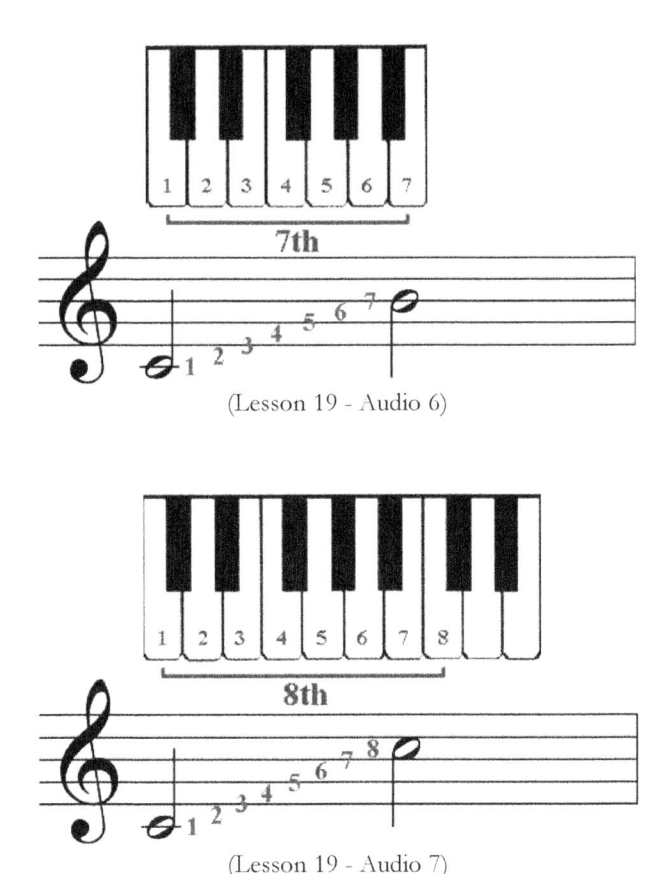

You may have noticed in the audio clips above, that the two pitches were first played consecutively and then played simultaneously. Pitches played consecutively are called **melodic intervals**; pitches played simultaneously are called **harmonic intervals**. Most music contains both types of intervals.

When harmonic intervals are written on the staff, the notes are placed vertically (one above the other). The one exception is the harmonic 2nd, which is written with the upper note placed slightly to the side (but touching the other note). This is due to the fact that the notes would overlap if placed vertically.

INTRODUCTION TO INTERVALS

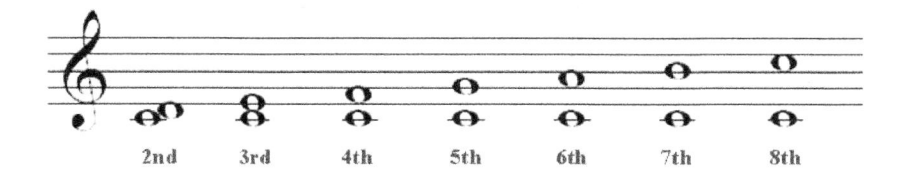

MUSICAL RATIOS

As we proceed through this course we will be measuring and comparing pitches. In order to do so, we need to understand **ratio**. A ratio is a comparison of two quantities. An example of a ratio can be seen in the mixing of concrete. If the instructions on a bag of concrete mix say that for every 4 pounds of cement you need to add 1 corresponding unit of water, then the ratio of cement to water is "4 to 1". This can also be written as 4:1.

In a previous lesson we mentioned the ancient Greek philosopher and mathematician, Pythagoras (570-495 BC). He is considered to be the first to discover that the pitches of an interval have mathematical ratios. Pythagoras discovered this by measuring and comparing different lengths of vibrating strings. The device he used in his experiments was called a **monochord**. (From the Greek; mono = one, chord = string) The monochord consists of a string stretched over a sound box and attached to both ends. A moveable bridge was used to mathematically divide and measure the vibrating string lengths.

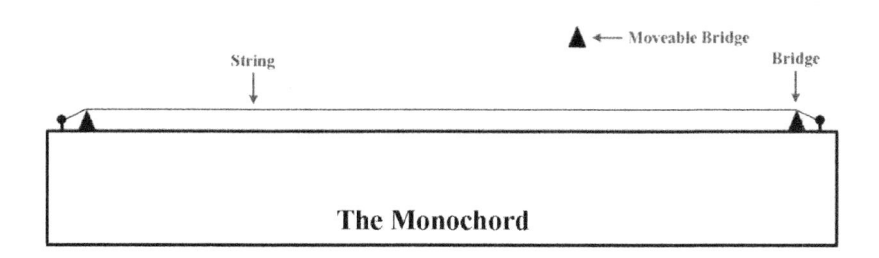

The Monochord

We will now illustrate in the following diagrams, the mathematical ratios of intervals that Pythagoras discovered.

If the string is divided into 2 equal parts, 1 part vibrating will produce a pitch twice the frequency of the entire string vibrating. To divide the string in half, the moveable bridge is placed directly in the center of the string. When the right side of the string is plucked we will hear the pitch that is twice the frequency of the entire string. To hear the entire string vibrating, the moveable bridge is removed and the string is plucked.

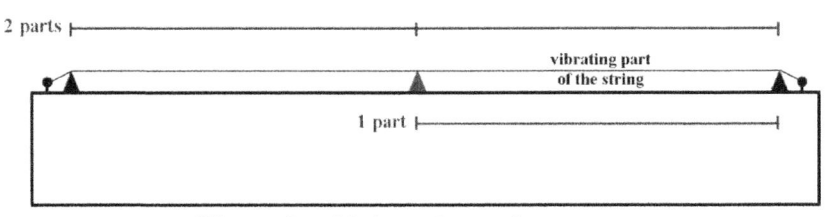

The ratio of 2:1 produces the octave.

The interval created through this division of the string is the 8th or "octave". We call this the ratio of 2:1; 2 equal parts of the string vibrating (the entire string) compared to 1 part of the string vibrating (half of the string).

Here is the ratio illustrated on the keyboard. (For this example, and all of the following examples, we are assuming that the entire length of vibrating string produces the pitch "C".)

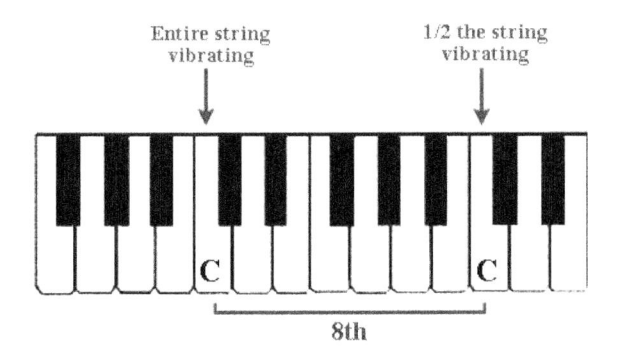

INTRODUCTION TO INTERVALS

Next, we divide the string into 3 equal parts. If the entire string vibrating produces a "C", then 2 of these parts vibrating will produce a "G" a 5th above "C". The ratio is called 3 to 2 because we are comparing 3 equal parts of the string vibrating (the entire string) to 2 of these parts vibrating (two-thirds of the string).

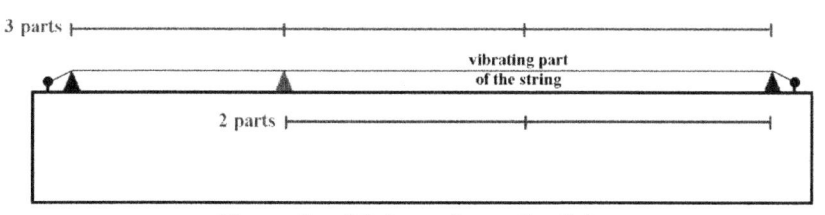

The ratio of 3:2 produces the 5th.

Here is the ratio illustrated on the keyboard.

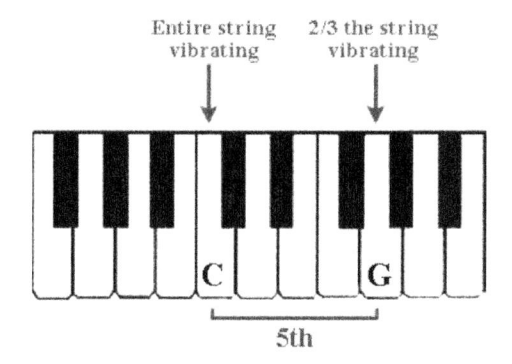

In terms of frequency, the "G" vibrates (completes one cycle) 3 times for every 2 times the "C" vibrates. <u>Note</u>: The ratio of the frequencies is the inverse ratio of the string lengths. For example, the ratio of the string lengths ("C" to "G") is 3 to 2; the ratio of the frequencies ("C" to "G") is 2 to 3. (Frequency = cycles per second. See lesson 13 for review.)

Next, we divide the string into 4 equal parts. If the entire string vibrating produces a "C", then 3 of these parts vibrating will produce an "F" a 4th above "C". The ratio is called 4 to 3 because we are comparing 4 equal parts of the string vibrating (the entire string) to 3 of these parts vibrating (three-fourths of the string).

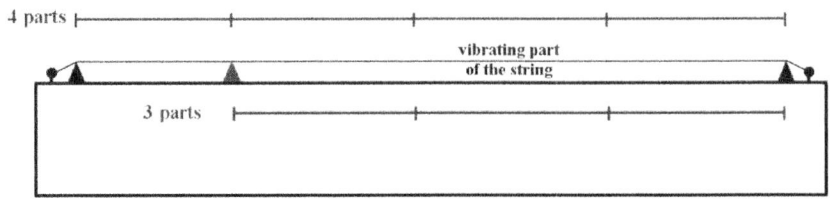

The ratio of 4:3 produces the 4th.

Here is the ratio illustrated on the keyboard.

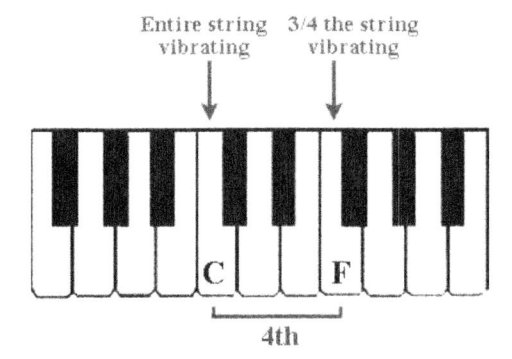

In terms of frequency, the "F" vibrates 4 times for every 3 times the "C" vibrates. The ratio of the string lengths ("C" to "F") is 4 to 3; the ratio of the frequencies ("C" to "F") is 3 to 4.)

The entire history of Western music might have been completely different if Pythagoras had not made his discovery. His findings also gave people the ability to objectively measure the **consonance** and **dissonance** of two pitches. (Pitches that sound well together are called consonances; pitches that do not sound well together are called dissonances.) During Pythagoras' time, the intervals that were considered consonant were the 8th, 5th, and 4th. The simplest whole number ratio and simplest division of the string (the 8th) was considered the most consonant; the second simplest whole number ratio and second simplest division of the string (the 5th) was considered the second most consonant; the third simplest whole number ratio and third simplest division of the string (the 4th) was considered the third most consonant. Thus, the beauty of a harmony was not a subjective reality determined by the listener, but an objective reality measured through mathematical proportions. We will study more about ratios, consonance and dissonance as we proceed through the course.

Note: You can try any of the experiments above by building your own monochord. There are many videos online that demonstrate how to build one from scratch, or you can purchase a kit. If you aren't handy with carpentry, you can also do these experiments using any stringed instrument (such as guitar or violin) and a measuring tape.

Memory Questions

What Latin word is the word interval derived from?
The word interval is derived from the Latin, "intervallum", meaning, "the space between two walls" (inter = between, vallum = wall)

What is an interval?
An interval is the distance from one pitch to another pitch.

How are intervals measured on the keyboard?
Intervals are measured on the keyboard by counting keys.

How are intervals measured on the staff?
Intervals are measured on the staff by counting lines and spaces.

What is a melodic interval?
A melodic interval is two distinct consecutive pitches.

What is a harmonic interval?
A harmonic interval is two distinct simultaneous pitches.

What is a ratio?
A ratio is a comparison of two quantities.

Who was Pythagoras?
Pythagoras was a Greek philosopher and mathematician who lived from 570-495 BC.

What is a monochord?
A monochord is an ancient one-stringed instrument used to measure and compare pitches.

What is Pythagoras credited for discovering?
Pythagoras is credited for discovering the mathematical ratios of pitches.

What is the ratio of an 8th? (in terms of string lengths)
The ratio of an 8th is 2:1.

What is the ratio of a 5th? (in terms of string lengths)
The ratio of a 5th is 3:2.

What is the ratio of a 4th? (in terms of string lengths)
The ratio of a 4th is 4:3.

What is the ratio of an interval's frequencies?
The ratio of an interval's frequencies is the inverse ratio of the string lengths.

What are pitches that sound well together called?
Pitches that sound well together are called consonances.

What are pitches that do not sound well together called?
Pitches that do not sound well together are called dissonances.

How can consonance and dissonance be objectively measured?
Consonance and dissonance can be objectively measured by an intervals' ratio.

Which ratios produce more consonant sounding intervals?
Simpler whole number ratios produce more consonant sounding intervals.

Lesson 19 Quiz

Log in to your course at www.udemy.com and take the quiz for this lesson.

20. INTRODUCTION TO THE SCALE

STEPS OF THE SCALE

In the last lesson we learned about Pythagoras' discovery regarding the ratios of pitches. In this lesson we are going to learn how his discovery played an important role in giving us the modern day scale.

There are many different types of scales that we will be studying in this course. In this lesson we are going to be learning about the **major scale**. The major scale is a particular sequence of whole steps and half steps encompassing 8 pitches. The sequence in ascending order is: whole step, whole step, half step, whole step, whole step, whole step, half step.

INTRODUCTION TO THE SCALE

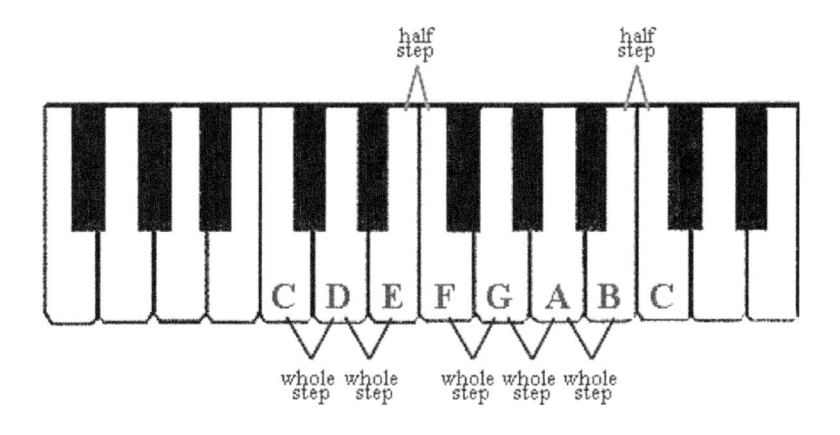

(Lesson 20 - Audio 1)

We call the preceding example a "C" major scale, since the sequence of whole steps and half steps begins and ends on "C". It is very important to understand that as long as the sequence of whole steps and half steps remains the same, a scale may begin on any pitch. Here is an example of a "G" major scale. It has the same sequence of whole steps and half steps, but because it begins and ends on "G" it is called a "G" major scale rather than a "C" major scale.

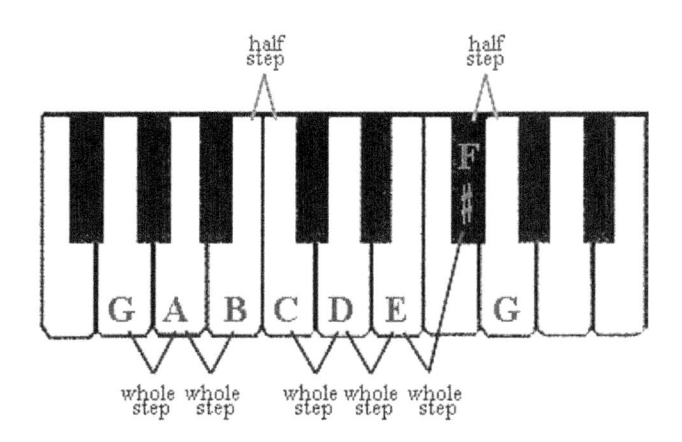

(Lesson 20 - Audio 2)

As you can see, the "C" major scale consisted of all white keys (no sharps or flats), whereas the "G" major scale contains one black key (an "F sharp"). A black key is used to maintain the sequence of whole steps and half steps. For example, if "F" was used instead of "F sharp", the sequence of whole steps and half steps would have been: whole, whole, half, whole, whole, half, whole. This would not be a major scale. It would also sound very different from a major scale due to the difference in the sequential order of whole steps and half steps.

Important: the pitches of the scale must be neighbor letters of the musical alphabet. For example, "F sharp" was used above rather than its enharmonic equivalent, "G flat", to avoid having two "G's" in a row. (G, A, B, C, D, E, G flat, G) Using "G flat" would be an incorrect "spelling" of the scale.

Here is the "G" major scale on the staff.

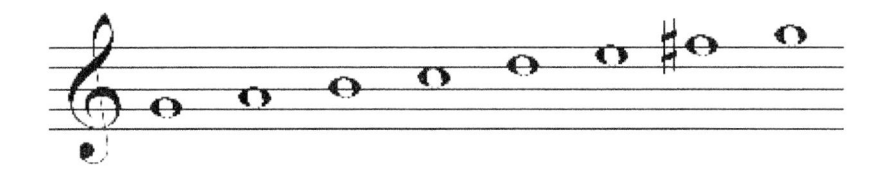

Note: Whole steps and half steps can be easily perceived on the keyboard. They are less apparent on the staff. Know your piano keyboard well so that when you see the notes on the staff you will have a mental image of the corresponding whole steps and half steps on the keyboard.

TETRACHORDS

The human ear is an amazing organ. It can perceive over one thousand distinct pitches. If we are able to hear so many pitches, why

INTRODUCTION TO THE SCALE

does a major scale contain only 8? Who chose 8 pitches and why? To answer this question, we must look at the octave (8th) and Pythagoras' discovery that we read about in the previous lesson.

The very basis for the scale is the octave. This is because the octave encompasses all possible pitches. Let's illustrate what is meant by this with an example. Imagine for a moment a fire engine racing to a fire with its siren blazing. Listen to the sound of the siren raising and falling in pitch. If you were to sing the pitch "C", and then slide (as a siren does) the pitch of your voice up to a "C" an octave higher, and then back down again to the "C" that you began with, you will have sung every possible pitch between those two "C"s. Any higher or lower than the two "C"s and you would simply be repeating the same pitches at higher or lower frequencies. These two pitches, an octave apart, are like natural boundaries; making the octave the obvious starting point for the scale.

With the boundaries of the scale firmly established, the next question is: how was it determined which of the countless pitches that fall between an octave should make up the musical scale? Should there be 4 pitches between each octave? 9? 12?

$$C \xleftrightarrow{?\ ?\ ?\ ?\ ?\ ?\ ?\ ?\ ?\ ?} C$$

The answer lies in the interval of a 2nd and Pythagoras' discovery of its ratio. After the octave, the next most consonant intervals were the 5th and the 4th. Through mathematics, Pythagoras found that the difference between these two intervals was the 2nd (a ratio of 9:8; or 8/9 of a string vibrating).

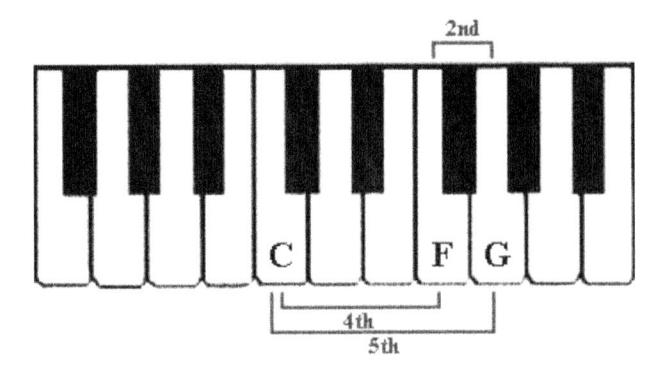

This may not seem like much of a discovery, since we can easily see the on the piano keyboard that the difference between a 5th and a 4th is a 2nd. But we must remember that the ancient Greeks did not have pianos; they figured this out using only mathematics. In fact, the reason the piano keyboard looks and sounds the way it does is actually a result of this discovery! Pythagoras had discovered a mathematical reason for the tuning of a **whole tone**. The whole tone would go on to become one of the intervals used to create the scale (which we will see below) and people from many cultures and times since then would use the whole tone in their music. (If you think the term "whole tone" sounds a lot like the term "whole step" that we learned about in a previous lesson, that's because the whole step is the modern day equivalent of the whole tone.)

To see how whole tones became part of the scale, we need to take a brief look at **tetrachords** (from the Greek, meaning "four strings"; tetra = four, chord = string). The Greeks used tetrachords to tune the strings of their instruments. One early Greek instrument was the "lyre". A lyre was like a small hand held harp and usually consisted of four to seven strings. These strings were tuned in a particular way. A lyre with four strings had the first and last strings tuned to the interval of a 4th. There were a number of different ways to tune the two middle strings, but the most common way was with the whole tone. So that you can better understand what we are talking about, here is what a tetrachord would look like on a piano keyboard.

INTRODUCTION TO THE SCALE

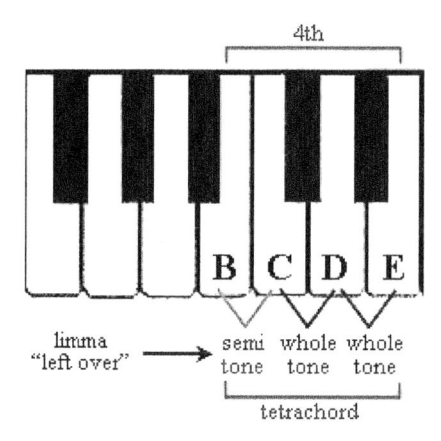

The Greeks found that if the strings were tuned so that each was a whole tone apart in pitch, then the first and last strings would not be a 4th apart in pitch. They discovered that a 4th is actually two whole tones and a remainder, rather than a total of 3 whole tones. The remainder became the very basis for the semi tone (the ancient Greek equivalent of our modern day half step)! They called the remainder "limma" (from the Greek, meaning "left over"). A tetrachord was therefore two whole tones and a semi tone (the ancient Greek equivalent of two whole steps and a half step).

The Greeks also used tetrachords to tune seven stringed lyres. To do so, they would use two tetrachords and "overlap" them (i.e., the highest string from the first tetrachord and the lowest string from the second tetrachord would be the same string). The pitch "E", in the following diagram, is the top pitch of one tetrachord and the bottom of the other tetrachord.

MUSIC THEORY

tetrachord   tetrachord

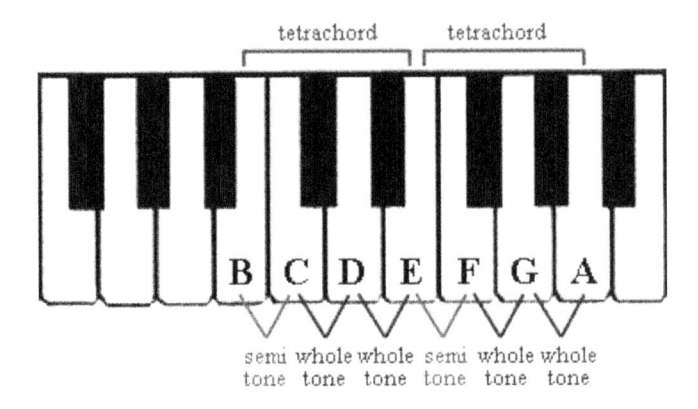

B C D E F G A

semi whole whole semi whole whole
tone tone tone tone tone tone

The Greeks were able to invent many different scales by placing the "limma" in various places. We call these various scales "modes". You will learn about modes in a later lesson.

There are no known surviving texts written directly by Pythagoras. What we know of Pythagoras comes from others writing about him. Because of this, historians differ in opinion on the exact method he used to create the scale. Another commonly held view is that Pythagoras created the scale using only the ratio of the 5th (3:2). Let's demonstrate how this would be done.

1. Choose any pitch. ("D" is used in the following example for ease of teaching.)
2. Starting from that pitch ("D"), find three pitches each a 5th higher than the previous.
3. Starting from the same pitch ("D"), find three pitches each a 5th lower than the previous.

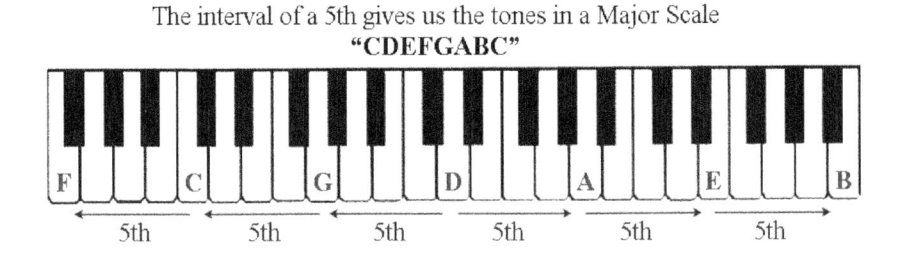

The interval of a 5th gives us the tones in a Major Scale
"CDEFGABC"

F   C   G   D   A   E   B

5th   5th   5th   5th   5th   5th

We now have a total of 7 pitches, each a 5th apart. By placing these 7 pitches into the space of one octave we get the 7 different pitches of the major scale: CDEFGAB(C).

Pythagoras could have continued the series of 5ths in either direction to include even more pitches in the scale, but he stopped with seven. Why seven? Seven was an important number to the Greeks, since they believed there to be seven heavenly bodies circling the earth (our sun and moon, Mercury, Venus, Mars, Saturn, and Jupiter). These heavenly bodies were each thought to emit a pitch. Together these pitches created what the Greeks called the "music of the spheres". They claimed that people couldn't hear the pitches because they were born hearing them and because they are constantly playing in the background of our lives.

As you can see from the discussion above, the discovery of the whole tone and semi tone, and the use of tetrachords are the origins of the modern day scale. This lesson was just an overview of the scale and its origin. We will learn much more about scales in later lessons.

Memory Questions

What is a major scale?
A major scale is a particular sequence of whole steps and half steps encompassing 8 pitches. The sequence in ascending order is: whole step, whole step, half step, whole step, whole step, whole step, half step.

What is the basis for the scale?
The basis for the scale is the octave.

Why is the octave the basis for the scale?
The octave is the basis for the scale because it is a natural boundary that encompasses all possible pitches.

What is the basis for the whole tone?
The basis for the whole tone is the difference between a 5th and a 4th.

What is the basis for the semi tone?
The basis for the semi tone is the difference between a 4th and two whole tones.

What is a tetrachord?
A tetrachord is a total of four pitches tuned in such a way that the result equals two whole tones and one semi tone.

What are the origins of the scale?
The origins of the scale are the discovery of the whole tone and semi tone by the Greeks, and their use of tetrachords in tuning their instruments.

Lesson 20 Exercises

Log in to your course at www.udemy.com and practice the exercises for this lesson.

Lesson 20 Quiz

Log in to your course at www.udemy.com and take the quiz for this lesson.

21. MAJOR KEYS

THE DEFINITION OF A "KEY"

Have you ever wondered how composers and songwriters decide which pitches to use in their music? The pitches they use are determined by the **key** they are writing in. A key is a specific group of pitches used to write a piece of music (or part of a piece of music).

Where does this specific group of pitches come from? The scale! Composers and songwriters use the 7 distinct pitches of scales to write their music. For example, if a song is made up from the pitches of the C major scale, we say that the song is written in the "key" of C major; if a song is made up from the pitches of the G major scale, we say that the song is written in the "key" of G major.

A key is comparable to an artist's palette of colors. If the artist's palette consists of the 3 colors, red, yellow and white, then the painting he creates will be made up of only those 3 colors. If the composer's palette consists of the 7 pitches, D, E, F sharp, G, A, B, and C sharp, then the song he writes will be made up of only those 7 pitches. (There are of course exceptions to this, which we will learn about at a later time.)

KEY SIGNATURES

The key a piece is written in is indicated through a **key signature**. A key signature is the sharps or flats placed on the staff at the beginning of each line of music. Here is an example.

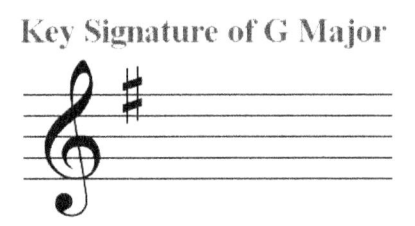

Key Signature of G Major

A performer who sees this one "F sharp" will know that the song is written in the key G major. There are two ways the performer will know this. The first way is through knowledge of scales; if they have learned their scales well, they will know that the G major scale consists of G, A, B, C, D, E, and F sharp. The second way is by memorizing the circle of 5ths. (We will learn about the circle of 5ths momentarily.)

In lesson 18 we learned that a sharped or flatted pitch remains sharped or flatted until the end of the measure. It is very important to understand that a sharp or flat in a key signature applies to the <u>entire song</u>. In the key signature of G major above, the "F sharp" indicates that every "F" (on any line or space) is to be played "F sharp" for the entire song.

Note: Sharps or flats placed throughout different measures in the music that are not part of the key are called "accidentals". A "C sharp" for example, is not part of the key of G major (G, A, B, C, D, E, F sharp) and would therefore be called an accidental. Accidental does not mean that they happened by accident. It refers to something being non-essential. For example, if you colored a piano purple, it would still be a piano. The color purple is an "accident" since it is not essential to what a piano is.

MAJOR KEYS

All key signatures are written with the sharps and flats in a particular order. (The reason for this will become apparent as we proceed). Sharps in a key signature are always placed in the following order on the staff. We call this, the **order of sharps**.

Flats in a key signature are always placed in the following order on the staff. We call this, the **order of flats**.

There are two useful mnemonic devices that will help you to remember the order of sharps and flats.

The order of sharps can be remembered with the following mnemonic device.

Father **C**hristmas **G**ave **D**ad **A**n **E**lectric **B**lanket

The order of flats can be remembered with the following mnemonic device.

Blanket **E**xplodes **A**nd **D**ad **G**ets **C**old **F**eet

Note: the order of flats is the reverse of the order of sharps.

Here are the order of sharps and the order of flats on the keyboard. Take note how every sharp or flat is a 5th (7 half steps) apart.

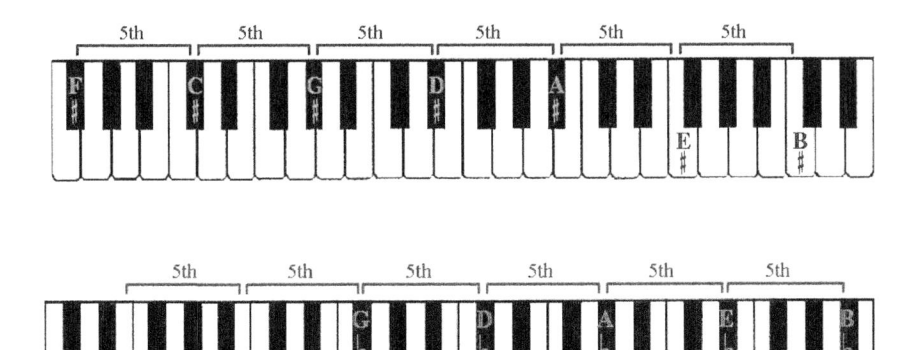

Note: the order of sharps goes from left to right on the keyboard while the order of flats goes from right to left.

MAJOR KEYS WITH SHARPS

Now that we have learned a little bit about what a key is, we are going to learn all the major keys that contain sharps. To do this we need to study the circle of 5ths. The circle of 5ths is a very useful tool that has many applications. Understanding and memorizing it will help you to know all of the different keys that songs may be written in. The keys that contain sharps are found on the right side of the circle of 5ths. (Remember, a 5th is equal to 7 half steps.)

MAJOR KEYS

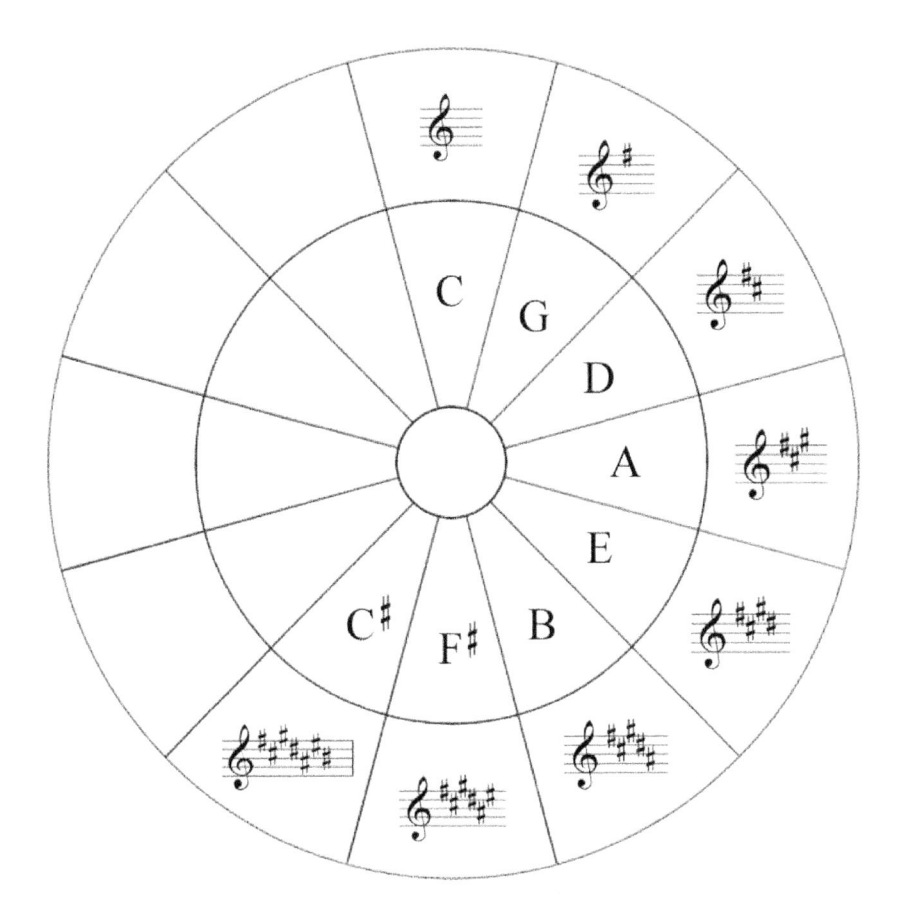

Here are a few important things to note about the preceding diagram.

1. Starting with the key of "C" and moving in a clockwise direction, each key is a 5th a part. ("G" is a 5th higher than "C", "D" is a 5th higher than "G", etc.)

2. Starting with the key of "C" and moving in a clockwise direction, each key has an additional sharp (1 sharp more than the previous key on the circle).

3. Each additional sharp follows the "order of sharps". ("F sharp" is the first sharp added; "C sharp" is the next sharp added; etc.)

Using the knowledge above, let's look at some practical applications of the circle of 5ths. Let's say you want to know how many sharps there are in the key of "A major". Start at "C" and count up by 5ths; when you reach "A", stop. (The key of "C" has 0 sharps, the key of "G" has 1 sharp, the key of "D" has 2 sharps, and the key of "A" has 3 sharps.) This is even clearer when using the piano keyboard.

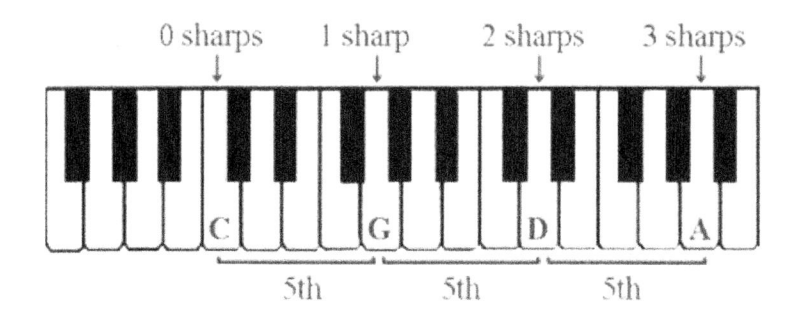

We now know that the key of "A major" has 3 sharps…but which 3 pitches are sharp? To find this out, simply list the order of sharps and stop at the third sharp. (Use the mnemonic device if needed.) **F**ather **C**hristmas **G**ave; the 3 sharps in the key of "A major" are therefore "F sharp", "C sharp", and "G sharp".

This is the most straight forward way to find how many and which sharps are in a particular major key. The other way involves finding the pitch one half step lower than the name of the key and then listing the order of sharps until you reach that pitch. Let's demonstrate using our example of "A major".

First, find the pitch one half step lower than the name of the key. One half step lower than "A", is "G sharp". Next, list the order of sharps until we reach "G sharp". **F**ather **C**hristmas **G**ave. The 3 sharps in the key of "A major" are therefore "F sharp", "C sharp", and "G sharp".

Above, we saw how starting from the name of a key, we could use the circle of 5ths to discover how many sharps were in that particular key. This also works in reverse. In other words, we can start with the number of sharps and discover the name of the key.

Let's say you are looking at a piece of music and the key signature has 3 sharps. You want to know what key this is. What do you do? Simply name the last sharp and then name the pitch one half step higher.

The last sharp in the key signature above is "G sharp". One half step higher than "G sharp", is "A". Therefore the name of the key is "A major". You can use this technique to find the name of any key signature that contains sharps.

MAJOR KEYS WITH FLATS

We are now going to study the other side of the circle of 5ths. The keys that contain flats are found on the left side of the circle. (Remember: a 5th is equal to 7 half steps.)

MUSIC THEORY

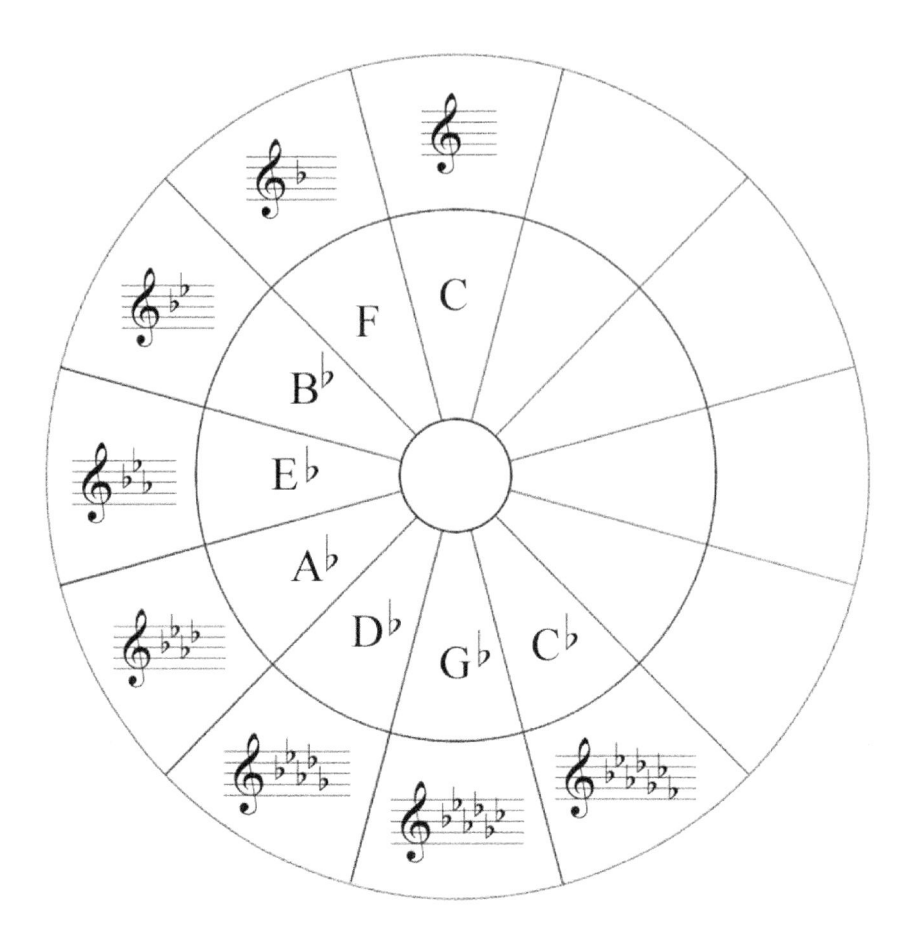

Here are a few important things to note about the preceding diagram.

1. Starting with the key of "C" and moving in a counterclockwise direction, each key is a 5th a part. ("F" is a 5th lower than "C", "B flat" is a 5th lower than "F", etc.)

2. Starting with the key of "C" and moving in a counterclockwise direction, each key has an additional flat (1 flat more than the previous key on the circle).

3. Each additional flat follows the "order of flats". ("B flat" is the first flat added; "E flat" is the next flat added; etc.)

Using the knowledge above, let's look at some practical applications of the circle of 5ths. Let's say you want to know how many flats there are in the key of "E flat major". Start at "C" and count down by 5ths; when you reach "E flat", stop. (The key of "C" has 0 flats, the key of "F" has 1 flat, the key of "B flat" has 2 flats, and the key of "E flat" has 3 flats.) This is even clearer when using the piano keyboard.

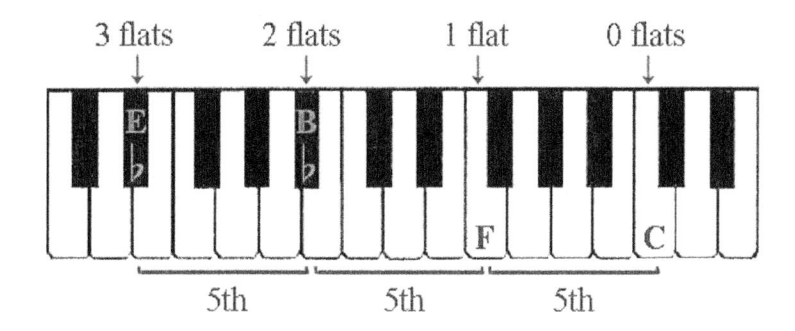

We now know that the key of "E flat major" has 3 flats...but which 3 pitches are flat? To find this out, simply list the order of flats and stop at the third flat. (Use the mnemonic device if needed.) **B**lanket **E**xplodes **A**nd. The 3 flats in the key of "E flat major" are therefore "B flat", "E flat", and "A flat".)

This is the most straight forward way to find how many and which flats are in a particular major key. The other way involves listing the order of flats until you reach the name of the key and then adding one more flat. Let's demonstrate using our example of "E flat major".

List the order of flats until we reach "E flat": **B**lanket **E**xplodes. Now we add one more flat: **B**lanket **E**xplodes **A**nd. The 3 flats in the key of "E flat major" are therefore "B flat", "E flat", and "A flat".

Above, we saw how starting from the name of a key, we could use the circle of 5ths to discover how many flats were in that particular key. This also works in reverse. In other words, we can start with the number of flats and discover the name of the key.

Let's say you are looking at a piece of music and the key signature has 3 flats. You want to know what key this is. What do you do? Simply name the second to last flat.

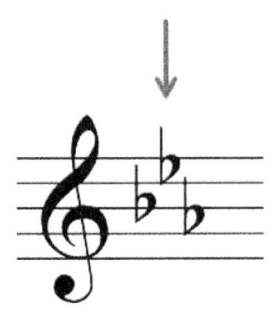

The second to last flat in the key signature above is "E flat". Therefore the name of the key is "E flat major".

You can use this technique to find the name of any key signature that contains flats. The one exception is the key of F major.

Since the key of F major only has one flat, there is no "second to last" flat. The key signature of F major must be memorized.

ENHARMONIC KEYS

When two different keys have the same sound but are spelled differently they are considered to be **enharmonic keys**. For example, a song written in the key of "F sharp major" will sound just like the exact same song written in the key of "G flat major" but the music on the page will look different, since the key signatures are different. Be sure to take note of the six enharmonic keys in the two preceding "circle of 5ths" diagrams. (The keys containing 5 to 7 sharps or flats)

"B major" is the enharmonic equivalent of "C flat major"
"F sharp major" is the enharmonic equivalent of "G flat major"
"C sharp major" is the enharmonic equivalent of "D flat major"

Because all major keys come from the pitches of the major scale, this means that there will also be six **enharmonic scales**. Enharmonic scales are scales that sound the same but are spelled differently. Here is an example of the enharmonic scales "F sharp major" and "G flat major".

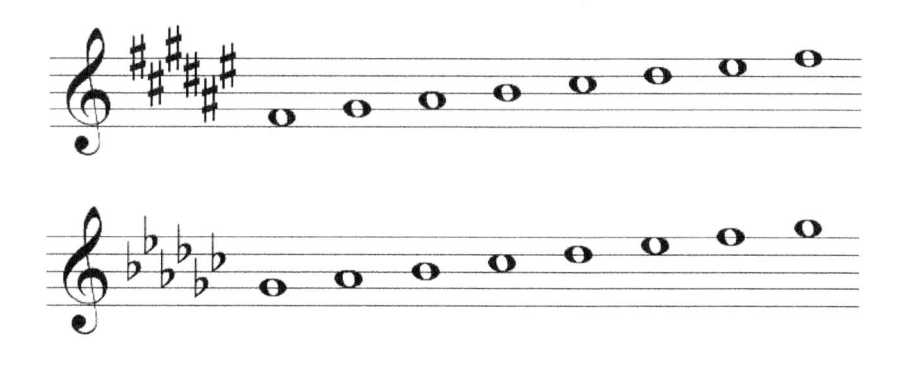

Both of the scales above will sound exactly the same when played. As you can see, the difference is in how they are spelled. One is spelled using sharps and the other is spelled using flats. Composers will choose one over the other depending on the musical context or the instrument they are writing for. This is more of a topic for a composition or orchestration class. The objective here is to know that these equivalents exist and to be able to recognize them.

Memory Questions

What is a key?
A key is a specific group of pitches used to write a piece of music (or part of a piece of music).

What is a key signature?
A key signature is the sharps or flats placed on the staff at the beginning of each line of music.

What does the key signature indicate?
The key signature indicates which key the piece of music (or part of a piece of music) is written in.

What is the order of sharps?
The order of sharps is FCGDAEB

What is the order of flats?
The order of flats is BEADGCF

What is the circle of fifths?
The circle of 5ths is a useful tool for understanding keys and key signatures.

What are enharmonic keys?
Enharmonic keys are keys that have the same sound but are spelled differently.

What are enharmonic scales?
Enharmonic scales are scales that have the same sound but are spelled differently.

Lesson 21 Exercises

Log in to your course at www.udemy.com and practice the exercises for this lesson.

Lesson 21 Quiz

Log in to your course at www.udemy.com and take the quiz for this lesson.

22. MAJOR, MINOR, & PERFECT INTERVALS

NUMBER VS. QUALITY

In lesson 19 we began studying intervals. We found that intervals receive their name from the amount of lines and spaces they span on the staff. For example, a "2nd" spans one line and one space (1+ 1 =2). This is called an interval's "number". In this lesson we are going to learn about an interval's "quality". The term "quality" refers to the amount of half steps the interval spans.

There are five types of interval qualities. In this lesson we will learn about the **major**, **minor** and **perfect** qualities. Let's begin by looking at the interval of a 2nd.

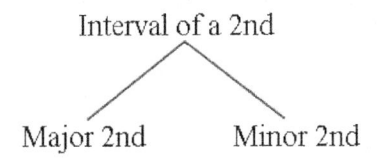

```
           Interval of a 2nd
              /       \
         Major 2nd   Minor 2nd
```

MAJOR, MINOR & PERFECT INTERVALS

The interval of a 2nd can either be major or minor. This is determined by the amount of half steps the interval spans. (Remember: a half step is the distance from one piano key to the very next piano key; higher or lower.) As you can see from the following diagram, a major 2nd is equal to two half steps.

major 2nd
(M2)

A minor 2nd is smaller than a major 2nd. A minor 2nd is equal to one half step. (This is the smallest in size that an interval may be.)

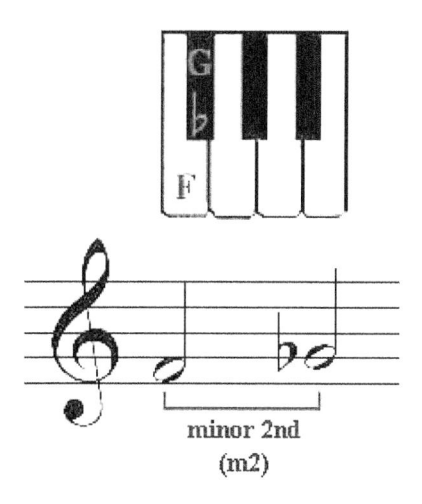

minor 2nd
(m2)

MUSIC THEORY

The following is a diagram showing the interval qualities from minor 2nd through octave. (M = major, m = minor, P = perfect)

> **m2** = 1 half step
> **M2** = 2 half steps
> **m3** = 3 half steps
> **M3** = 4 half steps
> P4 = 5 half steps
> ? = 6 half steps
> P5 = 7 half steps
> **m6** = 8 half steps
> **M6** = 9 half steps
> **m7** = 10 half steps
> **M7** = 11 half steps
> **P8** = 12 half steps

(Lesson 22 - Audio 1)

Here are a few important items that you should be aware of in the preceding diagram.

1. 2nds, 3rds, 6ths, and 7ths can be either major or minor.
2. 4ths, 5ths, and 8ths are perfect (very consonant).
3. Minor intervals are always one half step smaller than their major counterparts.
4. Moving top to bottom on the diagram, the number of half steps is increasing incrementally by "1". (This will help with memorization for the quiz.)

Note: The interval made up of six half steps will be learned about in the next lesson.

We are now going to demonstrate the steps to finding an interval's "number" and "quality".

Step 1
Determine the intervals' "number" by counting the total number of lines and spaces that the interval spans on the staff (including the lines or spaces that the two notes occupy). The interval in the preceding example spans a total of six staff lines and spaces (three lines and three spaces). It is therefore a 6th. (Notice that we ignored the flat sign and simply counted the lines and spaces.)

Step 2
Play the interval on a piano and determine the number of half steps from the bottom note to the top note. (Make sure that you do not include the first note in your count, but rather the first half step "away from" the first note.) The interval in the preceding example is equal to 9 half steps on the piano. Using the interval chart that we memorized in this lesson we find that 9 half steps is a major 6th. The preceding interval is therefore a major 6th.

INTERVALS AND THE SCALE

All of the major and perfect intervals can be formed from the pitches of the major scale. Although you cannot form the minor intervals from the pitches of the major scale, they can be formed by lowering the highest note of the major intervals one half step. Let's demonstrate this using the C major scale. Observe in the following diagram that by combining the starting pitch of the scale ("C") with any other pitch in the scale, we can form the major and perfect intervals.

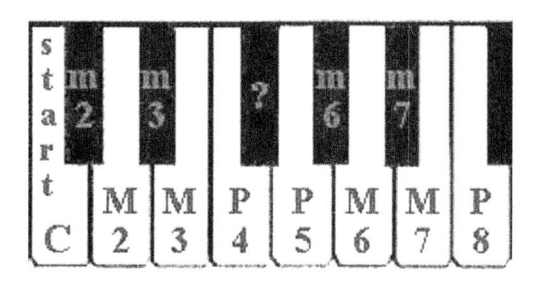

C to D = a major 2nd
C to E = a major 3rd
C to F = a perfect 4th
C to G = a perfect 5th
C to A = a major 6th
C to B = a major 7th
C to C = a perfect 8th

To form the minor intervals we simply lower the highest note of the major intervals one half step.

C to D flat = a minor 2nd
C to E flat = a minor 3rd
C to A flat = a minor 6th
C to B flat = a minor 7th

Note: We will learn about the pitch between the perfect 4th and perfect 5th in the next lesson.

Knowing that all of the major and perfect intervals can be formed from the pitches of the major scale is another helpful way of determining an interval's quality. Take the following example. First we count the amount of lines and spaces the interval spans to determine that the interval below is a 7th.

To determine if this 7th is major or minor we would use the D major scale (since the interval has "D" as its lowest pitch). As you know from a previous lesson, the D major scale is made up of the pitches D, E, F sharp, G, A, B, C sharp and D.

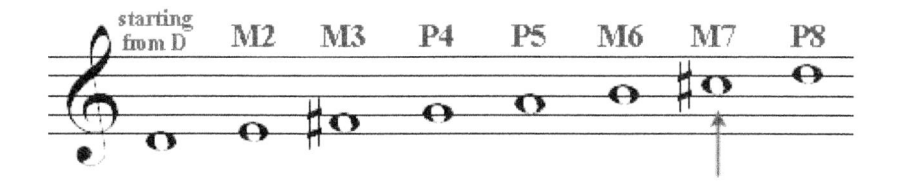

We also know that all of the major and perfect intervals can be formed with the pitches of the major scale. Therefore "D" to "C sharp" is a major 7th. Let's try another example.

To discover this interval's quality we would once again use the D major scale (since the interval has "D" as its lowest pitch). We know that the D major scale is made up of the pitches D, E, F sharp, G, A, B, C sharp and D. The top pitch of the interval ("C") is therefore not a pitch of the D major scale. It is however one half step lower than the 7th pitch of the D major scale ("C sharp"). The interval above is therefore a minor 7th.

This is just one of the important reasons for knowing each scale. If you have your scales memorized you should be able to quickly identify any interval's quality. If you can't remember a particular scale, you can always resort to counting half steps using the piano keyboard.

Memory Questions

How is an interval's number determined?
An interval's number is determined by the amount of lines and spaces it spans on the staff.

How is an interval's quality determined?
An interval's quality is determined by the amount of half steps it spans.

What three interval qualities were learned in this lesson?
The three interval qualities learned in this lesson were major, minor, and perfect.

Which intervals can be either major or minor?
The 2nd, 3rd, 6th, and 7th can be either major or minor.

Which intervals are perfect?
The 4th, 5th, and 8th are perfect.

How can the major and perfect intervals be formed?
The major and perfect intervals can be formed from the pitches of the major scale.

How can the minor intervals be formed?
The minor intervals can be formed by lowering the highest note of the major intervals one half step.

Lesson 22 Exercises

Log in to your course at www.udemy.com and practice the exercises for this lesson.

Lesson 22 Quiz

Log in to your course at www.udemy.com and take the quiz for this lesson.

23. AUGMENTED & DIMINISHED INTERVALS

AUGMENTED INTERVALS

In the last lesson we learned about the interval qualities: major, minor, and perfect. In this lesson we are going to learn two more interval qualities: **augmented** and **diminished**.

The word "augmented" comes from the Latin "augmentare", which means to increase. When we augment something we increase it. An augmented interval is any major or perfect interval that has been made larger by one half step.

There are two ways to turn a major or perfect interval into an augmented interval; we can either "raise" the top note by one half step, or "lower" the bottom note by one half step. (Either way we are increasing the size of the interval by one half step.) In all of the following examples we will augment the interval by raising the top note. This can be done by placing a sharp sign next to the top note. The abbreviation for augmented is "A" or "aug". (Remember: M=major, P=perfect)

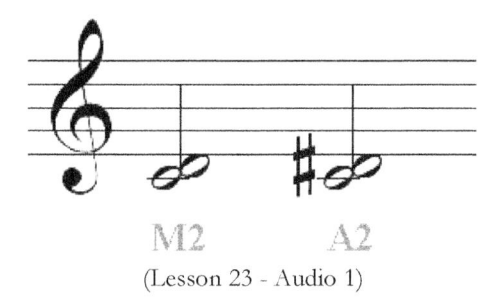

AUGMENTED & DIMINISHED INTERVALS

M2   A2
(Lesson 23 - Audio 1)

M3   A3
(Lesson 23 - Audio 2)

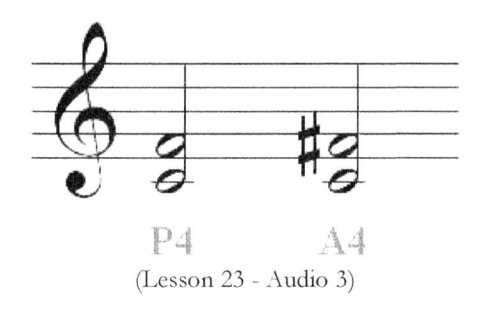

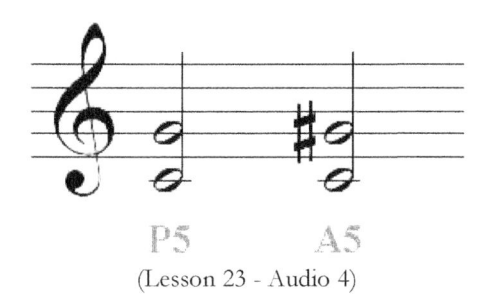

P4   A4
(Lesson 23 - Audio 3)

P5   A5
(Lesson 23 - Audio 4)

M6   A6
(Lesson 23 - Audio 5)

M7   A7
(Lesson 23 - Audio 6)

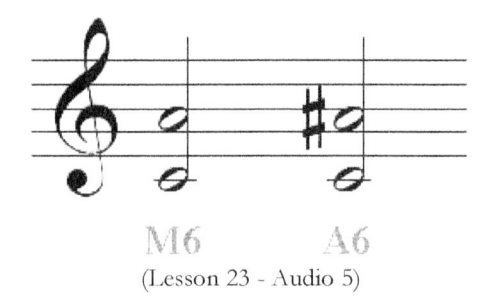

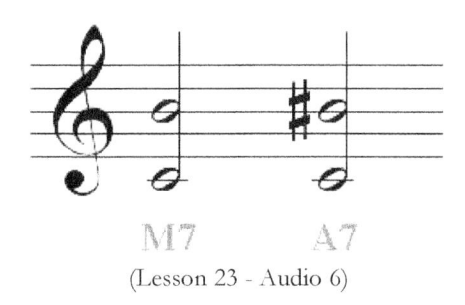

Many of the augmented intervals sound the same as other intervals that you have already learned. For example, the augmented 7th is the same sound as the perfect 8th when played on the piano. When two different intervals have the same sound but are spelled differently they are considered to be **enharmonic intervals**. Enharmonic intervals are a type of enharmonic equivalent. (We learned about enharmonic equivalents in lesson 17.)

Note: there is no augmented 8th in the preceding diagrams because an augmented 8th would be larger than an 8th. All pitches after the 8th are simply recurrences of the same pitches only an octave higher. We will learn about intervals larger than an octave in the next lesson.

THE DOUBLE SHARP

Not all intervals can be augmented by simply adding a sharp to the upper note (as in each of the preceding diagrams). For example, if we are in a key with flats we may have to use a natural sign.

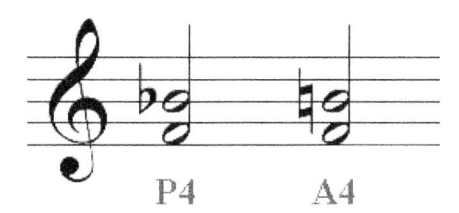

P4   A4

In order to raise the upper note by one half step we must get rid of the "B flat" and write "B natural".

If we are in a key with sharps, we may have to use something called a **double sharp**.

M3   A3

Since the upper note in the major 3rd is already sharp ("C sharp"), how do we raise it by one half step? The note one half step higher than "C sharp" is "D". We could write the interval as "A" and "D", but that would change the "number" of the interval from a 3rd into a 4th ("A" to "D" spans 4 lines/spaces). This is where the invention of the double sharp comes in. A double sharp looks similar to the letter "x". When placed next to a note it means to play the note 2 half steps higher. On the piano keyboard this would be the key two keys to the right.

C double sharp

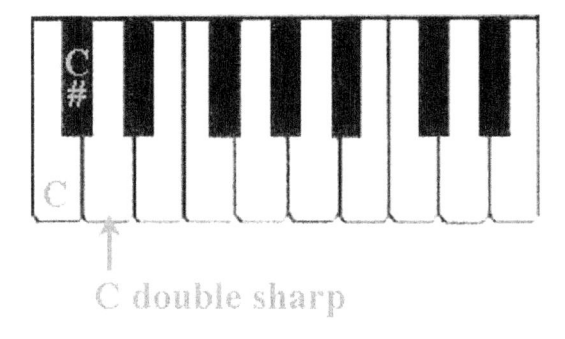

Note: "C double sharp" is the enharmonic equivalent of "D".

DIMINISHED INTERVALS

The word diminished comes from the Latin "diminutio" which means to decrease. When we diminish something we decrease it. A diminished interval is any minor or perfect interval that has been made smaller by one half step.

There are two ways to turn a minor or perfect interval into a diminished interval; we can either "lower" the top note by one half step or "raise" the bottom note by one half step. (Either way we are decreasing the size of the interval by one half step.) In all of the following examples we will diminish the interval by lowering the top note. This can be done by placing a flat sign next to the top note. The abbreviation for diminished is "d" or "dim". (Remember: m=minor, P=perfect)

AUGMENTED & DIMINISHED INTERVALS

m3   d3
(Lesson 23 - Audio 7)

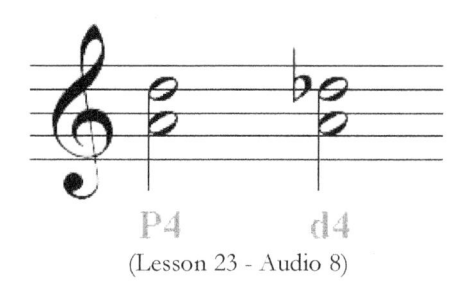

P4   d4
(Lesson 23 - Audio 8)

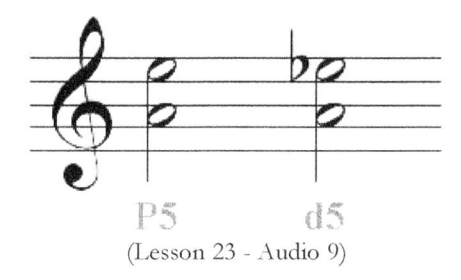

P5   d5
(Lesson 23 - Audio 9)

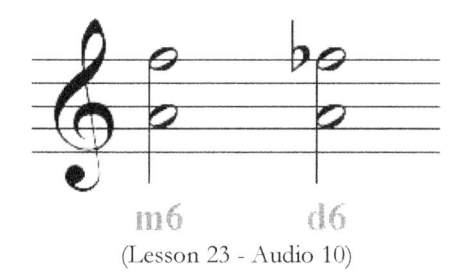

m6   d6
(Lesson 23 - Audio 10)

[musical notation: m7, d7]
(Lesson 23 - Audio 11)

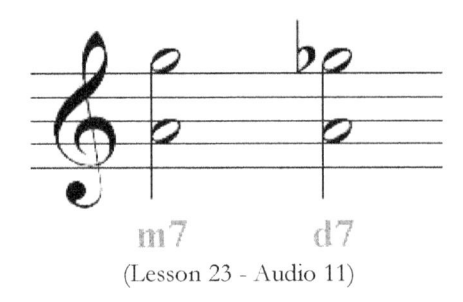

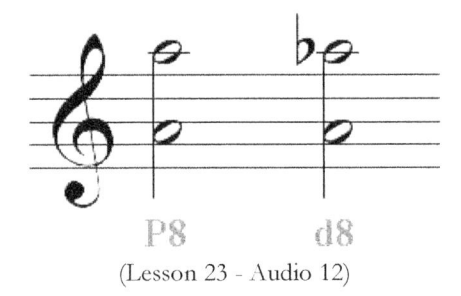

[musical notation: P8, d8]
(Lesson 23 - Audio 12)

Note: there is no diminished 2nd in the preceding diagrams because a diminished 2nd is not possible. A minor 2nd cannot be made any smaller (diminished) since it is already equal to one half step.

THE DOUBLE FLAT

Not all intervals can be diminished by simply adding a flat to the upper note (as in each of the preceding diagrams). For example, if we are in a key with flats we may have to use something called a **double flat**.

AUGMENTED & DIMINISHED INTERVALS

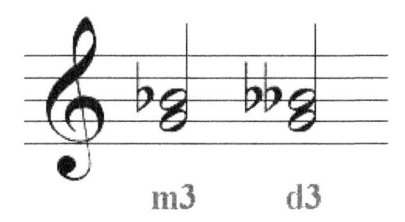

m3   d3

Since the upper note in this interval is already flat (B flat), how do we lower it by one half step? The note one half step lower than "B flat", is "A". We could write the interval as "G" and "A", but that would change the "number" of the interval from a 3rd into a 2nd ("G" to "A" spans 2 lines/spaces). This is where the invention of the double flat comes in. Unlike the double sharp, the double flat does not have its own symbol. It is simply written as two flat signs next to each other (see the second interval in the preceding diagram). When placed next to a note it means to play the note 2 half steps lower. On the piano keyboard this would be the key two keys to the left.

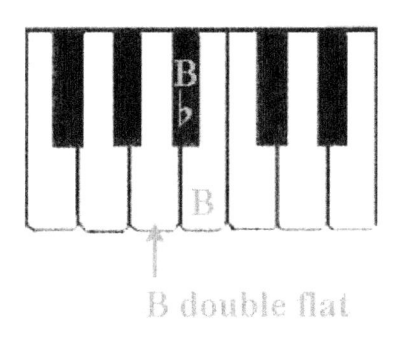

B double flat

Note: "B double flat" is the enharmonic equivalent of "A".

THE TRITONE

In the last lesson we memorized how many half steps there were in each interval quality. You may recall that the interval equal to 6 half steps was left blank and we did not give a name for it. Now that we have discussed augmented and diminished intervals we can finally give a name to this mystery interval. The interval equal to 6 half steps is called a **tritone**. It is called a tritone because it is made up of three whole steps. (tri = three)

m2 = 1 half step
M2 = 2 half steps

m3 = 3 half steps
M3 = 4 half steps

P4 = 5 half steps
Tritone ⎡ A4 = 6 half steps
         ⎣ d5 = 6 half steps
P5 = 7 half steps

m6 = 8 half steps
M6 = 9 half steps

m7 = 10 half steps
M7 = 11 half steps

P8 = 12 half steps

In the preceding diagram, you will notice that both the augmented 4th and the diminished 5th are called tritones. That is because both are equal to 6 half steps (or 3 whole steps). On the piano keyboard (or on the staff) the augmented 4th and the diminished 5th are considered enharmonic equivalents; they sound the same but are spelled differently.

AUGMENTED & DIMINISHED INTERVALS

Listen to the sound of the tritone played first as a melodic interval and then as a harmonic interval.

(Lesson 23 - Audio 13)

As you can plainly hear, the tritone is not very pleasant sounding. As you will learn later, the tritone is one of the most dissonant sounding intervals possible. In fact it was called "diabolus in musica" (the devil in music) and was avoided by musicians for centuries before slowly making its way into the composer's harmonic tool box. A skilled composer knows how to use the tritone in such a way as to add to the music rather than detract from it.

Tritones can be found by dividing any octave exactly in half.

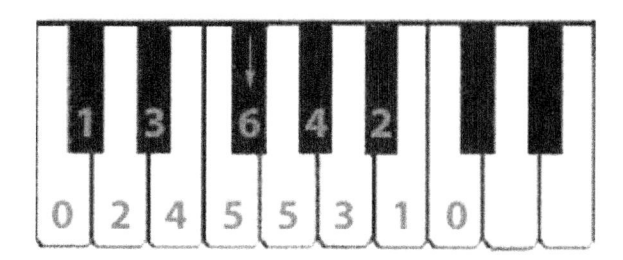

In the preceding diagram, the midway point between "C" and "C" is "F sharp" (or "G flat"). From either "C" it is 6 half steps to the center of the octave. The tritone is in fact the farthest you can travel away from any particular pitch before you start getting closer to the same pitch an octave higher (or lower).

In the lesson quiz you will be asked to identify the "number" and "quality" of various intervals. Here are some steps that will help you if you have trouble or are unclear on how to go about doing this.

Step 1
Determine the intervals' "number" by counting the total number of lines and spaces that the interval spans on the staff (including the lines or spaces that the two notes occupy).

Step 2
Play the interval on a piano and determine the number of half steps from the bottom note to the top note. (Make sure that you do not include the first note in your count, but rather the first half step "away from" the first note.)

Step 3
Locate the interval's "number" on the chart that you memorized. Compare the amount of half steps in the interval you are trying to determine to those on the chart with the same "number". If the number of half steps is one less than the minor or perfect interval it is a diminished interval. If the number of half steps is one more than the major or perfect interval it is an augmented interval.

Memory Questions

What is an augmented interval?
An augmented interval is any major or perfect interval that has been made larger by one half step.

What are the two ways to turn a major or perfect interval into an augmented interval?
To turn a major or perfect interval into an augmented interval we can either raise the top note by one half step, or lower the bottom note by one half step.

What is a diminished interval?
A diminished interval is any minor or perfect interval that has been made smaller by one half step.

What are the two ways to turn a minor or perfect interval into a diminished interval?
To turn a minor or perfect interval into a diminished interval we can either lower the top note by one half step, or raise the bottom note by one half step.

What is a double sharp?
A double sharp is an "x" shaped symbol placed next to a note indicating that the note be played 2 half steps higher than normal.

What is a double flat?
A double flat is two flat signs placed next to a note indicating that the note be played 2 half steps lower than normal.

What is a tritone?
A tritone is the augmented 4th or the diminished 5th and is equal to 6 half steps (or 3 whole steps).

What are enharmonic intervals?
Enharmonic intervals are intervals that have the same sound but are spelled differently.

Lesson 23 Exercises

Log in to your course at www.udemy.com and practice the exercises for this lesson.

Lesson 23 Quiz

Log in to your course at www.udemy.com and take the quiz for this lesson.

24. COMPLEMENTARY & COMPOUND INTERVALS

COMPLETMENTARY INTERVALS

In the previous lessons we learned about major, minor, perfect, augmented and diminished intervals. In this lesson we are going to learn about **complementary intervals** and **compound intervals**. We will begin with complementary intervals.

Two intervals that together equal an octave are called complementary intervals. We can find the complementary interval of any particular interval by simply "inverting" the interval. "Inversion" of an interval means moving the lowest pitch of the interval an octave higher so that it becomes the highest pitch. Let's demonstrate with examples.

The inversion of the perfect 5th is the perfect 4th. These two intervals together equal an octave, and are therefore complementary.

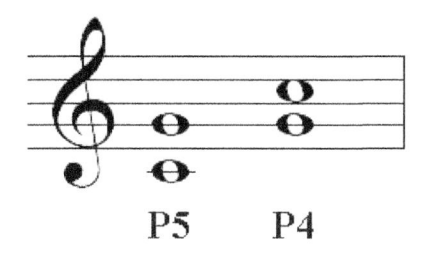

COMPLEMENTARY & COMPOUND INTERVALS

P5   P4

The inversion of the perfect 5th was formed by moving the lowest pitch ("C") an octave higher so that it becomes the highest pitch.

The inversion of the major 3rd is the minor 6th. These two intervals together equal an octave, and are therefore complementary.

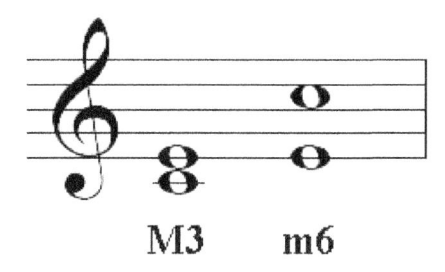

M3   m6

The inversion of the major 6th is the minor 3rd. These two intervals together equal an octave, and are therefore complementary.

M6   m3

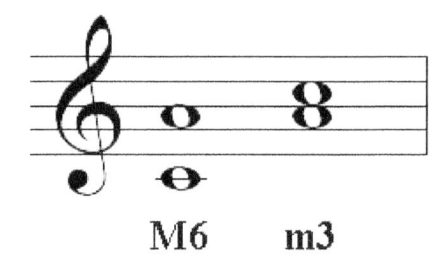

The inversion of the major 2nd is the minor 7th. These two intervals together equal an octave, and are therefore complementary.

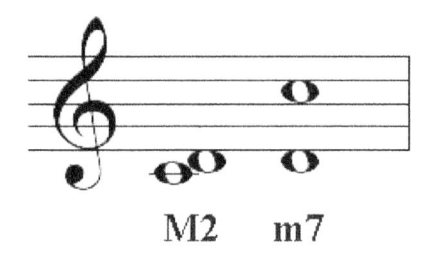

M2   m7

The inversion of the major 7th is the minor 2nd. These two intervals together equal an octave, and are therefore complementary.

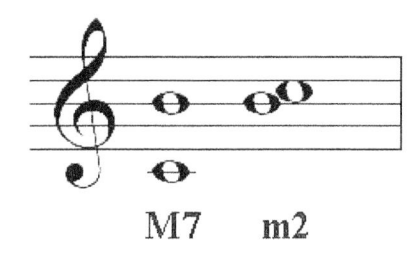

M7   m2

The inversion of the augmented 4th is the diminished 5th. These two intervals together equal an octave, and are therefore complementary.

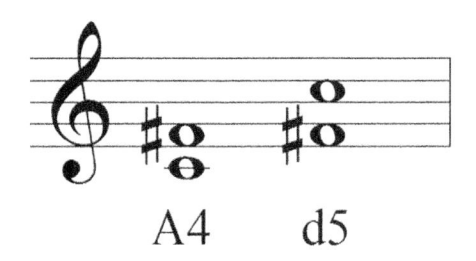

A4   d5

The inversion of the diminished 5th is the augmented 4th. These two intervals together equal an octave, and are therefore complementary.

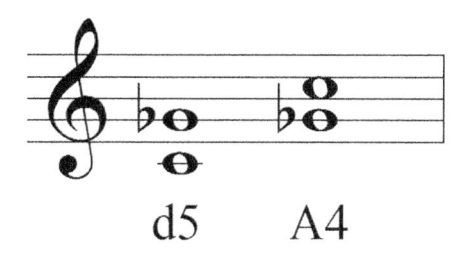

(A very easy way to remember which intervals are complementary is with the number 9. If you look back at each of the complementary intervals above, you will notice that each pair of intervals, when added together, equals the number 9.)

Here is a chart below that lists each interval quality and the corresponding complementary interval. Memorize it before taking the lesson quiz.

Interval	Complementary Interval
Major	Minor
Minor	Major
Perfect	Perfect
Augmented	Diminished
Diminished	Augmented

COMPOUND INTERVALS

Thus far we have only studied intervals that are an octave or smaller in size. Intervals that are an octave or smaller in size are called **simple intervals**. When an interval is larger than an octave it is called a **compound interval**. Compound intervals are formed by adding one or more octaves to a simple interval. Here is an example of adding one octave to a simple interval to form a compound interval.

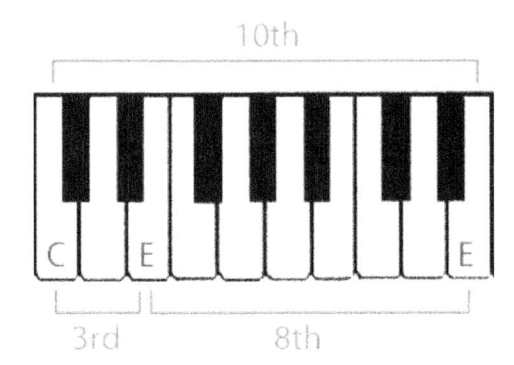

The interval from "C" to the highest "E" in the preceding diagram is a 10th. A 10th is a 3rd plus an 8th. ("C" to the lower "E" is a 3rd; the lower "E" to the higher "E" is an 8th.) Make sure not to add 3 plus 8 to get 11. If you do this you will be counting the lower "E" twice; once as part of the 3rd and once as part of the 8th.

To find out the number name of a compound interval which is made up of a simple interval plus one octave, simply add the numbers of the two intervals together and subtract 1. For example:

5 + 8 = 13
13 - 1 = 12
Therefore a 5th plus an 8th equals a 12th.

4 + 8 = 12
12 − 1 = 11
Therefore a 4th plus an 8th equals an 11th.

Here is an example of adding two octaves to a simple interval to form a compound interval.

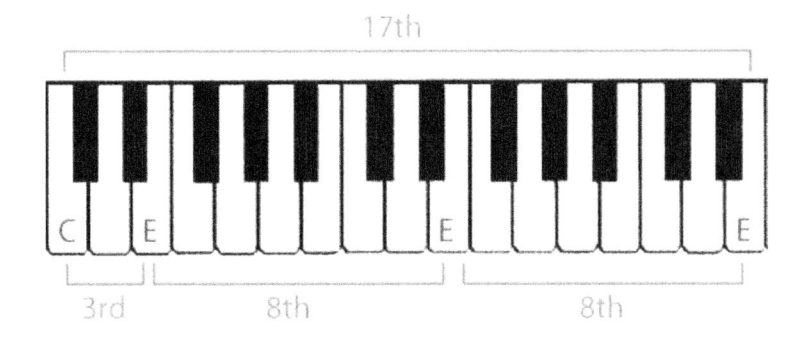

17th
3rd 8th 8th
C E E E

Again, make sure that you don't just add the numbers together. (3 + 8 + 8 = 19 and that would be incorrectly named.) If we want to add two octaves to a simple interval we must subtract the number 2 from the answer.

3 + 8 + 8 = 19
19 − 2 = <u>17</u>
Therefore a 3rd plus an 8th, plus an 8th, equals a 17th.

Why do we need to subtract 2? Because if we don't we will be counting certain pitches twice. (The lowest "E" will be counted once as part of the 3rd and once as part of the first 8th; the middle "E" will be counted once as part of the first 8th and once as part of the second 8th.)

REDUCING A COMPOUND INTERVAL

Because every compound interval is made up of a simple interval and one or more octaves, any compound interval can be reduced to its simple form by subtracting the octaves. To do this, drop the top note by 1 octave until you reach the interval's simplest form.

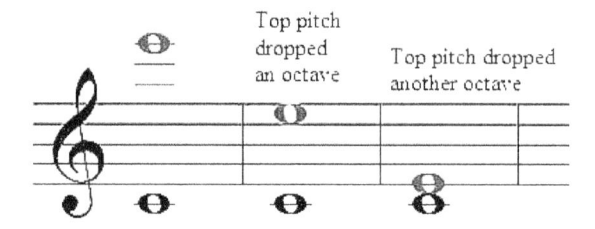

In the preceding example, the compound interval in the first measure is a 17th. In the second measure we have dropped the top pitch down an octave to get a 10th. In the third measure we have dropped the top pitch another octave to get a 3rd. Since we cannot drop the top pitch any further (without going lower than the bottom pitch), the interval is therefore now in its simplest form. We have discovered that the 17th is just a compound form of the 3rd.

OPEN & CLOSED HARMONY

When harmonies are made up of simple intervals we call this "closed" harmony. (Remember, harmony is pitches heard simultaneously.)

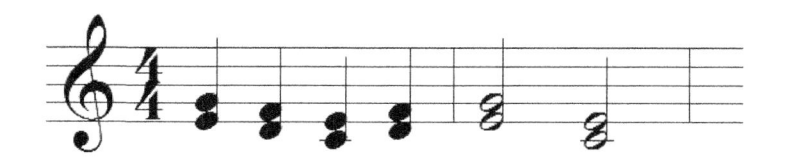

(Lesson 24 - Audio 1)

The preceding example used "closed" harmony; all of the intervals were simple (an octave or less).

When harmonies are made up of compound intervals we call this "open" harmony.

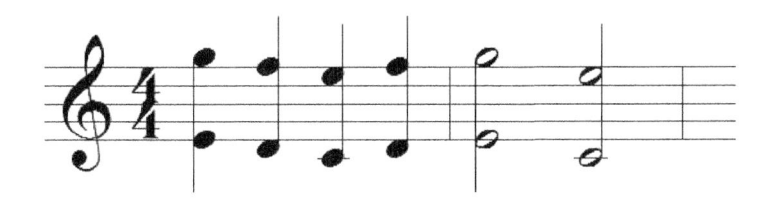

(Lesson 24 - Audio 2)

The preceding example used "open" harmony; all of the intervals were compounded (larger than an octave).

Did you notice that both examples used the exact same pitches even though the first was in simple form (3rds) and the second was in compound form (10ths)? Listen to the two preceding examples again. Can you hear the difference between them? Open harmony is much bigger and fuller sounding than closed harmony. That's part of what gives most choral and orchestral music its full sound.

QUALITY OF COMPOUND INTERVALS

The quality of a compound interval is the same as the quality of its simple form. In other words, since a 10th is a just a compound 3rd, whatever quality the 3rd is, the 10th will be of the same quality. Here are some examples:

A "major" 3rd will become a "major" 10th
A "minor" 3rd will become a "minor" 10th
A "perfect" 5th will become a "perfect" 12th
A "diminished" 5th will become a "diminished" 12th
An "augmented" 5th will become an "augmented" 12th

As you can see, major intervals will remain major, minor intervals will remain minor, diminished intervals will remain diminished, and augmented intervals will remain augmented in their corresponding compound forms. Why is this? It is because we are adding an octave(s) to the simple interval. Adding an octave(s) isn't changing the top pitch of the interval; it is the same pitch, only higher.

Memory Questions

What are complementary intervals?
Complementary intervals are any two intervals that together equal an octave.

How can we discover an interval's complement?
We can discover an interval's complement by inverting the interval.

What does "inversion" of an interval mean?
Inversion of an interval means moving the lowest pitch of the interval an octave higher so that it becomes the highest pitch.

What is the complementary interval of a major interval?
The complementary interval of a major interval is a minor interval.

What is the complementary interval of a minor interval?
The complementary interval of a minor interval is a major interval.

What is the complementary interval of a perfect interval?
The complementary interval of a perfect interval is a perfect interval.

COMPLEMENTARY & COMPOUND INTERVALS

What is the complementary interval of an augmented interval?
The complementary interval of an augmented interval is a diminished interval.

What is the complementary interval of a diminished interval?
The complementary interval of a diminished interval is an augmented interval.

What is a simple interval?
A simple interval is any interval an octave or smaller in size.

What is a compound interval?
A compound interval is any interval larger than an octave.

How are compound intervals formed?
Compound intervals are formed by adding one or more octaves to a simple interval.

How are compound intervals reduced to their simplest form?
Compound intervals are reduced to their simplest form by subtracting octaves.

What is closed harmony?
Closed harmony is harmony made up of simple intervals.

What is open harmony?
Open harmony is harmony made up of compound intervals.

How do we determine the quality of a compound interval?
The quality of a compound interval is the same as the quality of the interval in its simple form.

Lesson 24 Quiz

Log in to your course at www.udemy.com and take the quiz for this lesson.

25. INTRODUCTION TO CHORDS

MAJOR & MINOR CHORDS

In previous lessons we learned about intervals. Over the next few lessons we are going to learn about **chords**. One of the differences between an interval and a chord is that an interval consists of two distinct pitches, whereas a chord consists of three or more distinct pitches. In fact, chords are actually made up of multiple intervals as we shall see below.

Most chords have three distinct pitches. We call these chords **triads** (tri = three). The chords we will be studying over the next few lessons will all be triads, so they will all consist of three distinct pitches.

The first chord we are going to look at is the **major chord**. The major chord is made up of two intervals: the lower interval is a major 3rd and the upper interval is a minor 3rd. (Remember, a major 3rd is equal to 4 half steps, while a minor 3rd is equal to 3 half steps.)

The following diagram is an example of a "C major" chord on the keyboard and on the staff. In the audio clip you will hear each pitch played sequentially (we call this a broken chord), followed by the pitches played simultaneously (we call this a block chord).

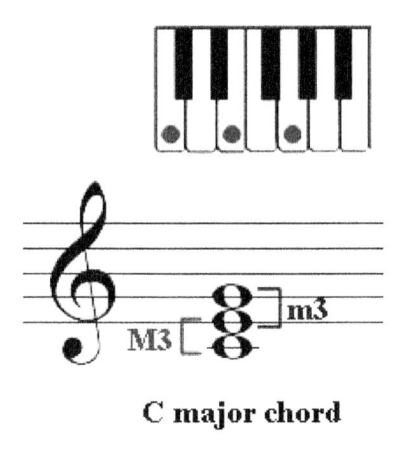

C major chord

(Lesson 25 - Audio 1)

It is important to note that the pitches of a chord must skip letters in the alphabet (**C**D**E**F**G**). The pitches on the staff must skip lines or spaces; in the preceding example, spaces are being skipped (**line**-space-**line**-space-**line**).

The letter name of a chord is determined by the letter name of the lowest pitch in the chord. The chord above is called a "C" chord because its lowest pitch is "C". (There are exceptions to this which we will learn about in another lesson.) The quality "major" can be represented with a capital letter "M" or as an abbreviation. For example, the C major chord can be written as "CM" or "Cmaj".

Now, let's look at the **minor chord**. A minor chord is in a sense the opposite of a major chord. The minor chord is also made up of two intervals: the lower interval is a minor 3rd and the upper interval is a major 3rd. (Remember, a major 3rd is equal to 4 half steps, while a minor 3rd is equal to 3 half steps.) The following diagram is an example of a "D minor" chord on the keyboard and on the staff.

INTRODUCTION TO CHORDS

D minor chord

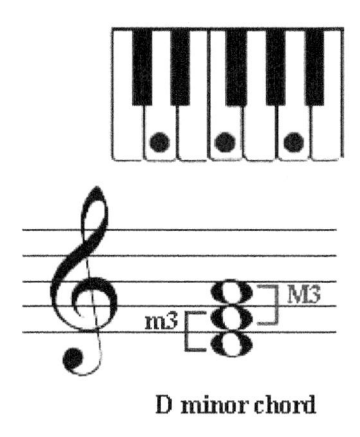

(Lesson 25 - Audio 2)

Did you notice the difference in the sound between the two chords above? The sound of major chords are often referred to as "happy", while the sound of minor chords are often referred to as "sad".

The quality "minor" can be represented with a lowercase letter "m" or as an abbreviation. For example, the D minor chord can be written as "Dm" or "Dmin".

RATIO OF MAJOR 3RDS & MINOR 3RDS

In this next section of the lesson (and over the next few lessons) we are going to show that the pitches in chords were not simply chosen randomly, but that there is a mathematical and natural reason that chords developed the way they did. To do this we need to first discover the ratio of the major 3rd using the monochord and Pythagoras' experiment.

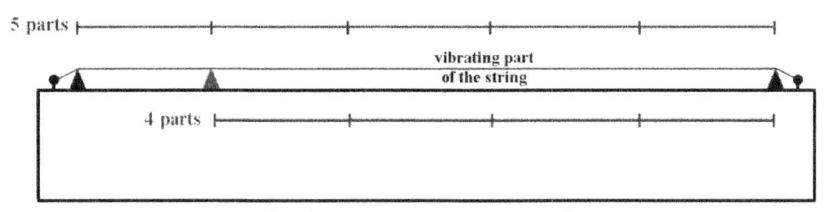

The ratio of 5:4 produces the Major 3rd.

The string in this diagram has been divided into 5 equal parts. We find that if the entire string vibrating produces the pitch "C", then 4 of these parts vibrating will produce the pitch "E", a major 3rd higher. The ratio is called 5 to 4 because we are comparing 5 equal parts of the string vibrating (the entire string) to 4 of these parts vibrating (four-fifths of the string).

While we are looking at the ratio of the major 3rd, we should also briefly look at the ratio of the minor 3rd, since we will need both ratios in the coming lessons.

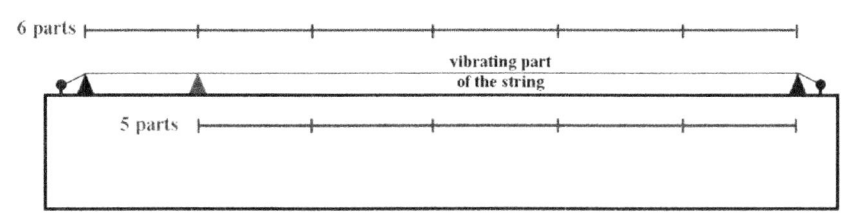

The ratio of 6:5 produces the Minor 3rd.

The string in this diagram has been divided into 6 equal parts. We find that if the entire string vibrating produces the pitch "C", then 5 of these parts vibrating will produce the pitch "E flat", a minor 3rd higher. The ratio is called 6 to 5 because we are comparing 6 equal parts of the string vibrating (the entire string) to 5 of these parts vibrating (five-sixths of the string).

From the time of Pythagoras until around the 14th century, 3rds were considered dissonant. Today, 3rds are considered to be consonant.

INTRODUCTION TO CHORDS

Without the 3rd, almost all of the music of the past few hundred years would not have been impossible.

We will now proceed to demonstrate through mathematics and physics that the pitches of a major chord are not random, but in fact very natural and obvious choices. You can try this for yourself on a monochord or any stringed instrument, using the first four simplest mathematical divisions of a vibrating string. (You may begin on any pitch, but "C" has been chosen in the following example for ease of understanding.)

Step 1
Starting with the pitch "C", divide the length of string in 1/2. The pitch that results is the "C" an 8th higher.

Step 2
Take 2/3 of this new length of string. The pitch that results is the "G" a 5th higher.

Step 3
Take 3/4 of this new length of string. The pitch that results is the "C" a 4th higher.

Step 4
Take 4/5 of this new length of string. The pitch that results is the "E" a major 3rd higher.

Here is the experiment illustrated on the piano keyboard.

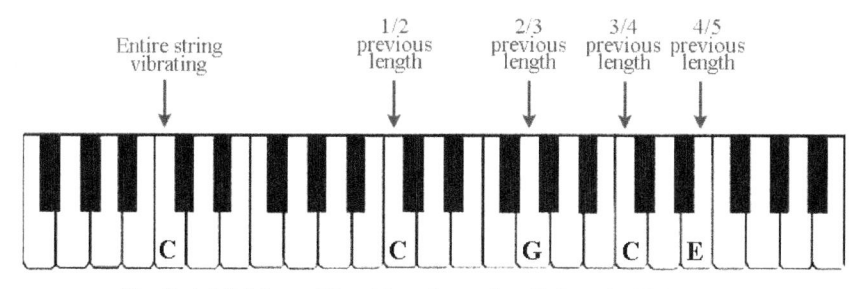

The first 4 divisions of the string give us the pitches of a Major chord!

Memory Questions

What is the difference between an interval and a chord?
An interval is made up of two distinct pitches; a chord is made up of three or more distinct pitches.

How many distinct pitches is the most common type of chord made up of?
The most common type of chord is made up of three distinct pitches.

What is a chord with three distinct pitches called?
A chord with three distinct pitches is called a triad.

What is the term used to describe a chord in which the pitches are heard simultaneously?
The term used to describe a chord in which the pitches are heard simultaneously is "block chord".

What is the term used to describe a chord in which the pitches are heard sequentially?
The term used to describe a chord in which the pitches are heard sequentially is "broken chord".

What is a chord?
A chord is a combination of intervals.

What intervals form a major chord?
Two intervals form a major chord: the lower interval is a major 3rd and the upper interval is a minor 3rd.

What intervals form a minor chord?
Two intervals form a minor chord: the lower interval is a minor 3rd and the upper interval is a major 3rd.

How many half steps does a major 3rd consist of?
A major 3rd consists of four half steps.

INTRODUCTION TO CHORDS

How many half steps does a minor 3rd consist of?
A minor 3rd consists of three half steps.

What is the ratio of a major 3rd? (in terms of string lengths)
The ratio of a major 3rd is 5:4.

What is the ratio of a minor 3rd? (in terms of string lengths)
The ratio of a minor 3rd is 6:5.

Why are the pitches of a major chord a natural choice?
The pitches of a major chord are a natural choice because they can be produced through the rational and mathematical division of a vibrating string.

Lesson 25 Quiz

Log in to your course at www.udemy.com and take the quiz for this lesson.

26. AUGMENTED & DIMINISHED CHORDS

THE AUGMENTED CHORD

Chords, just like intervals, can have qualities. In the last lesson we learned about major and minor chord qualities. In this lesson we are going to learn about two other chord qualities: **augmented** and **diminished**. We have already learned how intervals can be augmented or diminished by increasing or decreasing the size of the interval by one half step. In a similar way, we can also augment and diminish chords.

An augmented chord is formed by taking a major chord and raising the top note one half step. Augmented chords can be represented by the word "aug" or by a superscript plus sign (+).

AUGMENTED & DIMINISHED CHORDS

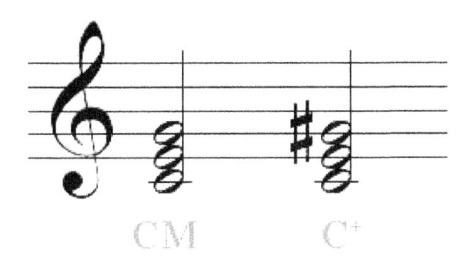

CM   C+

(Lesson 26 - Audio 1)

The first chord in the preceding diagram is a "C major" chord. The second chord is a "C augmented" chord. As you can see, the top note "G" was raised one half step to "G sharp".

One characteristic that differentiates the major and augmented chords is the size of the 5th in the chord. In a major chord, the interval from the bottom note to the top note is a perfect 5th. In an augmented chord, the interval from the bottom note to the top note is an augmented 5th.

Another important characteristic that differentiates the major and augmented chords is the size of the 3rds in the chord. We know from the previous lesson that a major chord is composed of a major 3rd with a minor 3rd added on top. An augmented chord is composed of a major 3rd with another major 3rd added on top.

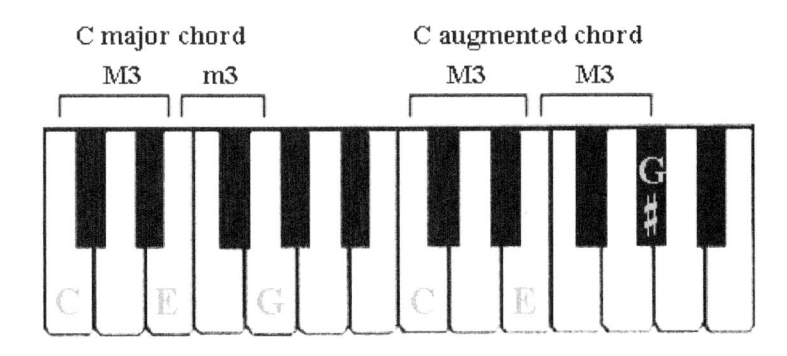

C major chord — M3, m3 — C E G
C augmented chord — M3, M3 — C E G#

The use of the double sharp is sometimes needed when augmenting certain chords, just as it was when augmenting certain intervals.

Since the top note of a "B major" chord is already sharped, we need to place a double sharp next to the top note in order to raise it one half step. Even though "F double sharp" is the same key as "G" on the piano keyboard, we cannot write the top note as "G". This would be an incorrect spelling of the chord. Why? Because as you learned above, an augmented chord is composed of a major 3rd with another major 3rd added on top. If we wrote the top note as "G" we would be notating a "4th" on the staff. ("D sharp" to "G" spans 4 staff lines & spaces, whereas "D sharp" to "F double sharp" spans 3 staff lines & spaces).

In the previous lesson we saw that different chord qualities evoke different emotions when heard. The major chord evokes happy or joyous emotions. The minor chord evokes sorrowful emotions. The augmented chord is often described as "anxious", or "unsure". (Of course sometimes emotion will depend on context; we are speaking in general here.) Listen again to the "C augmented" chord above and decide what type of emotion you think the augmented chord evokes.

THE DIMINISHED CHORD

A diminished chord is formed by taking a minor chord and lowering the top note one half step. Diminished chords can be represented by the word "dim" or by a superscript degree sign (°).

AUGMENTED & DIMINISHED CHORDS

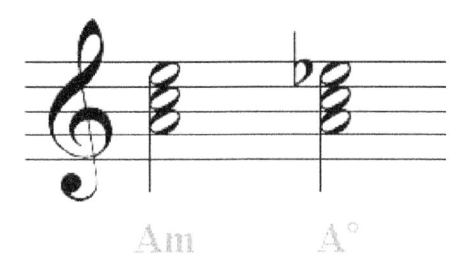

(Lesson 26 - Audio 2)

The first chord in the preceding diagram is an "A minor" chord. The second chord is an "A diminished" chord. As you can see, the top note "E" was lowered one half step to "E flat".

One characteristic that differentiates the minor and diminished chords is the size of the 5th in the chord. In a minor chord, the interval from the bottom note to the top note is a perfect 5th. In a diminished chord, the interval from the bottom note to the top note is a diminished 5th.

Another important characteristic that differentiates the minor and diminished chords is the size of the 3rds in the chord. We know from the previous lesson that a minor chord is composed of a minor 3rd with a major 3rd added on top. A diminished chord is composed of a minor 3rd with another minor 3rd added on top.

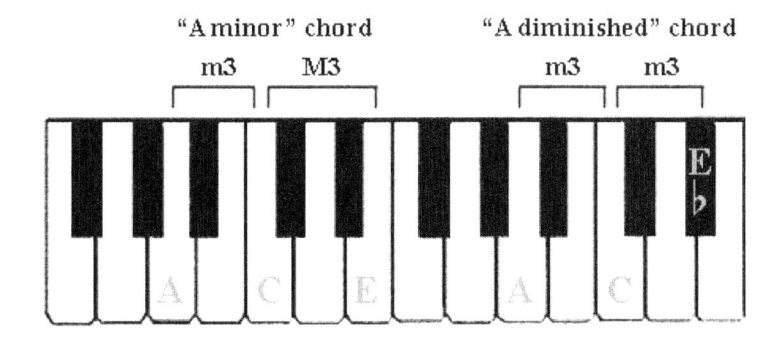

The use of the double flat is sometimes needed when diminishing certain chords, just as it was when diminishing certain intervals.

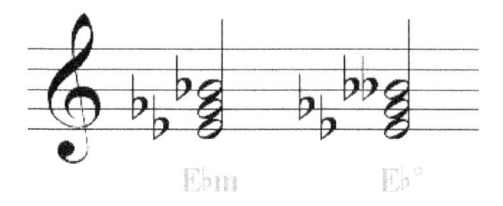

[musical notation: E♭m chord and E♭° chord]

Since the top note of an "E flat minor" chord is already flat, we need to place a double flat next to the top note in order to lower it one half step. Even though "B double flat" is the same key as "A" on the piano keyboard, we cannot write the top note as "A". This would be an incorrect spelling of the chord. Why? Because as you learned above, a diminished chord is composed of a minor 3rd with another minor 3rd added on top. If we wrote the top note as "A" we would be notating a 2nd on the staff. ("G flat" to "A" spans 2 staff lines & spaces, whereas "G flat" to "B double flat" spans 3 staff lines & spaces).

The diminished chord is often described as "angry" or "frustrated". (Again, sometimes emotion will depend on context; we are speaking in general here.) Listen again to the "A diminished" chord above and decide what type of emotion you think the diminished chord evokes.

Here is a list of the four chord qualities. Compare them and memorize the intervals that make them up.

Major triad = 4 half steps + 3 half steps (M3+m3)
Minor triad = 3 half steps + 4 half steps (m3+M3)
Augmented triad = 4 half steps + 4 half steps (M3+M3)
Diminished triad = 3 half steps + 3 half steps (m3+m3)

Memory Questions

What is an augmented chord?
An augmented chord is a chord composed of a major 3rd with another major 3rd added on top.

How does the size of the 5th differ in the major and augmented chords?
In a major chord the interval from the bottom note to the top note is a perfect 5th; in an augmented chord the interval from the bottom note to the top note is an augmented 5th.

How can a major chord become augmented?
A major chord can become augmented by raising the top note of the chord one half step.

What is a diminished chord?
A diminished chord is a chord composed of a minor 3rd with another minor 3rd added on top.

How does the size of the 5th differ in the minor and diminished chords?
In a minor chord the interval from the bottom note to the top note is a perfect 5th; in a diminished chord the interval from the bottom note to the top note is a diminished 5th.

How can a minor chord become diminished?
A minor chord can become diminished by lowering the top note of the chord one half step.

Lesson 26 Quiz

Log in to your course at www.udemy.com and take the quiz for this lesson.

27. THE MATHEMATICAL PROPORTIONS OF TRIADS

THE HARMONIC MEAN

Around the 16th century music began shifting from mostly horizontal in nature (single lines of melody) to more vertical in nature (use of chords). One man strove to explain this shift, and to make mathematical arguments for the use of chords in music. His name was Gioseffo Zarlino (1517-1590). Zarlino was an Italian music theorist, musician, composer, and Franciscan priest.

Using mathematics, Zarlino found that a major chord is the musical manifestation of the **harmonic mean** (one of the three Pythagorean means: harmonic mean, arithmetic mean, and geometric mean). A harmonic mean is a single number with a specific mathematical ratio to two other numbers. When the ratio between the largest and the smallest number is the same as the ratio between the "difference" of the two largest numbers and the "difference" of the two smallest numbers, it results in a harmonic mean. As you can see, the definition is a very long and confusing one. Let's use an example that will help make the definition clearer.

THE MATHEMATICAL PROPORTIONS OF TRIADS

$$15 : 12 : 10$$

The number 12 is the harmonic mean between the numbers 15 and 10. This is because the ratio of 15 to 10 (the largest and smallest numbers) is the same as the ratio of 3 to 2 (the difference between the two largest numbers, "15 minus 12", and the two smallest numbers, "12 minus 10"). The following diagram will help to illustrate.

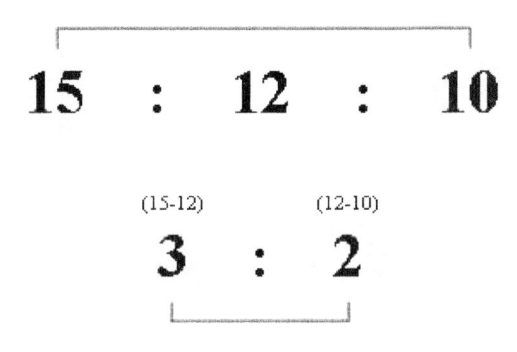

$$15 : 12 : 10$$

$$(15-12) \quad (12-10)$$
$$3 : 2$$

To see that the ratio of 15:10 is the same as the ratio of 3:2, we can write the ratio 15:10 as a fraction and divide by 5.

$$\frac{15}{10} \begin{array}{c} \div \ 5 \ = \ 3 \\ \div \ 5 \ = \ 2 \end{array}$$

This may all seem very abstract, so let's go ahead and apply these numbers to music. Let's measure out three lengths of string; one 15 inches in length, one 12 inches in length, and one 10 inches in length. Assuming that the 15 inch string produces the pitch "C", the 12 inch string will produce an "E" (a major 3rd higher), and the 10 inch string will produce a "G" (a minor 3rd higher than that). We have just created a major chord using the harmonic mean!

```
    C         E         G
    |         |         |
    |         |         |
    |         |         |
    |         |        10
    |        12
   15
```

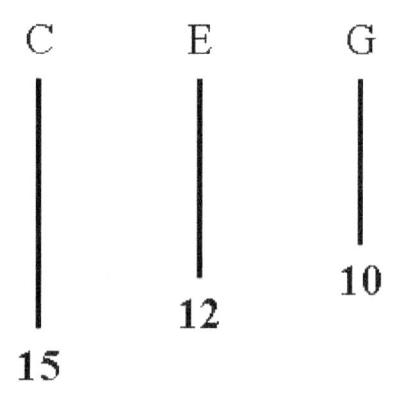

In lesson 25 we used a monochord to discover that the ratio of the major 3rd is 5:4 and the ratio of the minor 3rd is 6:5. At first glance, the numbers 15, 12, and 10 above, may not seem like the correct ratios for the intervals C-E-G, but they are. All we need to do is write them as fractions and simplify.

15 over 12 simplifies to 5 over 4; the ratio of the major 3rd.

$$\frac{15}{12} \div \frac{3}{3} = \frac{5}{4}$$

12 over 10 simplifies to 6 over 5; the ratio of the minor 3rd.

$$\frac{12}{10} \div \frac{2}{2} = \frac{6}{5}$$

The pitch "E" is therefore the harmonic mean between the pitches "C" and "G". Because of this fact, the major chord was termed "the harmonic division of the 5th" by Zarlino.

THE ARITHMETIC MEAN

Once again, using mathematics, Zarlino found that a minor chord is the musical manifestation of the **arithmetic mean**. What is the arithmetic mean? An arithmetic mean is a single number with a specific mathematical ratio to two other numbers. When the difference between the largest number and the middle number is the same as the difference between the middle number and the smallest number, it results in an arithmetic mean. Let's use an example that will help make the definition clearer.

$$6 : 5 : 4$$

The number 5 is the arithmetic mean between the numbers 6 and 4. This is because the difference between 6 and 5 and the difference between 5 and 4 is the same difference, namely "1". (6 - 5 = 1 and 5 - 4 = 1)

Now let's measure out three lengths of string; one 6 inches in length, one 5 inches in length, and one 4 inches in length. Assuming that the 6 inch string produces the pitch "A", the 5 inch string will produce a "C" (a minor 3rd higher), and the 4 inch string will produce an "E" (a major 3rd higher than that). We have just created a minor chord using the arithmetic mean!

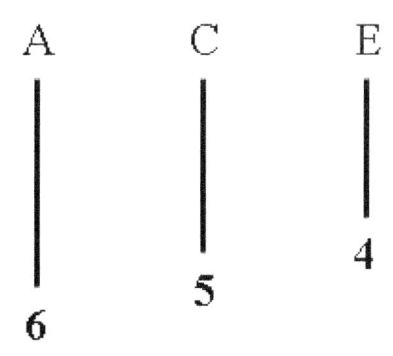

Notice the string lengths are the same as the ratios discovered on the monochord; the ratio of 6:5 creates the minor 3rd; the ratio of 5:4 creates the major 3rd.

The pitch "C" is therefore the arithmetic mean between the pitches "A" and "E". Because of this fact, the minor chord was termed "the arithmetic division of the 5th" by Zarlino.

THE GEOMETRIC MEAN

Although Zarlino didn't take this next step, we are now going to look at the ratios of the pitches in augmented and diminished chords. We know from our division of string lengths on the monochord that the ratio of the major 3rd is 5:4. Since the augmented chord is composed of two major 3rds, the ratio of the bottom pitch to the middle pitch will be 5:4 and the ratio of the middle pitch to the top pitch is also 5:4. Let's demonstrate this with string lengths.

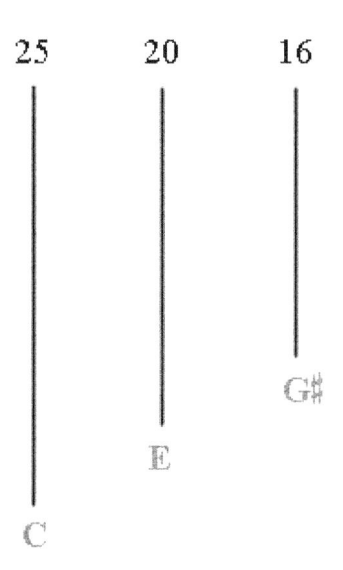

25   20   16

G♯

E

C

Let's say that a 25 inch length of string produced the pitch "C" when plucked. To produce the pitch "E", a major 3rd above "C", we would need a string length of 20 inches. (The ratio of 25:20 is the same ratio as 5:4; the ratio of the major 3rd.)

$$\frac{25}{20} \begin{array}{c} \div \\ \div \end{array} \begin{array}{c} 5 \\ 5 \end{array} \begin{array}{c} = \\ = \end{array} \frac{5}{4}$$

To produce the pitch "G sharp", a major 3rd above "E", we would need a string length of 16 inches. (The ratio of 20:16 is the same ratio as 5:4; the ratio of the major 3rd.)

$$\frac{20}{16} \begin{array}{c} \div \\ \div \end{array} \begin{array}{c} 4 \\ 4 \end{array} \begin{array}{c} = \\ = \end{array} \frac{5}{4}$$

Because 25:20 and 20:16 both have the ratio of 5:4, we can say that they are a continuous proportion.

$$25 : 20 :: 20 : 16$$

We read the above as follows: 25 is to 20, as 20 is to 16. What this means is that 20 is the geometric mean between 25 and 16. A geometric mean occurs when the first number has the same ratio to the middle number as the middle number has to the last number. In terms of pitches this means that "E" is the geometric mean between "C" and "G sharp", making the augmented chord the musical manifestation of the geometric mean.

Next let's look at the diminished chord. We know from our division of string lengths on the monochord that the ratio of the minor 3rd is 6:5. Since the diminished chord is composed of two minor 3rds, the ratio of the bottom pitch to the middle pitch will be 6:5 and the ratio of the middle pitch to the top pitch is also 6:5. Let's demonstrate this with string lengths.

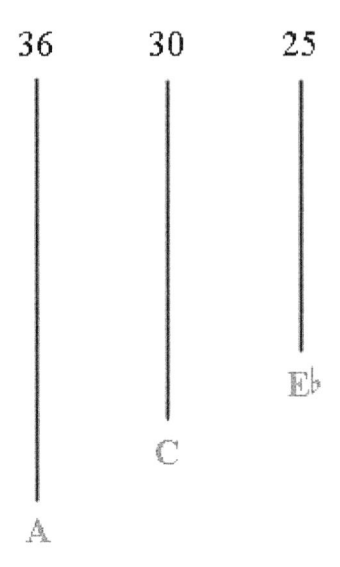

```
36        30        25
 |         |         |
 |         |         |
 |         |         |
 |         |         |
 |         |        Eb
 |         |
 |         C
 |
 A
```

Let's say that a 36 inch length of string produced the pitch "A" when plucked. To produce the pitch "C", a minor 3rd above "A", we would need a string length of 30 inches. (The ratio of 36:30 is the same ratio as 6:5; the ratio of the minor 3rd.)

$$\frac{36 \div 6}{30 \div 6} = \frac{6}{5}$$

To produce the pitch "E flat", a minor 3rd above "C", we would need a string length of 25 inches. (The ratio of 30:25 is the same ratio as 6:5; the ratio of the minor 3rd.)

$$\frac{30 \div 5}{25 \div 5} = \frac{6}{5}$$

THE MATHEMATICAL PROPORTIONS OF TRIADS

Because 36:30 and 30:25 both have the ratio of 6:5, we can say that they are a continuous proportion.

$$36 : 30 :: 30 : 25$$

We read the above as follows: 36 is to 30, as 30 is to 25. What this means is that 30 is the geometric mean between 36 and 25. In terms of pitches this means that "C" is the geometric mean between "A" and "E flat", making the diminished chord another example of the musical manifestation of the geometric mean.

To sum up what we have learned in this lesson:

> **The Harmonic Mean gives us the Major Triad**
> **The Arithmetic Mean gives us the Minor Triad**
> **The Geometric Mean gives us the Augmented Triad**
> **The Geometric Mean gives us the Diminished Triad**

Would you have ever guessed that music was so mathematical?

Memory Questions

Who was Gioseffo Zarlino?
Gioseffo Zarlino was an Italian music theorist, musician, composer, and Franciscan priest.

What did Zarlino discover about major and minor chords?
Zarlino discovered that major and minor chords had particular mathematical proportions.

The major chord is the musical manifestation of what Pythagorean mean?
The major chord is the musical manifestation of the harmonic mean.

The minor chord is the musical manifestation of what Pythagorean mean?
The minor chord is the musical manifestation of the arithmetic mean.

The augmented and diminished chords are musical manifestations of what Pythagorean mean?
The augmented and diminished chords are musical manifestations of the geometric mean.

Lesson 27 Quiz

Log in to your course at www.udemy.com and take the quiz for this lesson.

28. CHORDS OF THE MAJOR SCALE

CHORD ROOTS

In this lesson we are going to learn about the correlation that chords have to the scale. We will begin by looking at how composers and songwriters decide which chords to use in their pieces. Most of the time, they are using chords that come directly from the scale. Let's explain what is meant by this.

If we take a major scale and build a chord on each note of the scale, we can form seven different chords. The pitch of the scale that the chord is built upon is called the **root**. The root also corresponds with the chord's letter name. (The root of the "C" chord is "C"; the root of the "D chord" is "D"; etc.)

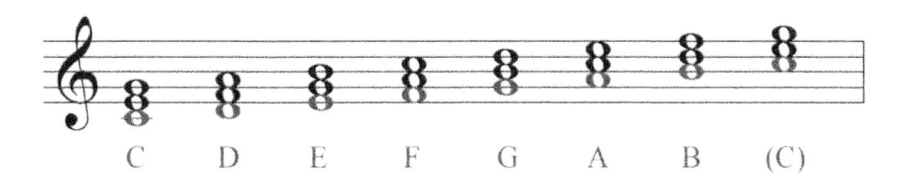

C D E F G A B (C)

It is important to note that each of the chords above is formed using only pitches from the C major scale (i.e., no other pitches are used in the chords other than C, D, E, F, G, A, and B).

CHORD QUALITIES OF THE MAJOR SCALE

Next let's look at the "quality" of each chord that can be formed using only the pitches of the major scale.

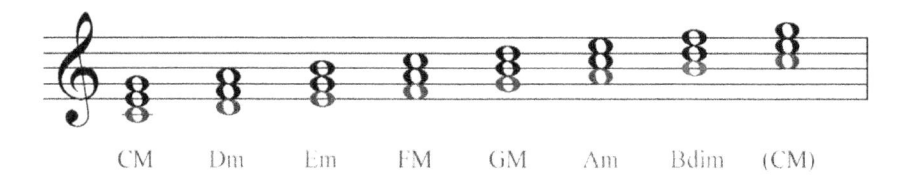

CM   Dm   Em   FM   GM   Am   Bdim   (CM)

As you can see in the preceding diagram, there are a total of three major chords, three minor chords, and one diminished chord.

It is important to understand that the chord qualities found in the major scale always appear in the same order no matter what the scale. Here is an example of the chords that can be formed using only the pitches of the D major scale.

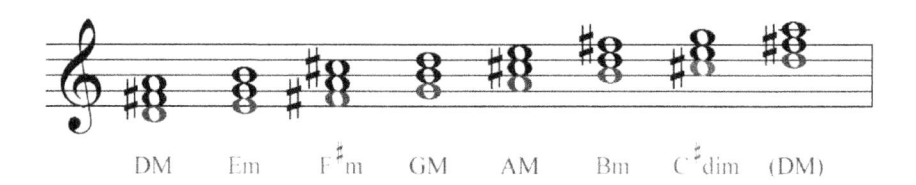

DM   Em   F#m   GM   AM   Bm   C#dim   (DM)

Notice that once again there are three major chords, three minor chords, and one diminished chord, and that they all occur in the same order. (M-m-m-M-M-m-dim)

The reason so many of the notes in the preceding diagram have sharps next to them is because the chords are formed using only the pitches of the D major scale: D, E, F sharp, G, A, B, and C sharp. Therefore all "F's" and "C's" in any of the chords must be sharp.

When a composer or songwriter is writing music in the key of "D major" they will most likely be using any of the seven chords above. If you are reading and playing music, having knowledge of each of the chords found in a scale will be a tremendous help in reading and processing the music much faster and also in understanding what it is you are playing.

This portion of the lesson was just an introduction into the correlation between chords and the scale. We will delve deeper in subsequent lessons.

ROOTS OF SCALES AND KEYS

At the beginning of this lesson we learned that every chord has a root. Scales and keys also have roots. The **root of a scale** is the pitch that the scale is built upon. For example, a "C major" scale will have "C" as its root.

The root of a scale (or key) is also sometimes referred to as the "key-note" or "home note". It is the pitch where the music feels most peaceful and at rest (most at home). To demonstrate this, listen to the C major scale with the final root omitted.

(Lesson 28 - Audio 1)

Did you hear how omitting the final root leaves you hanging? Our ears are not at rest until we hear the "home note".

The **root of a key** is the tonal center of a piece of music (or section of music). A tonal center is a specific pitch which the piece (or section) centers around. For example, a piece of music in the key of "G major" will have "G" as its tonal center, i.e., "G" will be the pitch which the music is centered around. There are numerous ways a piece of music can be centered around the pitch "G":

- "G" may be the first and last pitch of the song.
- "G" may be the most frequently heard pitch.
- The chord built on "G" may be the most frequently heard chord.
- Chords with strong relationships to the "G" chord will be used to refer the listener back to the tonal center "G". (We will learn about chord relationships in a later lesson.)

Note: Since the key of a piece originates from the pitches of the scale, the root of the scale and the root of the key will always be the same pitch.

Memory Questions

How many chords can be formed using only the pitches of the major scale?
Seven chords can be formed using only the pitches of the major scale.

How many major chords can be formed using only the pitches of the major scale?
Three major chords can be formed using only the pitches of the major scale.

How many minor chords can be formed using only the pitches of the major scale?
Three minor chords can be formed using only the pitches of the major scale.

How many diminished chords can be formed using only the pitches of the major scale?
One diminished chord can be formed using only the pitches of the major scale.

What is the order of the chord qualities found in the major scale?
The order of the chord qualities found in the major scale is: Major - Minor - Minor - Major - Major - Minor – Diminished.

What is the root of a chord?
The root of a chord is the particular pitch of the scale from which a chord has been built, and also the pitch from which the chord takes its name.

What is the root of a scale?
The root of a scale is the pitch that the scale is built upon.

What is the root of a key?
The root of a key is the tonal center of a piece of music (or section of music).

Lesson 28 Quiz

Log in to your course at www.udemy.com and take the quiz for this lesson.

29. THE NATURAL MINOR SCALE

COMPARING MAJOR AND MINOR SCALES

In lesson 20 we learned about the major scale and its origin. In this lesson we are going to learn about the **minor scale**. There are three forms of minor scales. The form that we will be studying in this lesson is called the **natural minor scale**.

Note: the term "natural" has nothing to do with the natural sign that cancels out a sharp or a flat. Here, "natural" denotes that the scale is in its "natural" form. The meaning of "natural" form will become clear when we study the other two forms of minor scales in the next lesson.

Just like the major scale, minor scales originated from Greek tetrachords. The natural minor scale is made up of two tetrachords, each consisting of two whole steps and one half step. The difference between the major scale and the natural minor scale is the order in which the whole steps and half steps occur. Let's compare each.

THE NATURAL MINOR SCALE

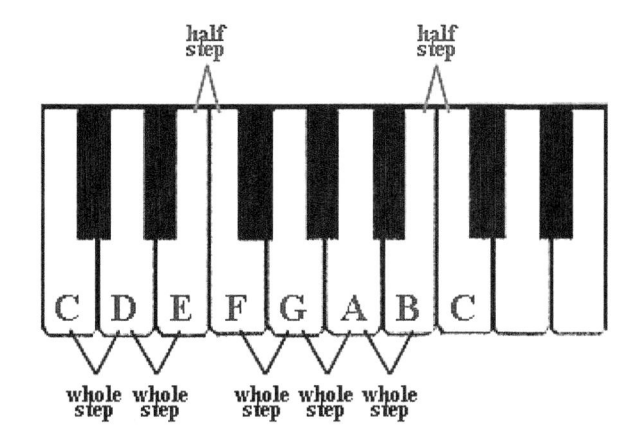

"C major" scale (Lesson 29 - Audio 1)

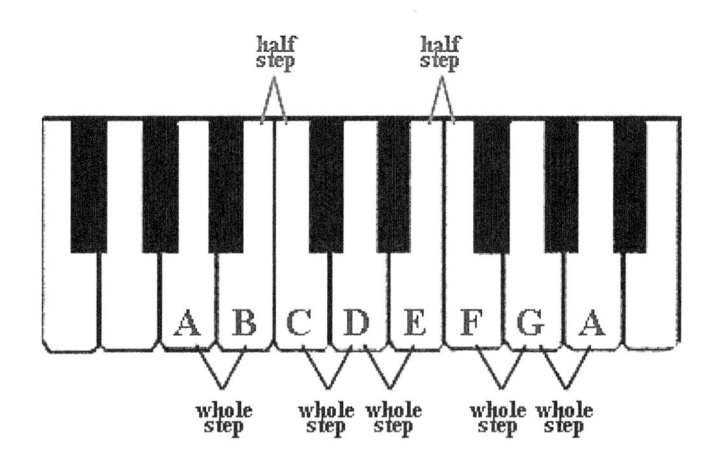

"A natural minor" scale (Lesson 29 - Audio 2)

Notice that the half steps in the natural minor scale occur at different places than in the major scale. The half steps are located between pitches 3 & 4 and 7 & 8 in the major scale, and between pitches 2 & 3 and 5 & 6 in the natural minor scale.

The natural minor scale above is called an "A natural minor" scale because it begins and ends on "A". If we had begun the scale on a pitch other than "A", certain pitches would need to be sharped or flatted to maintain the order of whole steps and half steps. Here is an example of a "D natural minor" scale. As you can see, a "B flat" is needed to maintain the half step between the 5th and 6th pitches.

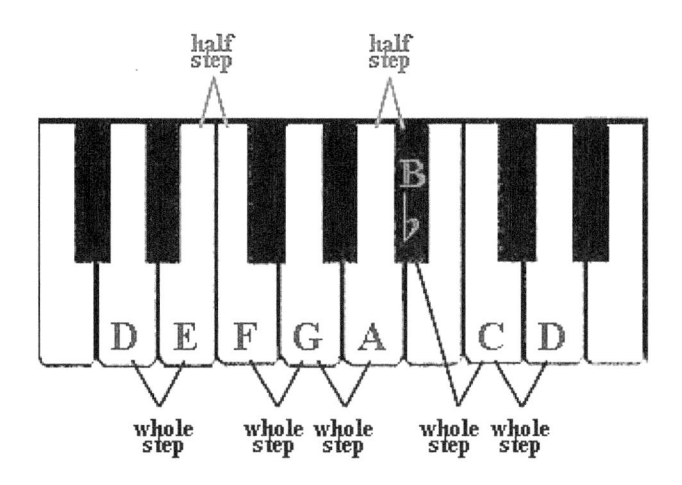

Important: the pitches of the scale must be neighbor letters of the musical alphabet. For example, "B flat" was used above rather than its enharmonic equivalent, "A sharp", to avoid having two "A's" in a row. (D, E, F, G, A, A sharp, C, D) Using "A sharp" would be an incorrect spelling of the scale.

Memory Questions

Where did minor scales originate?
Minor scales originated from Greek tetrachords.

How many forms of the minor scale are there?
There are three forms of the minor scale.

What is a natural minor scale?
A natural minor scale is a particular sequence of whole steps and half steps encompassing 8 pitches. The sequence in ascending order is: whole - half - whole - whole - half - whole - whole.

Where are the half steps in the natural minor scale located?
The half steps in the natural minor scale are located between pitches 2 & 3 and pitches 5 & 6.

Lesson 29 Exercises

Log in to your course at www.udemy.com and practice the exercises for this lesson.

Lesson 29 Quiz

Log in to your course at www.udemy.com and take the quiz for this lesson.

30. HARMONIC & MELODIC MINOR SCALES

THE HARMONIC MINOR SCALE

In the previous lesson we learned about the natural minor scale. In this lesson we are going to be studying the other two forms of minor scales: the **harmonic minor scale** and **melodic minor scale**. Let's begin with the harmonic minor scale and compare it with the natural minor scale.

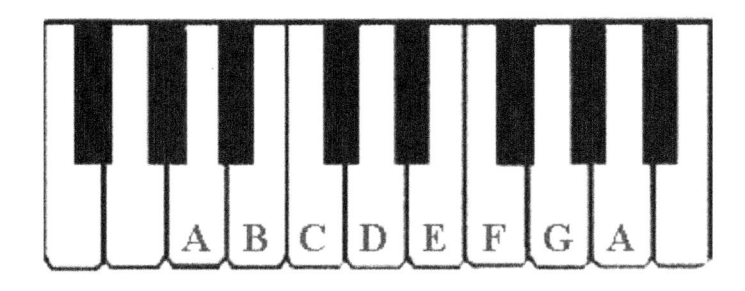

"A natural minor" scale (Lesson 30 - Audio 1)

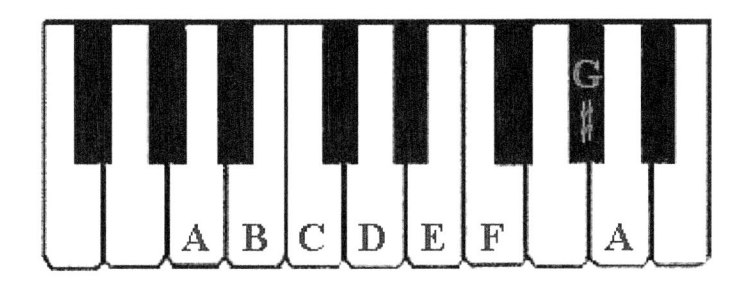

HARMONIC & MELODIC MINOR SCALES

"A harmonic minor" scale (Lesson 30 - Audio 2)

As you can see in the preceding diagrams, there is only one difference between the natural minor scale and the harmonic minor scale. The 7th pitch of the harmonic minor scale is raised one half step. Because of this, the order of whole steps and half steps is different. In fact the distance between the 6th and 7th pitches of the scale ("F" to "G sharp") is neither a whole step nor a half step; it is three half steps! This makes the harmonic minor scale the only scale that is not made up entirely of single whole steps and half steps.

Important: the pitches of the scale must be neighbor letters of the musical alphabet. For example, "G sharp" was used above rather than its enharmonic equivalent, "A flat", to avoid having two "A's" in a row. (A, B, C, D, E, F, A flat, A) Using "A flat" would be an incorrect spelling of the scale.

Of the three forms of minor scales, the harmonic minor scale is the most commonly used by composers and songwriters. One of the reasons for this is the raised 7th. The raised 7th produces a larger distance between the 6th & 7th pitches of the scale and a smaller distance between the 7th & 8th pitches. This creates a stronger "pull" towards the key's tonal center "A". In other words, hearing the root "A" becomes even more satisfying, and the sense of being at rest on the "home note" is even stronger.

THE MELODIC MINOR SCALE

The third and final form of minor scale is the **melodic minor scale**. We can best understand it by comparing it to the natural minor scale.

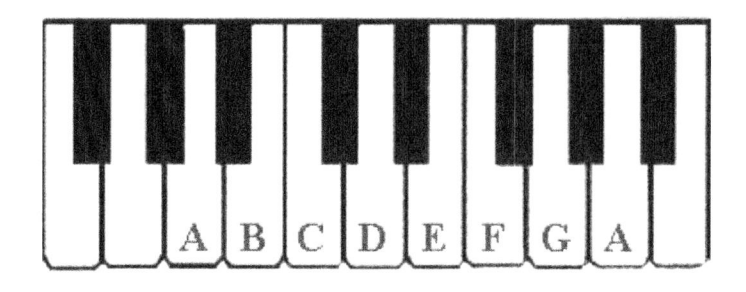

"A natural minor" scale (Lesson 30 - Audio 1)

"A melodic minor" scale (Lesson 30 - Audio 3)

As you can see in the preceding diagrams, there are only two differences between the natural minor scale and the melodic minor scale. The 6th and 7th pitches of the melodic minor scale are raised one half step. Because of this, the order of whole steps and half steps is different.

It is important to note that the melodic minor scale is played one way when ascending and another way when descending. It is only the ascending version that contains the raised 6th & 7th pitches; the descending version is played exactly like a descending "natural" minor scale (without the raised 6th & 7th pitches).

HARMONIC & MELODIC MINOR SCALES

The ascending melodic minor scale also has a similarity to the major scale. The sequence of whole steps and half steps formed by the last four pitches are the same in each scale (whole - whole - half).

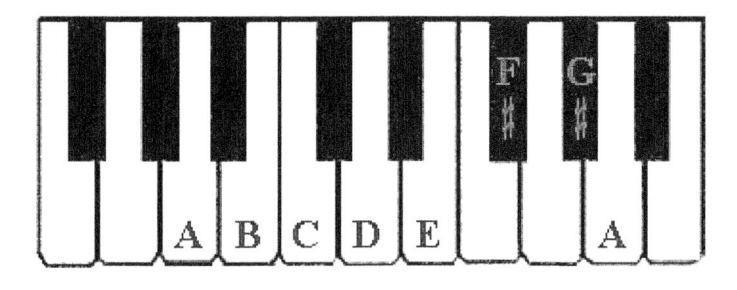

Ascending "A melodic minor" scale (Lesson 30 - Audio 3)

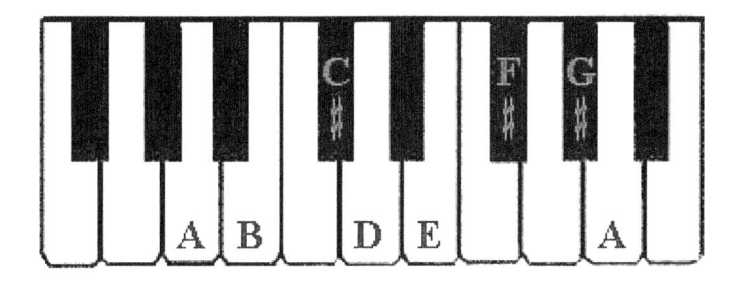

"A major" scale (Lesson 30 - Audio 4)

(Due to the ascending melodic minor's similarity to the major scale, music that uses the pitches of the ascending melodic minor scale is not as "sad" sounding as music that uses the pitches of the natural or harmonic minor scales.)

Memory Questions

What are the three forms of the minor scale?
The three forms of the minor scale are natural, harmonic and melodic.

Of the three forms of minor scales, which is the most commonly used by composers and songwriters?
Of the three forms of minor scales, the harmonic minor scale is the most commonly used by composers and songwriters.

How is the harmonic scale formed?
The harmonic minor scale is formed by raising the 7th pitch of the natural minor scale.

How is the "ascending" melodic scale formed?
The "ascending" melodic minor scale is formed by raising the 6th & 7th pitches of the natural minor scale.

How does the "descending" melodic minor scale differ from the "ascending" melodic minor scale?
The "descending" melodic minor scale does not have the 6th and 7th pitches raised; it is the same as the descending natural minor scale.

What do the ascending melodic minor scale and the major scale have in common?
The ascending melodic minor scale and the major scale have the sequence of whole steps and half steps formed by the last four pitches in common (whole - whole - half).

Lesson 30 Exercises

Log in to your course at www.udemy.com and practice the exercises for this lesson.

Lesson 30 Quiz

Log in to your course at www.udemy.com and take the quiz for this lesson.

31. MINOR KEYS

RELATIVE KEYS

In lesson 21 we learned that a key is a specific group of pitches used to write a piece of music (or part of a piece of music). The specific group of pitches is determined by a particular scale. Pieces written using the pitches from major scales are said to be in a major key. Pieces written using the pitches of minor scales are said to be in a minor key.

We also learned about major key signatures in lesson 21. A key signature is the sharps or flats placed on the staff at the beginning of each line of music. It indicates which key the piece of music (or part of a piece of music) is written in.

In this lesson we are going to learn about minor keys. Every major key has a corresponding minor key. We call this corresponding minor key the **relative minor**. Every minor key has a corresponding major key. We call corresponding major key the **relative major**. Keys that are "relative" share the same pitches and therefore the same key signature. This can be illustrated with the "circle of 5ths". The uppercase letters represent the relative major keys; the lowercase letters represent the relative minor keys.

MINOR KEYS

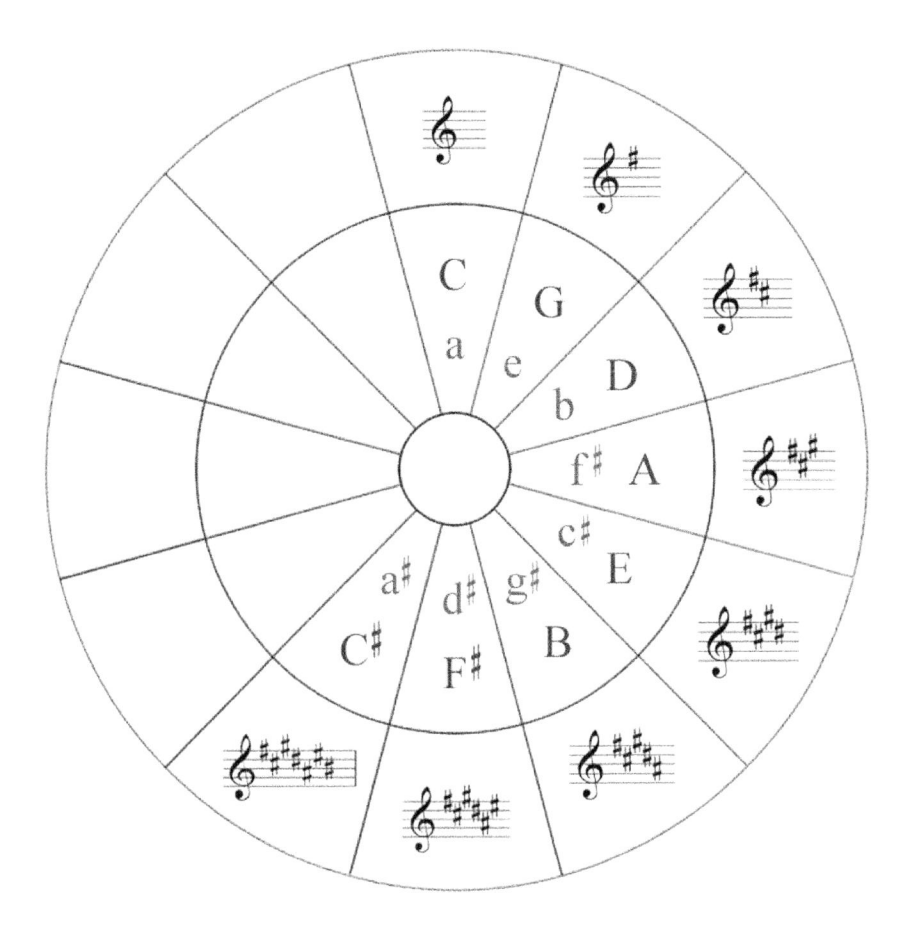

To find the relative minor of a particular major key, name the pitch a minor 3rd lower than that major key's name. This will be the relative minor. Let's test this useful little trick out. Find the key of "C major" on the circle of 5ths above. The pitch a minor 3rd lower than "C", is "A". "C major" and "A minor" are relative keys; neither of them contains any sharps or flats. Next, find the key of "G major" on the circle of 5ths above. The pitch a minor 3rd lower than "G", is "E". "G major" and "E minor" are relative keys; they both contain one sharp ("F sharp").

Note: Everything mentioned above also works in reverse, that is, it works for finding the relative major of a minor key. To find the relative major of a particular minor key, name the pitch a minor 3rd higher than that minor key's name.

MUSIC THEORY

<u>Important</u>: A minor 3rd is equal to 3 half steps. When you count three half steps, be sure to skip one letter of the musical alphabet otherwise you will end up with an incorrect musical spelling. For example, three half steps lower than "A" in the preceding diagram, is "F sharp", not the enharmonic equivalent, "G flat".

The other way to find the relative minor of a particular major key is by naming the sixth pitch of that major scale. For example, the sixth pitch of the C major scale is "A". Therefore, "A minor" is the relative minor of "C major".

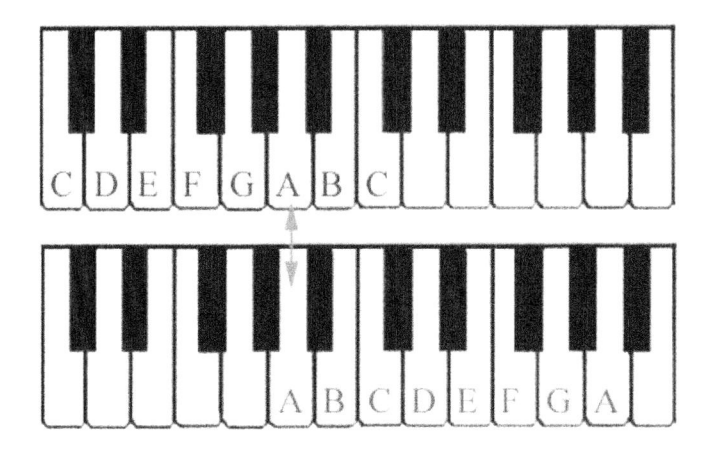

Although this way of finding the relative key is more difficult (it involves memorizing every possible major scale), it makes the relationship between the relative major and minor keys very apparent. Both of the scales above are made up of the exact same pitches, and this is the reason that they share the same key signature. A song written in "C major" uses the exact same pitches as a song written in the key of "A minor". The only difference is that the song in "C major" has "C" as its tonal center, while the song in "A minor" has "A" as its tonal center.

Note: When using the scale to find the relative major of a particular minor key, name the third pitch of that minor scale. For example, the third pitch of the "A minor" scale is "C". "C major is therefore the relative major to "A minor".

MINOR KEYS

Here is the other half of the circle of 5ths for you to study. This side of the circle shows the relative minor keys that contain flats. The relative minor of a particular major key is once again found by naming the pitch that is a minor 3rd lower than that major key's name.

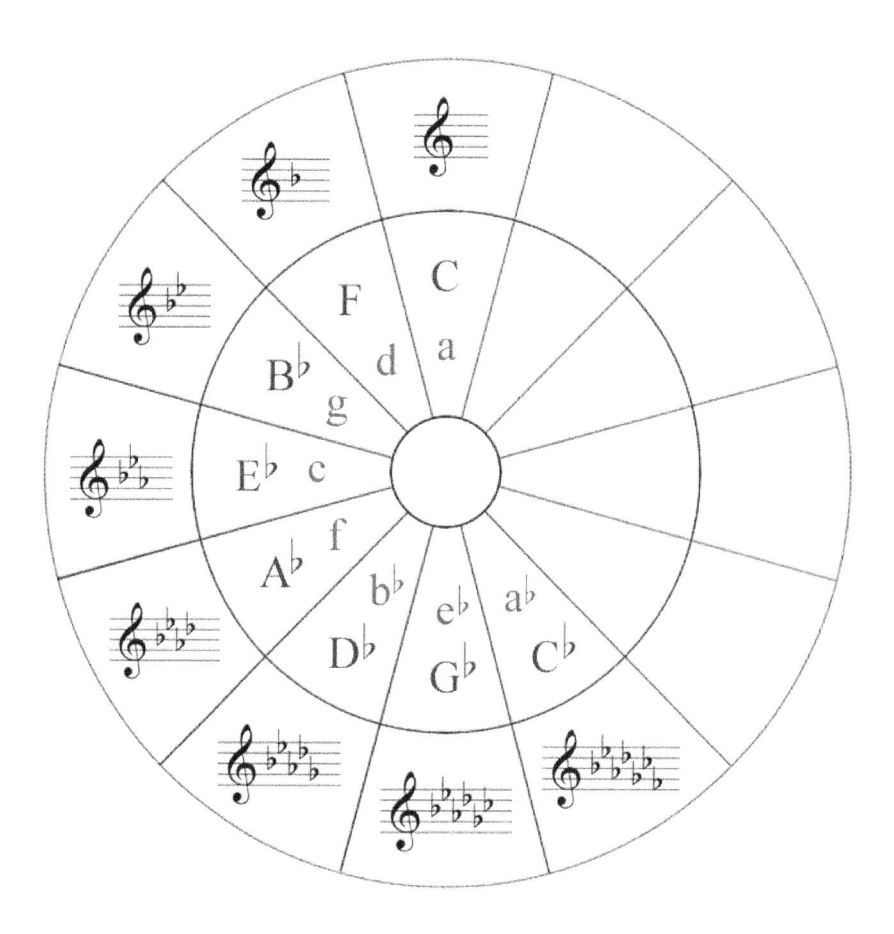

(Be sure to take note of the six enharmonic keys in the two preceding "circle of 5ths" diagrams. "A sharp minor" is the enharmonic equivalent of "B flat minor"; "D sharp minor" is the enharmonic equivalent of "E flat minor"; "G sharp minor" is the enharmonic equivalent of "A flat minor".)

SHARED KEY SIGNATURES

Let's say that you were given a piece of music and the key signature had no sharps and flats. How would you determine if the piece was in "C major" or in its relative minor "A minor"? Since relative keys share the same key signature, there is no way to tell by looking only at the key signature. We must also look at the pitches in the music. Listen to the following example.

(Lesson 31 - Audio 1)

Since the preceding example is written in a key signature with no sharps or flats, we know that it is either in "C major" or its relative "A minor". To determine the key we must:

1) Use our ears. Does the music have a minor quality (sad sounding), or does it have a major quality (happy sounding)? This example definitely has a minor quality.

2) Find the tonal center. Measures 1, 2, and 4 have a downward motion ending on the pitch "A". "A" is a frequently repeated pitch. "A" is also the final note. These three aspects point to the music being in the key of "A minor" rather than "C major".

PARALLEL KEYS

Keys that have the same tonal center are called **parallel keys**. Because they share the same tonal center, parallel keys will therefore also have the same letter name. Parallel keys do not however have the same key signatures. Here is an example of "C major" and its parallel minor, "C minor".

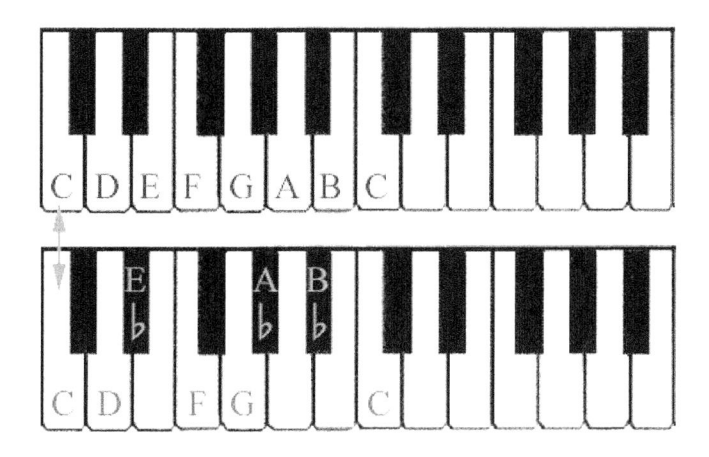

As you can see, both keys have the same tonal center (or root), "C". All of the pitches have the same letter names, but three of the pitches are flat in C minor. The key signature of "C major" and the key signature of "C minor" will therefore be different.

Relative and parallel keys are very important in music, because it is very easy to transition from a major key to the relative minor key, or from a major key to the parallel minor key (or vice versa).

Memory Questions

What are relative keys?
Relative keys are keys that have the same pitches but different tonal centers. They also share the same key signature.

Do all major keys have a corresponding relative minor key?
Yes, all major keys have a corresponding relative minor key (and vice versa).

How do we find the relative minor of a particular major key?
To find the relative minor of a particular major key, name the pitch a minor 3rd lower than that major key's name; or name the sixth pitch of that major scale.

How do we find the relative major of a particular minor key?
To find the relative major of a particular minor key, name the pitch a minor 3rd higher than that minor key's name; or name the third pitch of that minor scale.

What are parallel keys?
Parallel keys are keys that have the same tonal center but different pitches. They do not share the same key signature.

Do all major keys have a corresponding parallel minor key?
Yes, all major keys have a corresponding parallel minor key (and vice versa).

Lesson 31 Quiz

Log in to your course at www.udemy.com and take the quiz for this lesson.

32. CHORDS OF THE MINOR SCALE

NATURAL MINOR SCALE CHORDS

In lesson 28 we learned which chords could be formed using only the pitches of the major scale. In this lesson we are going to learn which chords can be formed using only the pitches of the minor scale. Starting with an "A natural minor" scale, and building a chord on each pitch of the scale, we end up with the following chord qualities:

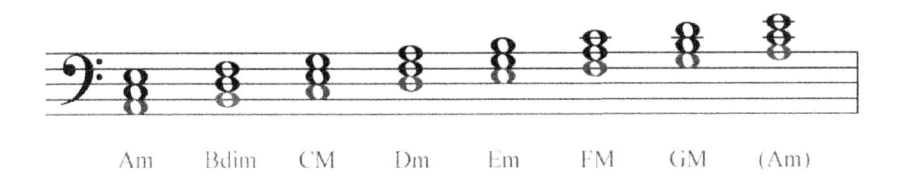

Am   Bdim   CM   Dm   Em   FM   GM   (Am)

It is important to note that each of the chords above is formed using only pitches from the A natural minor scale (no other pitches are used in the chords other than A, B, C, D, E, F, and G).

As you can see in the preceding diagram, there are a total of three major chords, three minor chords, and one diminished chord. They will always appear in the order above no matter the scale. For example, the chords built on an "A natural minor" scale will have the same order as the chords built on a "D natural minor" scale (m-dim-M-m-m-M-M).

Furthermore, the natural minor scale has the same number of major, minor, and diminished chords as the major scale; only they are in a different order. Here are the chords built on the C major scale for your review. (Compare the order found in the major scale below, with the order found in the natural minor scale above.)

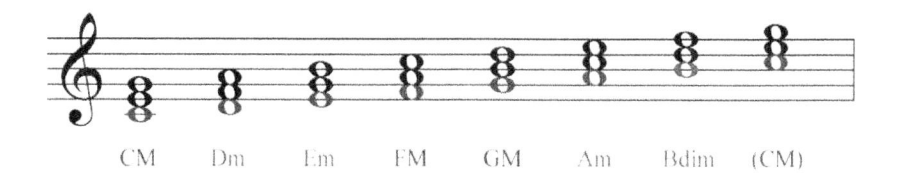

CM   Dm   Em   FM   GM   Am   Bdim   (CM)

HARMONIC MINOR SCALE CHORDS

In lesson 30 we learned that the harmonic minor scale is formed by raising the 7th pitch of the natural minor scale one half step. The pitches of the "A harmonic minor" scale are therefore A, B, C, D, E, F, and G sharp. If we build a chord on each of these pitches we get the following chord qualities:

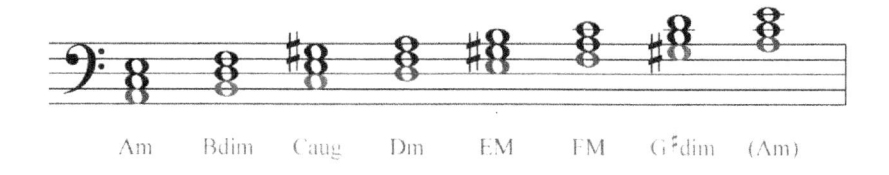

Am   Bdim   Caug   Dm   EM   FM   G#dim   (Am)

As you can see in the preceding diagram, there are a total of two major chords, two minor chords, two diminished chords, and one augmented chord. They will always appear in the order above no matter the scale. For example, the chords built on an "A harmonic minor" scale will have the same order as the chords built on an "E harmonic minor" scale (m-dim-aug-m-M-M-dim). The reason some of the chords in the preceding diagram contain a "G sharp" is because all of the chords are formed using only the pitches of the "A harmonic minor" scale (which includes a "G sharp)". By using the harmonic minor scale rather than the natural minor scale, composers and songwriters can have a different set of chords to work with when writing music.

Memory Questions

How many major, minor, and diminished chords can be formed using only the pitches of the natural minor scale?
Three major chords, three minor chords, and one diminished chord can be formed using only the pitches of the natural minor scale.

What is the order of the chord qualities found in the natural minor scale?
The order of the chord qualities found in the natural minor scale is: Minor - Diminished - Major - Minor - Minor - Major - Major.

How many major, minor, diminished, and augmented chords can be formed using only the pitches of the harmonic minor scale?
Two major chords, two minor chords, two diminished chords, and one augmented chord can be formed using only the pitches of the harmonic minor scale.

What is the order of the chord qualities found in the harmonic minor scale?

The order of the chord qualities found in the harmonic minor scale is: Minor - Diminished - Augmented - Minor - Major - Major - Diminished.

Lesson 32 Quiz

Log in to your course at www.udemy.com and take the quiz for this lesson.

33. DEGREES OF THE SCALE

NAMING WITH ROMAN NUMERALS

Thus far we have named the pitches of the scale and the chords built upon them using letter names. In this lesson we are going to learn how to name the pitches of the scale and the chords built upon them using Roman numerals. Naming with Roman numerals is actually the preferred method of naming. The reason for this will become clear as we proceed.

In case you are not familiar with Roman numerals, here are the first seven Roman numerals and their modern equivalents.

I (1)
II (1+1=2)
III (1+1+1=3)
IV (1 taken from 5 = 4)
V (5)
VI (5+1=6)
VII (5+1+1=7)

In the following diagram, the Roman numerals are placed under each degree of the scale. ("Degree" is another term for "pitches" of the scale, or "steps" of the scale.)

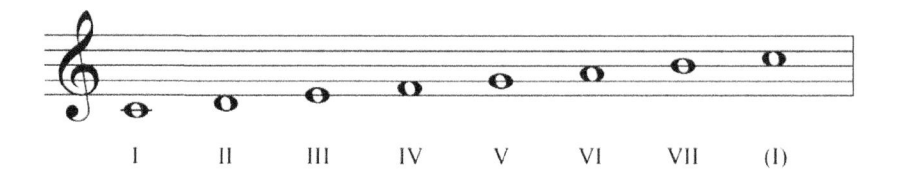

[musical staff: C major scale with degrees labeled I, II, III, IV, V, VI, VII, (I)]

It is very important to understand that Roman numerals are not specific to a certain pitch, but rather they are specific to the degrees of the scale. Let's explain what is meant by this. In the preceding diagram, "C" is the 1st pitch of the C major scale, and so it is named using the Roman numeral "I". In the following diagram, "C" is the 4th pitch of the G major scale, and so it is named using the Roman numeral "IV".

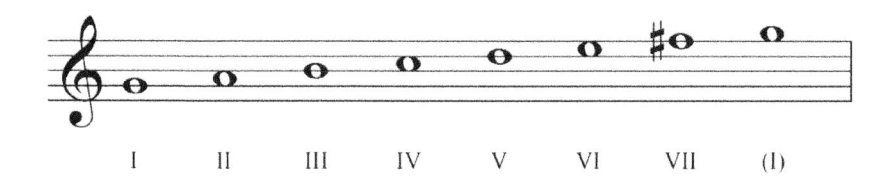

[musical staff: G major scale with degrees labeled I, II, III, IV, V, VI, VII, (I)]

As mentioned above, Roman numerals are not only used to name each pitch of the scale, but also the chords built upon them. Major chords are indicated with an uppercase Roman numeral while minor, diminished, and augmented chords are indicated with a lowercase Roman numeral.

DEGREES OF THE SCALE

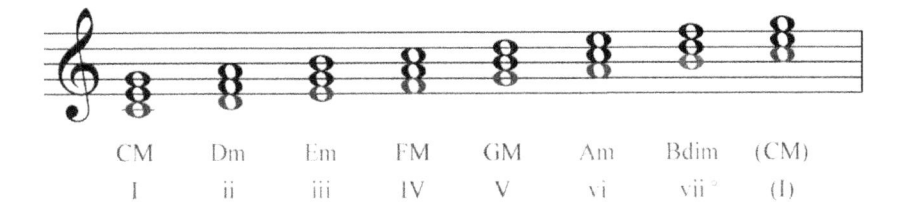

CM	Dm	Em	FM	GM	Am	Bdim	(CM)
I	ii	iii	IV	V	vi	vii°	(I)

Just as Roman numerals are not specific to certain pitches, so too, they are not specific to certain chords. Rather, they are specific to the degrees of the scale. For example, in the preceding diagram, the "A minor" chord is the 6th chord of the scale, and so it is named using the Roman numeral "vi". In the following diagram, the "A minor" chord is the 2nd chord of the scale, and so it is named using the Roman numeral "ii".

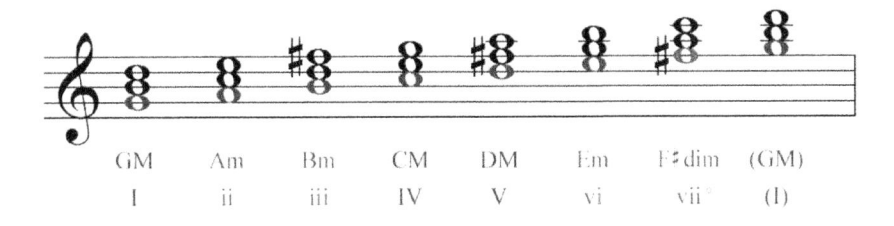

GM	Am	Bm	CM	DM	Em	F#dim	(GM)
I	ii	iii	IV	V	vi	vii°	(I)

Calling chords by their letter names is very useful in identifying them, but calling chords by their Roman numeral has an even greater benefit; it tells us about a chord's positional relationship to the other chords in the scale. The relationship between chords is an important aspect of music. We will learn more about the relationships between certain chords as we proceed through the course.

Note: Although only major scales were used in the diagrams for this lesson, the degrees of the minor scale can also be named using Roman numerals.

Memory Questions

What are the degrees of the scale?
The degrees of the scale are the pitches of the scale.

What are two ways of naming the degrees of the scale and the chords built upon them?
The degrees of the scale and the chords built upon them may be named using letters of the alphabet or Roman numerals.

What are uppercase Roman numerals used to indicate?
Uppercase Roman numerals are used to indicate major chords.

What are lowercase Roman numerals used to indicate?
Lowercase Roman numerals are used to indicate minor, diminished, and augmented chords.

Does a chord's Roman numeral name correspond with its letter name?
No, a chord's Roman numeral name does not correspond with its letter name; the Roman numeral name is specific to its place in the scale.

What is the benefit of naming chords with Roman numerals?
The benefit of naming chords with Roman numerals is to know a chord's positional relationship to other chords in the scale.

Lesson 33 Quiz

Log in to your course at www.udemy.com and take the quiz for this lesson.

34. PRIMARY CHORDS

CHORD RELATIONSHIPS

In the last lesson we learned how the pitches of the scale and the chords built upon them can be named with Roman numerals. In this lesson we are going to take a closer look at the "I", "IV", and "V" chords. We call these three chords **primary chords**.

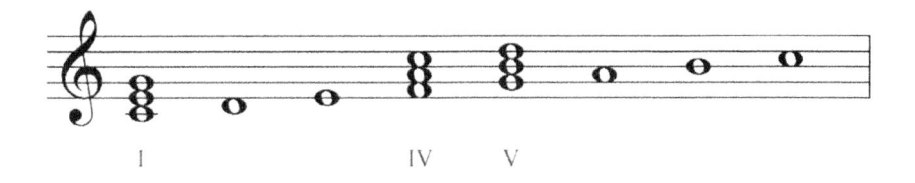

The primary chords are the chords most frequently used in music. There are two reasons for this. The first is their ability to harmonize with the pitches of the scale. Using only the primary chords, a composer or songwriter is able to create harmonies that will blend with any pitch of the scale. This is because every pitch of the scale can be found in the primary chords.

C (lowest pitch in the "I" chord, highest pitch in the "IV" chord)
D (highest pitch in the "V" chord)
E (middle pitch in the "I" chord)
F (lowest pitch in the "IV" chord)
G (highest pitch in the "I" chord, lowest pitch in the "V" chord)
A (middle pitch in the "IV" chord)
B (middle pitch in the "V" chord)

The second reason the primary chords are the chords most frequently used in music is their strong relationship to the root of the scale (or key). Let's explain this by looking at each of the primary chords in turn.

The "I" chord has the strongest relationship to the root of the scale because it is built upon the root of the scale. In fact, the root of the "I" chord and the root of the scale are the same pitch.

The "V" chord is the chord with the second strongest relationship to the root of the scale. The reason for this can be seen from Pythagoras' experiment on the monochord, the mathematical ratios of pitches, and the physics of sound waves (we will study the physics of sound waves in a subsequent lesson). We know that the first and fifth pitches of the scale (a 5th) have a very strong relationship to one another (i.e., a 5th is a very consonant interval). Therefore, the chords built on these pitches of the scale will also have a strong relationship to one another.

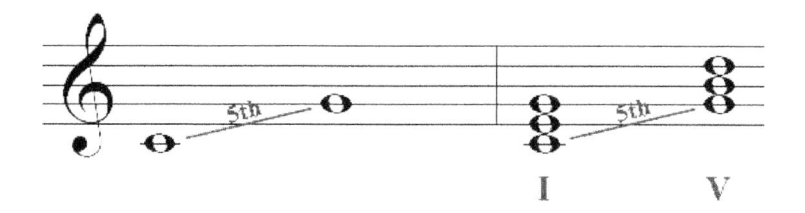

What do we mean when we say that the "V" chord has a strong relationship to the "I" chord? Do we mean that they sound well together the same way a 5th sounds consonant? No. We what we mean is that the "V" chord has a strong tendency towards the "I" chord. In other words, after hearing the "V" chord, our ear desires to hear the "I" chord. (More on this in subsequent lessons)

The "IV" chord is the chord with the third strongest relationship to the root of the scale. Once again, the reason for this can be seen from Pythagoras' experiment on the monochord, the mathematical ratios of pitches, and the physics of sound waves. We know that the first and fourth pitches of the scale (a 4th) have a strong relationship to one another (i.e., a 4th is a consonant interval). Therefore, the chords built on these pitches of the scale will also have a strong relationship to one another.

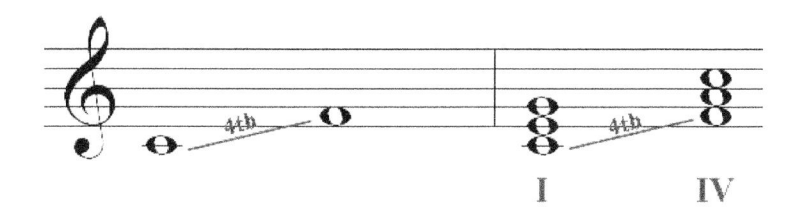

What do we mean when we say that the "IV" chord has a strong relationship to the "I" chord? Do we mean that they sound well together the same way a 4th sounds consonant? No. We what we mean is that the "IV" chord has a strong tendency towards the "I" chord (Not as strong as the tendency that "V" has to "I". You will be able to hear this distinction when we learn about cadences in a subsequent lesson.)

Because chords "IV" and "V" have a strong tendency towards "I", they are often used to refer the ear back the root of the scale, thus helping to create a tonal center in the music.

Note: Everything regarding primary chords and chord relationships mentioned above, also applies to the primary chords in minor keys. While the primary chords of the major scale are all major chords, the primary chords of the minor scale are all minor.

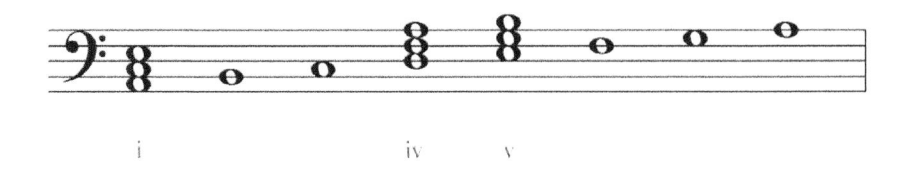

If however, the chords are built upon the harmonic minor form of the scale, the "V" chord will become major. We observed this in lesson 32 but it is mentioned again here for your review, since it specifically relates to the concept of primary chords.

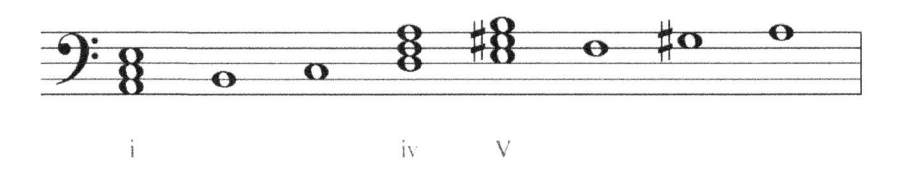

Memory Questions

What are primary chords?
Primary chords are the chords built upon the 1st, 4th, and 5th pitches of the scale.

Why are the primary chords the most frequently used chords in music?
The primary chords are the most frequently used chords in music because of their ability to harmonize with the pitches of the scale, and because of their relationship to the root of the scale.

What is the "I" chord's relationship to the root of the scale?
The "I" chord is built upon the root of the scale.

What is the "IV" chord's relationship to the root of the scale?
The "IV" chord is related to the root of the scale by way of a 4th.

What is the "V" chord's relationship to the root of the scale?
The "V" chord is related to the root of the scale by way of a 5th.

Which chord has the strongest tendency to the "I" chord?
The "V" chord has the strongest tendency to the "I" chord.

Which chord has the second strongest tendency to the "I" chord?
The "IV" chord has the second strongest tendency to the "I" chord.

What qualities are the primary chords of the major scale?
The primary chords of the major scale are all major.

What qualities are the primary chords of the natural minor scale?
The primary chords of the natural minor scale are all minor.

What qualities are the primary chords of the harmonic minor scale?
The primary chords of the harmonic minor scale are all minor, with the exception of the "V" chord, which is major.

Lesson 34 Quiz

Log in to your course at www.udemy.com and take the quiz for this lesson.

35. CHORD INVERSIONS

REORDERING CHORD PITCHES

In lesson 24 we learned that intervals may be inverted by moving the lowest pitch of the interval an octave higher so that it becomes the highest pitch. Chord inversions are formed in the exact same way. Let's illustrate this using a C major chord on the piano keyboard.

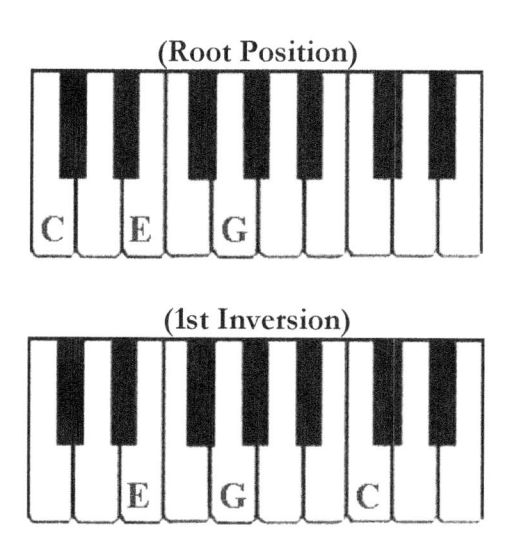

(Root Position)

C E G

(1st Inversion)

E G C

CHORD INVERSIONS

In the first diagram of this lesson, the C major chord is in its natural state (a minor 3rd added to the top of a major 3rd). We call this ordering of the pitches **root position**. You may recall from lesson 28, that "C" is called the "root" of the chord, since "C" is the pitch of the scale which the chord is built upon. It is also the pitch from which the chord takes its name. The second diagram in this lesson shows an inversion of the C major chord. The lowest pitch, "C", has been moved an octave higher so that it is now the highest pitch. We call this ordering of pitches **1st inversion**.

This new C major chord in 1st inversion also has an inversion.

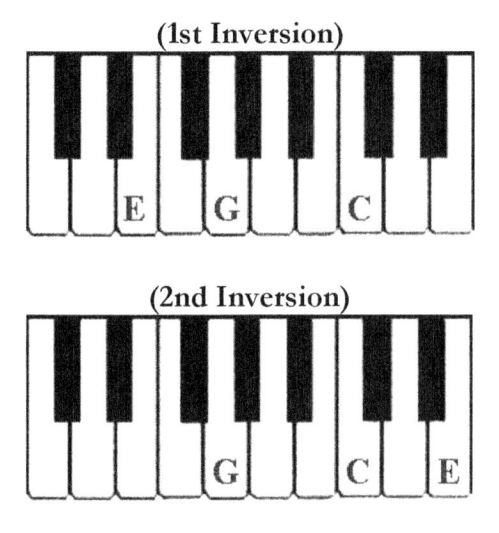

(1st Inversion)

E   G   C

(2nd Inversion)

G   C   E

The first diagram shows the C major chord in 1st inversion. In the second diagram, the lowest pitch, "E", has been moved an octave higher so that it is now the highest pitch. We call this ordering of pitches **2nd inversion**.

Note: no other inversions are possible; moving the "G" in the 2nd inversion an octave higher would result in root position once again.

Although a major chord was used in all of the preceding examples, any quality of chord may be inverted; major, minor, augmented or diminished.

LOCATION OF THE ROOT

An important aspect of chord inversions are the intervals formed due to the inverting of the chord's root position. In the following diagram you will notice that only the root position chord is made up of 3rds; the 1st and 2nd inversions are made up of 3rds and 4ths.

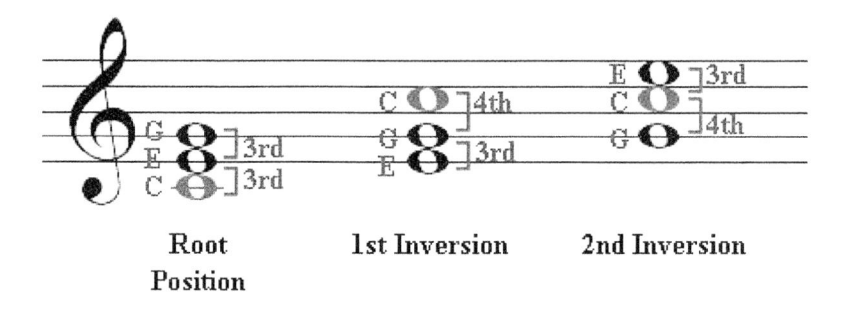

Root Position: C–E (3rd), E–G (3rd)
1st Inversion: E–G (3rd), G–C (4th)
2nd Inversion: G–C (4th), C–E (3rd)

(Lesson 35 - Audio 1)

Knowing where the interval of a 4th is situated is very important; this will help you to determine the location of the chord's root. The chord's root is always the upper pitch of the 4th. Each of the chords in the preceding diagram is a C major chord. When the C major chord is in 1st inversion, the root, "C", is the upper pitch in the interval of a 4th. When the C major chord is in 2nd inversion, the root, "C", is also the upper pitch in the interval of a 4th.

Here is a helpful way to remember which inversion is which. If the root is the "1st" pitch from the top, the chord is in "1st" inversion. If the root is the "2nd" pitch from the top, the chord is in "2nd" inversion.

HOW TO IDENTIFY CHORD INVERSIONS

Once we know which of the three chord pitches the root is, we can then 1) identify which inversion the chord is in, and 2) name the chord. Here are some steps to help you properly identify chord inversions. Memorize them before taking the lesson quiz.

Step 1
Locate the interval of a 4th.

Step 2
Name the upper pitch in the 4th. (This is the root and also the name of the chord).

Step 3
Reorder the pitches so that the root is on the bottom (i.e. so that the chord is in root position).

Step 4
Count the number of half steps between each pitch to determine if the chord is major, minor, augmented, or diminished.

Let's practice these steps with some examples.

First, we locate the 4th. Second, we name the upper pitch of the 4th. In this example, the upper pitch of the 4th is "F". We now know that "F" is the root and the name of the chord. Third, we reorder the pitches so that the root, "F", is on the bottom (i.e., so that the chord is in root position).

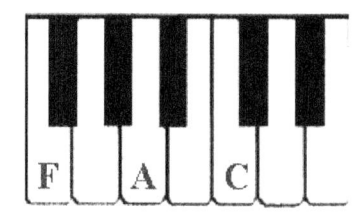

Last, we count the number of half steps between each pitch. "F" to "A" is four half steps (a major 3rd), and "A" to "C" is three half steps (a minor 3rd). The chord inversion on the staff above is therefore an "F major" chord.

Let's try identifying one more chord before taking the lesson quiz.

First, we locate the 4th. Second, we name the upper pitch of the 4th. In this example, the upper pitch of the 4th is "A". We now know that "A" is the root and the name of the chord. Third, we reorder the pitches so that the root, "A", is on the bottom (i.e., so that the chord is in root position).

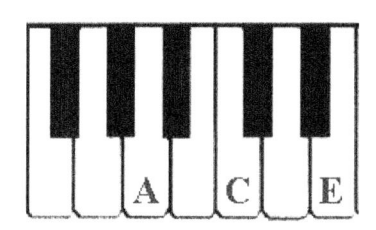

Last, we count the number of half steps between each pitch. "A" to "C" is three half steps (a minor 3rd), and "C" to "E" is four half steps (a major 3rd). The chord inversion on the staff above is therefore an "A minor" chord.

Memory Questions

How are chords inverted?
Chords are inverted by moving the lowest pitch of the chord an octave higher so that it becomes the highest pitch.

How many ways can the three pitches of a chord be reordered?
The three pitches of a chord can be reordered in three different ways; they are root position, 1st inversion, and 2nd inversion.

When is a chord in root position?
A chord is in root position when the root of the chord is the lowest pitch.

When is a chord in 1st inversion?
A chord is in 1st inversion when the root of the chord is the 1st pitch from the top.

When is a chord in 2nd inversion?
A chord is in 2nd inversion when the root of the chord is the 2nd pitch from the top.

How do we locate the root of chords in 1st or 2nd inversion?
We locate the root of chords in 1st or 2nd inversion by naming the upper pitch of the 4th.

Which chord qualities may be inverted?
Major, minor, augmented, and diminished chord qualities may be inverted.

Lesson 35 Exercises

Log in to your course at www.udemy.com and practice the exercises for this lesson.

Lesson 35 Quiz

Log in to your course at www.udemy.com and take the quiz for this lesson.

36. VOICE LEADING

TRANSITION BETWEEN CHORDS

In this lesson we are going to look at the different ways one chord can transition to another. The transition or "movement" from one chord to another is called a **chord progression**.

But before we can talk about chord progressions, we first need to define **voice** and **voice leading**. Each pitch of a chord is sometimes referred to as a "voice". The top pitch is called the top voice, the middle pitch is called the middle voice, and the bottom pitch is called the bottom voice. "Voice leading" is the manner in which each voice in one chord transitions to the corresponding voice in the subsequent chord.

Here is an example of a "IV" chord moving to a "I" chord. Notice, each voice in the "IV" chord moves to the corresponding voice in the "I" chord by way of a 4th. ("F" to "C", "A" to "E", and "C" to "G") The reason for this is that both chords are in root position. Listen to what a "IV" chord moving to a "I" chord sounds like when both chords are in root position.

MUSIC THEORY

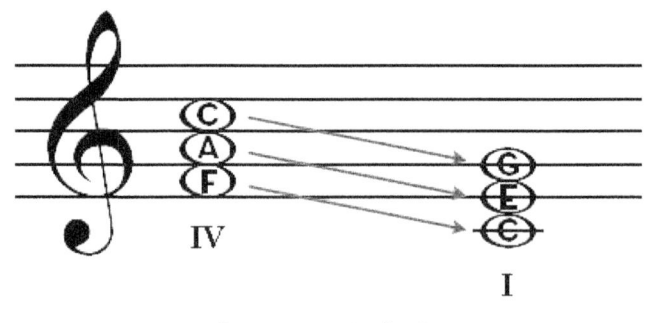

[Musical notation showing chord progression IV to I with notes C-A-F moving to G-E-C]

(Lesson 36 - Audio 1)

This chord progression sounds okay, but there are even better ways to transition between these two chords. This is where the use of inversions comes into play. Let's use the 2nd inversion of the "IV" chord and compare the sound of the transition to the preceding example, which uses only root position chords.

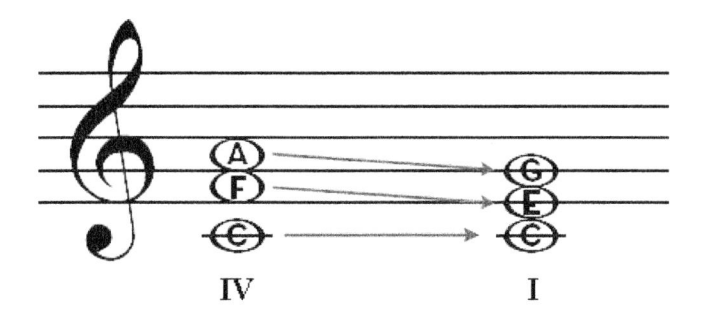

[Musical notation showing chord progression IV to I with notes A-F-C moving to G-E-C]

(Lesson 36 - Audio 2)

Although we have used the exact same two chords ("IV" and "I"), this chord progression sounds more pleasant. There are two reasons for this which can be summed up in the following rule of voice leading: the transition between chords is most pleasant when one (or more) of the voices remains on the same pitch, and when one (or more) of the other voices moves by a step. Let's analyze the preceding diagram and see how this particular chord progression follows the rule just stated.

VOICE LEADING

1) The bottom voice in the "IV" chord remains on the same pitch, "C", when it moves to the "I" chord.

2) The other voices in the "IV" chord (top and middle voices) move by steps to the "I" chord. ("A" to "G" is a whole step; "F" to "E" is a half step.)

Next, let's look at an example of a "V" chord moving to a "I" chord. Notice, each voice in the "V" chord moves to the corresponding voice in the "I" chord by way of a 5th. ("G" to "C", "B" to "E", and "D" to "G") The reason for this is that both chords are in root position. Listen to what a "V" chord moving to a "I" chord sounds like when both chords are in root position.

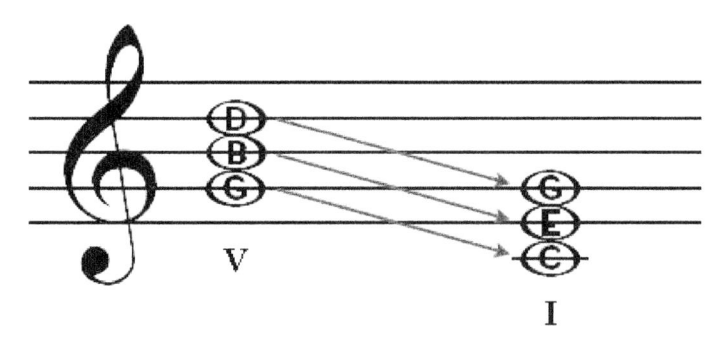

(Lesson 36 - Audio 3)

Again, this chord progression sounds okay, but with the use of inversions we can make the transition between the chords sound even better. Let's use the 1st inversion of the "V" chord and compare the sound of the transition to the preceding example, which uses only root position chords.

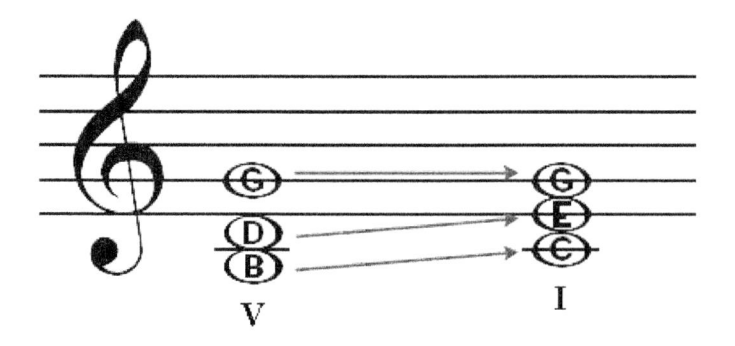

(Lesson 36 - Audio 4)

This is a much better voice leading. Although we have used the exact same two chords ("V" and "I"), this chord progression sounds much nicer since we have stayed true to our rule of voice leading: transition between chords is most pleasant when one (or more) of the voices remains on the same pitch, and when one (or more) of the other voices moves by a step. Let's analyze the diagram.

1) The top voice in the "V" chord remains on the same pitch, "G", when it moves to the "I" chord.

2) The other voices in the "V" chord (middle and bottom voices) move by steps to the "I" chord. ("D" to "E" is a whole step; "B" to "C" is a half step)

Why does following this rule make the sound of the transition more pleasant? First of all, by keeping one pitch the same in each chord we create continuity between the two chords. Second, movement by steps is the most melodic form of movement. It is both natural to the human voice and the movement that we find present in the scale.

Note: inversions can be used to improve the transition between any type of chord; major, minor, augmented or diminished. The "I", "IV" and "V" chords were only used as illustrations for this lesson.

Memory Questions

What is the movement from one chord to another called?
The movement from one chord to another is called a chord progression.

What are chord "voices"?
Chord "voices" are the different pitches of a chord.

What is "voice leading"?
"Voice leading" is the manner in which each voice in one chord transitions to the corresponding voice in the subsequent chord.

How can we create better voice leading between two chords?
We can create better voice leading between chords through the use of chord inversions.

What does the voice leading rule state?
The voice leading rule states: the transition between chords is most pleasant when one (or more) of the voices remains on the same pitch, and when one (or more) of the other voices moves by a step.

Lesson 36 Quiz

Log in to your course at www.udemy.com and take the quiz for this lesson.

37. FUNCTIONS

NAMING SCALE DEGREE "ROLES"

In previous lessons we learned how to name the scale degrees and the chords built upon them using both letters and Roman numerals. In this lesson we will learn yet another way of naming the degrees of the scale and the chords that can be built upon them. We will learn how to name them by their "function" (i.e., by their role). In the following diagram of the C major scale you will see the function name under each scale degree.

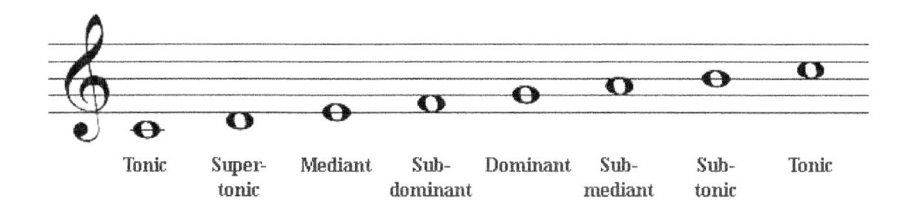

Tonic — Super-tonic — Mediant — Sub-dominant — Dominant — Sub-mediant — Sub-tonic — Tonic

These names may look very foreign right now, but by the end of this lesson they will make more sense. Each pitch (and each chord built

FUNCTIONS

on that pitch) is named for its particular function (role) in music and for its relation to the root of the scale.

Some of the names in the preceding diagram are a little misleading. For example, the word "sub" means "under". If you look at the diagram, the submediant is not "under" the mediant; it is much higher. The reason for this is because the Greek scale did not start and end with the root. Instead their scale had the root as the center of the scale. If we take the root (tonic), "C", and place it in the middle of the scale, the names will become clearer. Let's take a look at them one at a time, starting with dominant.

The **dominant** scale degree is a 5th above the tonic. The word dominant means "prominent". We know from Pythagoras and his mathematical discovery about intervals, that the 5th is a very prominent interval (because it is one of the most consonant sounding intervals). The chord built upon the dominant pitch is called the dominant chord.

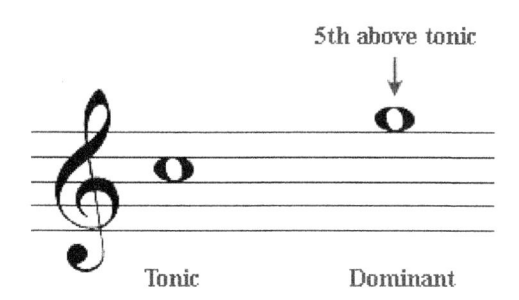

Next, let's look at the **mediant**. The word comes from the Latin, "mediare", "to be in the middle". The mediant is the mid-point between the tonic and the dominant. The chord built on the mediant pitch is called the mediant chord.

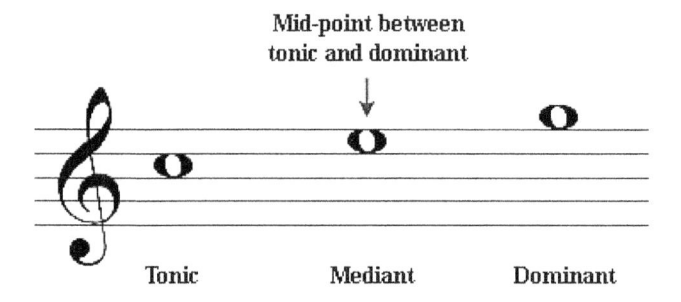

[Staff diagram: Tonic, Mediant (mid-point between tonic and dominant), Dominant]

Our next scale function is the **subdominant**. Just as the dominant was a 5th "above" the tonic, so the subdominant is a 5th "below" the tonic. The chord built on the subdominant pitch is called the subdominant chord.

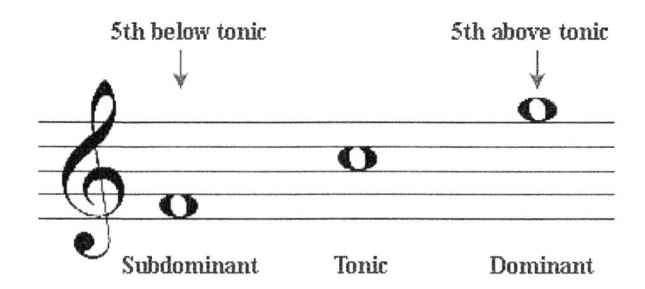

[Staff diagram: Subdominant (5th below tonic), Tonic, Dominant (5th above tonic)]

Next, let's take a look at the **submediant**. Just as the mediant was the mid-point between the tonic and dominant, so the submediant is the mid-point between the tonic and the subdominant. The chord built on the submediant pitch is called the submediant chord.

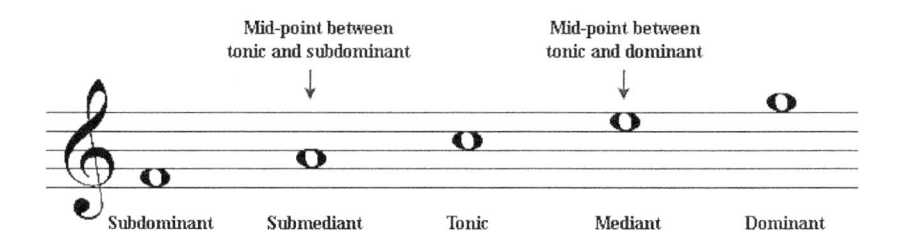

[Staff diagram: Subdominant, Submediant (mid-point between tonic and subdominant), Tonic, Mediant (mid-point between tonic and dominant), Dominant]

FUNCTIONS

Last of all we will look at the **supertonic** and **subtonic**. We can gather from their names that the supertonic is "above" the tonic, and the subtonic is "below" the tonic.

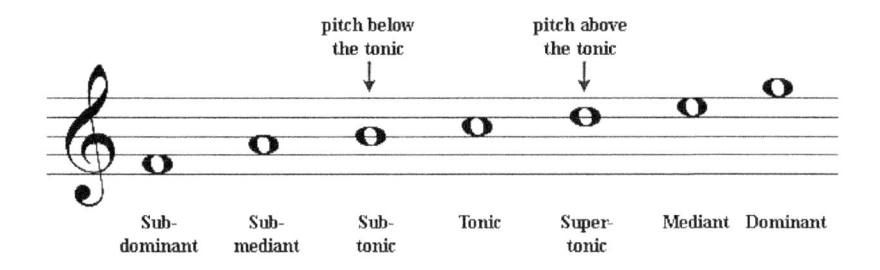

The chord built on the supertonic pitch is called the supertonic chord, while the chord built upon the subtonic pitch is called the subtonic chord. It should be noted that the subtonic is also more commonly known as the **leading tone**. In the modern day scale, it is the pitch that "leads" back to the tonic.

Here are all the chords from the scale in its modern form with the functions and Roman numerals labeled.

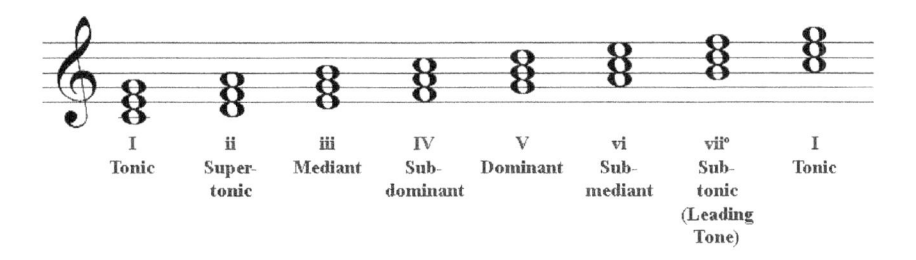

This was just an introduction to functions and a demonstration of how each function relates to the root of the scale. Understanding the actual "role" that each scale degree (or chord built upon each scale degree) plays in music falls outside of the scope of a music theory course. This topic can be studied in more depth in a music composition course.

Memory Questions

Besides letter names and Roman numerals, what is another way of naming the degrees of the scale (and the chords built upon them)?
Besides letter names and Roman numerals, another way of naming the degrees of the scale (and the chords built upon them) is by their function.

What does the word "function" refer to?
The word "function" refers to the role each pitch (or chord built upon that pitch) plays in music and how each relates to the root of the scale.

What is the tonic?
The tonic is the first scale degree (or chord built on that degree).

What is the dominant?
The dominant is the fifth scale degree (or chord built on that degree).

What is the mediant?
The mediant is the third scale degree (or chord built on that degree).

What is the subdominant?
The subdominant is the fourth scale degree (or chord built on that degree).

What is the submediant?
The submediant is the sixth scale degree (or chord built on that degree).

What is the supertonic?
The supertonic is the second scale degree (or chord built on that degree).

What is the subtonic?
The subtonic is the seventh scale degree (or chord built on that degree).

What is the subtonic more commonly known as?
The subtonic is more commonly known as the leading tone (because of its tendency to "lead" back to the tonic).

Lesson 37 Quiz

Log in to your course at www.udemy.com and take the quiz for this lesson.

38. THE DOMINANT SEVENTH CHORD

EXTENSION OF THE TRIAD

Up to this point in the course we have studied chords made up of three distinct pitches (triads). In this lesson we will learn about chords made up of four distinct pitches. Chords with four or more distinct pitches are called **extended chords**.

There are a few different kinds of extended chords. The extended chord we will be studying in this lesson is the **dominant seventh chord**. Dominant seventh chords are formed by adding a minor 3rd to the top of a major chord in root position.

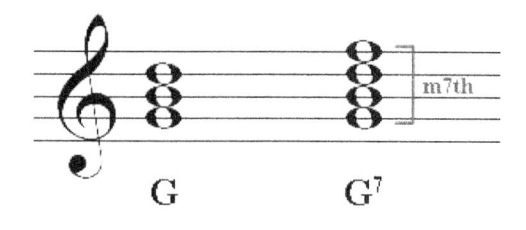

(Lesson 38 - Audio 1)

THE DOMINANT SEVENTH CHORD

In the preceding diagram, a minor 3rd ("D" to "F") was added to the top of a "G major" chord in root position. The name "dominant seventh", comes from the fact that the chord is built on the fifth pitch of the scale (the dominant pitch), and from the fact that the interval between the top and bottom pitches is a 7th. Note: the 7th in a dominant seventh chord is always a minor 7th (10 half steps).

The dominant seventh chord is abbreviated with a superscript 7. We pronounce the chord as "G seven", <u>not</u> "G seventh".

The following diagram illustrates how the dominant seventh chord is built on the fifth pitch of the scale (the dominant pitch). When we name this chord by its scale degree, we call it "V^7" rather than "G^7".

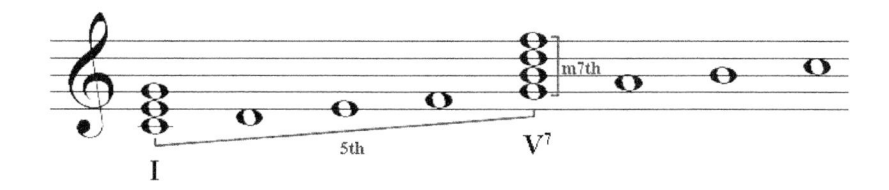

As you can see, the Roman numeral "V" signifies the chord's place in the scale. The superscript 7 signifies the interval between the top and bottom pitches. It is very important that you understand this moving forward.

We learned in a previous lesson, that the "V" chord has a strong tendency to return to the "I" chord. The same holds true for the "V^7" chord, since it is an extended version of the "V" chord. (Extending the chord does not change the underlying major chord; it only adds flavor to the existing sound.)

Note: The voices of the dominant seventh chord (from bottom to top) are called the root, 3rd, 5th, and 7th.

DOMINANT SEVENTH INVERSIONS

When we studied chord inversions, we found that a chord with three pitches could have three different arrangements of its pitches: root position, 1st inversion, and 2nd inversion. Since dominant seventh chords have an added pitch, a "3rd inversion" is now possible. (Remember, inversions are formed by moving the lowest pitch of the chord an octave higher so that it becomes the highest pitch.)

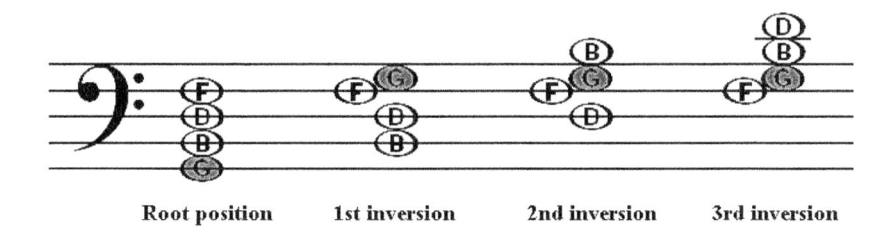

Root position   **1st inversion**   **2nd inversion**   **3rd inversion**

(Lesson 38 - Audio 2)

The root of the dominant seventh chord is the lowest pitch when it is in root position. To determine the location of the root in the inversions, identify the interval of a 2nd. The root will always be the upper pitch in the 2nd. ("F" and "G" in this example) <u>Important</u>: Do not confuse this with locating the root in a chord with three pitches. Remember, with triads, the root is always the upper pitch in the 4th.

Here is a helpful way to remember which inversion is which. If the root is the "1st" pitch from the top, the chord is in "1st" inversion. If the root is the "2nd" pitch from the top, the chord is in "2nd" inversion. If the root is the "3rd" pitch from the top, the chord is in "3rd" inversion.

Sometimes a dominant seventh chord will occur in music with one of its pitches missing in order to make it easier to play. Generally it is the 5th pitch that is left out, as in the following example.

THE DOMINANT SEVENTH CHORD

(Lesson 38 - Audio 3)

Through a process of elimination we can see the reason why the 5th pitch is the pitch generally left out. The 7th pitch cannot be left out, since the 7th pitch is what makes the chord a dominant seventh. The 3rd pitch cannot be left out, since the 3rd pitch is what gives the chord its major quality. The root pitch cannot be left out, since the root pitch is the foundation on which the chord is built. This leaves us with only the 5th pitch as an option.

Here is the inversion of the seventh chord with the missing 5th.

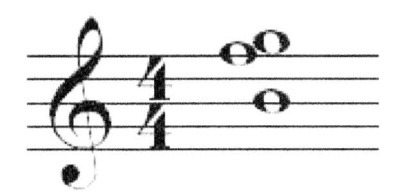

(Lesson 38 - Audio 4)

Because this chord only has three pitches, it could easily be mistaken as something other than a dominant seventh chord. The interval of the 2nd tells us otherwise. The upper note in the 2nd is "G". This chord is therefore a G^7 chord.

Note: Just like any other chord, the dominant seventh chord can occur in music as a block chord (pitches heard simultaneously) or as a broken chord (pitches heard sequentially).

Memory Questions

What is an extended chord?
An extended chord is a chord with four or more distinct pitches.

What is a dominant seventh chord?
A dominant seventh chord is one of many types of extended chords.

How is a dominant seventh chord formed?
A dominant seventh chord is formed by adding a minor 3rd to the top of a major chord in root position.

How are dominant seventh chords abbreviated?
Dominant seventh chords are abbreviated with a superscript 7.

Where does the name "dominant seventh", come from?
The name "dominant seventh" comes from the fact that the chord is built on the fifth pitch of the scale (the dominant pitch), and from the fact that the interval between the top and bottom pitches is a 7th.

What does the Roman numeral "V" in V^7 signify?
The Roman numeral "V" signifies the dominant seventh chord's place in the scale.

What does the superscript "7" in V^7 signify?
The superscript "7" signifies the interval between the top and bottom pitches of the dominant seventh chord.

What are the voices of the dominant seventh chord (from bottom to top) called?
The voices of the dominant seventh chord (from bottom to top) are called: the root, 3rd, 5th, and 7th.

How many possible inversions does the dominant seventh chord have?
The dominant seventh chord has three possible inversions: 1st inversion, 2nd inversion and 3rd inversion.

How do we locate the root in an inversion of a dominant seventh chord?
We locate the root in an inversion of a dominant seventh chord by naming the upper pitch of the 2nd.

When is a dominant seventh chord in root position?
A dominant seventh chord is in root position when the root of the chord is the lowest pitch.

When is a dominant seventh chord in 1st inversion?
A dominant seventh chord is in 1st inversion when the root of the chord is the 1st pitch from the top.

When is a dominant seventh chord in 2nd inversion?
A dominant seventh chord is in 2nd inversion when the root of the chord is the 2nd pitch from the top.

When is a dominant seventh chord in 3rd inversion?
A dominant seventh chord is in 3rd inversion when the root of the chord is the 3rd pitch from the top.

Lesson 38 Quiz

Log in to your course at www.udemy.com and take the quiz for this lesson.

39. OTHER FORMS OF SEVENTH CHORDS

THE MAJOR 7TH CHORD

In the last lesson we learned about the dominant 7th chord. In this lesson we are going to learn about three other types of 7th chords: the **major 7th chord**, the **minor 7th chord**, and the **diminished 7th chord**. Note: All 7th chords are types of extended chords.

The major 7th chord is the most similar to the dominant 7th chord. If you recall, the dominant 7th chord is formed by adding a minor 3rd to the top of a major chord in root position. (Thus the distance from the bottom pitch to the top pitch is a minor 7th.) A major 7th chord on the other hand is formed by adding a major 3rd to the top of a major chord in root position. (Thus the distance from the bottom pitch to the top pitch is a major 7th.)

Listen to the major 7th chord played first as a broken chord and then as a block chord.

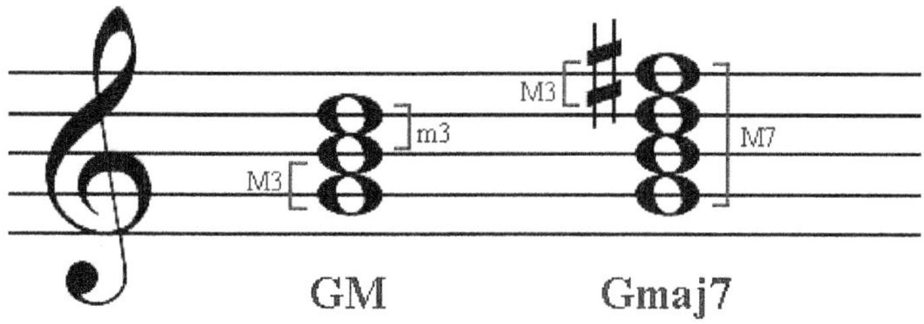

(Lesson 39 - Audio 1)

Because the major 7th chord is comprised of a major chord and a major seventh, it is also known as the major/major seventh. Today the name has been shortened to simply "major 7th" chord. It is abbreviated as M7 or maj7.

Note: the 3rds in the major 7th chord (from bottom to top) are M3, m3, M3.

THE MINOR 7TH CHORD

The minor 7th chord is formed by adding a minor 3rd to the top of a minor chord in root position. (Thus the distance from the bottom pitch to the top pitch is a minor 7th.)

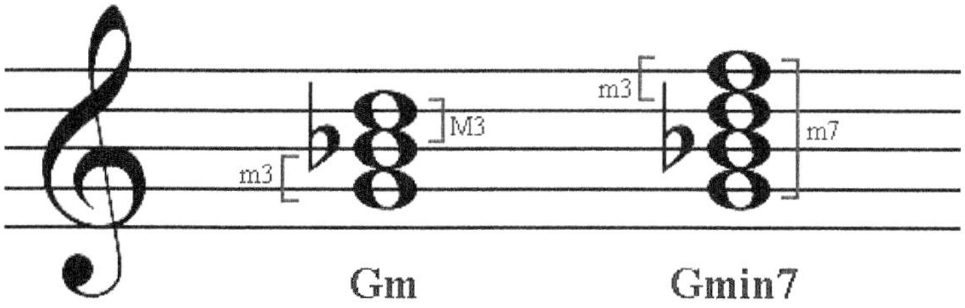

(Lesson 39 - Audio 2)

Because it is comprised of a minor chord and a minor seventh, it is also known as the minor/minor seventh. Today the name has been shortened to simply "minor 7th" chord. It is abbreviated as m7 or min7.

Note: the 3rds in the minor 7th chord (from bottom to top) are m3, M3, m3. This is the opposite of the 3rds in the major 7th chord (M3, m3, M3).

THE DIMINISHED 7TH CHORD

The diminished 7th chord is formed by adding a minor 3rd to the top of a diminished chord in root position. (Thus the distance from the bottom pitch to the top pitch is a diminished 7th.)

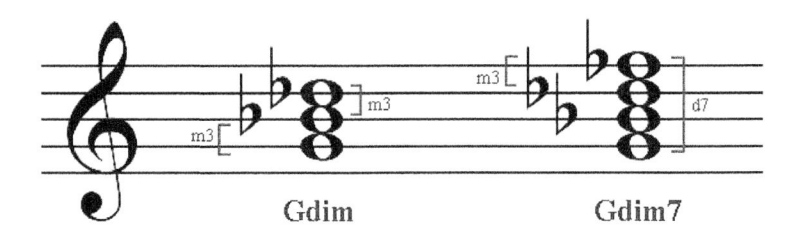

(Lesson 39 - Audio 3)

Because the diminished 7th chord is comprised of a diminished chord and a diminished seventh, it is also known as the diminished/diminished seventh. Today the name has been shortened to simply "diminished 7th" chord. It is abbreviated as °7 or dim7.

Note: all of the 3rds in the diminished 7th chord are minor. (m3, m3, m3)

OTHER FORMS OF SEVENTH CHORDS

Do you hear how the diminished 7th chord sounds much more intense than the diminished chord? This is because of the interlocked diminished 5ths created by the addition of a fourth pitch.

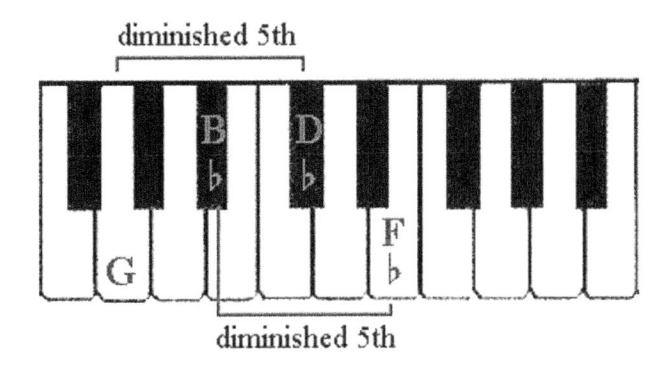

If you recall from lesson 23, the diminished 5th is also known as the "tritone" and is one of the most dissonant sounding intervals. By interlocking two tritones we create a very unstable chord.

Note: As with any chord, each of the 7th chords above can be inverted. Since there are four notes in each chord there can be four possible arrangements: root position, 1st inversion, 2nd inversion, and 3rd inversion.

Memory Questions

How are 7th chords classified?
7th chords are classified as extended chords.

How is a dominant 7th chord formed?
A dominant seventh chord is formed by adding a minor 3rd to the top of a major chord in root position.

How is a major 7th chord formed?
A major 7th chord is formed by adding a major 3rd to the top of a major chord in root position.

How is a minor 7th chord formed?
A minor 7th chord is formed by adding a minor 3rd to the top of a minor chord in root position.

How is a diminished 7th chord formed?
A diminished 7th chord is formed by adding a minor 3rd to the top of a diminished chord in root position.

From bottom to top, what is the order of 3rds in a major 7th chord?
From bottom to top, the order of 3rds in a major 7th chord is: M3, m3, M3.

From bottom to top, what is the order of 3rds in a minor 7th chord?
From bottom to top, the order of 3rds in a minor 7th chord is: m3, M3, m3.

From bottom to top, what is the order of 3rds in a diminished 7th chord?
From bottom to top, the order of 3rds in a diminished 7th chord is: m3, m3, m3.

Lesson 39 Quiz

Log in to your course at www.udemy.com and take the quiz for this lesson.

40. CADENCES

MUSICAL PUNCTUATION

In lesson 36 we learned about chord progressions and how one chord can transition more smoothly to another chord through use of chord inversions. In this lesson we are going to learn about a specific type of chord progression called a **cadence**. A cadence is a chord progression that expresses a sense of finality. This sense of finality can be stronger or weaker depending on certain factors which will be discussed below. Musicians and music theorists often liken cadences to punctuation in language. A cadence that is weaker might be likened to a comma in a sentence. It communicates that the musical sentence or "musical phrase" is briefly stopping but will continue on. A cadence that is stronger might be likened to a period in a sentence. It communicates that the musical sentence is finished. There are four types of cadences: **authentic**, **half**, **plagal** and **deceptive**. We will go over each one below.

THE AUTHENTIC CADENCE

An authentic cadence is movement from "V" to "I" (or "V^7" to "I"). This is the strongest type of cadence, since "V" has the strongest tendency towards "I". Authentic cadences can be further classified into **perfect** and **imperfect**. Both are considered to be strong cadences, but the perfect is slightly stronger than the imperfect as you will see below.

A "perfect" authentic cadence is movement from "V" to "I", with two additional criteria that must be met. 1) Each chord must have its root as the lowest pitch, and 2) the final chord must also have its root as the highest pitch. When either of these two criteria is not met, it is considered an "imperfect" authentic cadence. Here is an example of a **perfect authentic cadence**.

Note: The following chords might look confusing since there are four pitches in each and one of the pitches is a duplicate (GDGB and CEGC). In actual pieces of music, the pitches of a chord may be duplicated and heard in many different octaves depending on the number and type of instruments playing. In this case, the left hand of the piano is duplicating the pitches "G" and "C" in the bass clef.

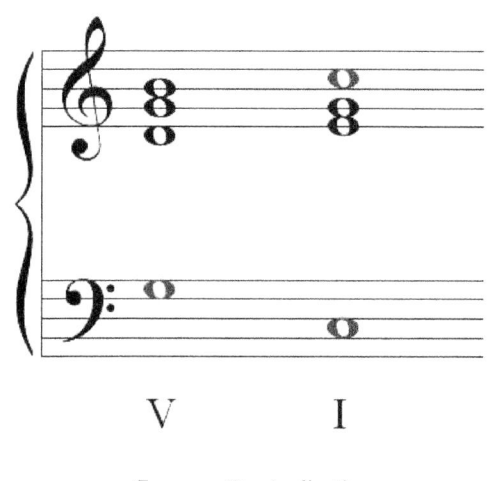

(Lesson 40 - Audio 1)

The preceding example is in the key of C major; where the G major chord is the "V" chord (GDGB) and the C major chord (CEGC) is the "I" chord. As you can see, the root of the "V" chord ("G") is the lowest pitch in the "V" chord, and the root of the "I" chord ("C") is the lowest pitch in the "I" chord; thus, criteria #1 is met. The root of the "I" chord is also the highest pitch of the "I" chord; thus criteria #2 is met. Do you hear how the sound of this cadence is very final and absolute? This is mainly due to the root of the "I" chord being both the lowest and the highest pitch of the final chord.

Here is an example of an **imperfect authentic cadence**.

        V   I

(Lesson 40 - Audio 2)

The preceding example is considered an "imperfect" authentic cadence because criteria #2 is not met. The root of the "V" chord ("G") is the lowest pitch in the "V" chord, and the root of the "I" chord ("C") is the lowest pitch in the "I" chord; thus, criteria #1 is met. But the root of the "I" chord ("C") is not also the highest pitch of the "I" chord; thus criteria #2 is not met.

This cadence is still very strong, but because the root of the "I" chord is not in both the highest and lowest positions of the chord, it is not as final and absolute sounding as the perfect authentic cadence. Authentic cadences are a great way to establish a tonal center for a piece of music (or section of music). In either of the preceding audio examples you definitely feel like you are in the key of C major; in other words, "C" feels like home.

THE HALF CADENCE

The half cadence is in a sense the opposite of the authentic cadence. The authentic cadence was movement from "V" to "I", whereas the half cadence is movement from "I" to "V". Because it is movement away from the "tonic" chord (the "I" chord), the half cadence is considered to be a weak cadence. This type of cadence is usually found at the end of a section of music because it creates the sense of coming to a temporary stopping place before moving on to another section.

I   V

(Lesson 40 - Audio 3)

This example is also in the key of C major; where the G major chord is the "V" chord and the C major chord is the "I" chord. Do you hear how there is some sense of closure but that the music wants to continue on to something more?

THE PLAGAL CADENCE

The plagal cadence is movement from "IV" to "I". It is often referred to as the "Amen cadence" because of its frequent occurrence in hymns on the syllables "A-men". It is not quite as strong as the authentic cadence.

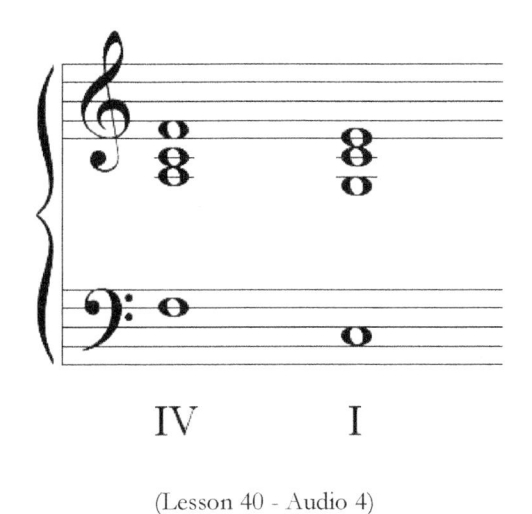

IV   I

(Lesson 40 - Audio 4)

THE DECEPTIVE CADENCE

With the authentic cadence we had movement from "V" (or "V^7") to "I". The deceptive cadence is movement from "V" (or "V^7") to a chord other than "I". It is called "deceptive" because the ear is expecting to hear the resolution to the "I" chord, then a chord other than the "I" is played. These types of cadences create a sense of suspension and are more like commas, or even question marks in a sentence. Here is an example of a typical deceptive cadence.

$$\text{V7} \quad \text{vi}$$

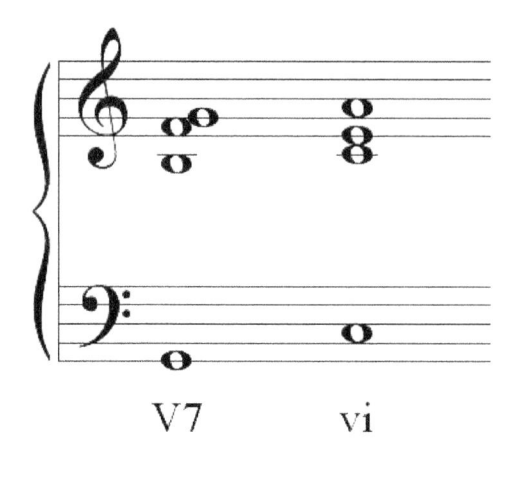

(Lesson 40 - Audio 5)

The notes in the bass clef (left hand) give you the feel of moving from "V" ("G") to "I" ("C"), but if you take a look at the top three notes in the last chord you will see it is an "A minor" chord (or "vi" chord in the key of C major).

Memory Questions

What is a cadence?
A cadence is a chord progression that expresses a sense of finality.

What are the four types of cadences?
The four types of cadences are the authentic, half, plagal, and deceptive cadences.

What is an authentic cadence?
An authentic cadence is movement from a "V" chord to a "I" chord (or "V7" to "I").

CADENCES

What are the two classifications of authentic cadences?
The two classifications of authentic cadences are perfect and imperfect.

In order for an authentic cadence to be called "perfect", what two criteria must be met?
In order for an authentic cadence to be called "perfect", both the "V" and the "I" chords must have their respective roots as the lowest pitch, and the "I" chord must also have its root as the highest pitch.

What is an imperfect authentic cadence?
An imperfect authentic cadence is an authentic cadence that does not meet both the criteria of a perfect authentic cadence.

What is a half cadence?
A half cadence is movement from a "I" chord to a "V" chord; it is the opposite of the authentic cadence.

What is a plagal cadence?
A plagal cadence is movement from a "IV" chord to a "I" chord.

What is a deceptive cadence?
The deceptive cadence is movement from a "V" chord to a chord other than "I".

Lesson 40 Quiz

Log in to your course at www.udemy.com and take the quiz for this lesson.

41. OTHER FORMS OF SCALES

THE WHOLE TONE SCALE

Besides the diatonic scale (major and minor scales), there are many other forms of scales that are used to create music. In this lesson we are going to learn about some of the more common forms. The first is the **whole tone scale**. A whole tone scale is exactly what it sounds like…it is made up entirely of whole tones (whole steps). There are no half steps present in this scale.

(Lesson 41 - Audio 1)

The whole tone scale is called a **hexatonic** scale because it is made up of six ("hexa"= six) tones. On the piano keyboard it is the set of 3 white keys and 3 black keys.

OTHER FORMS OF SCALES

It can also be written as 2 black keys and 4 white keys.

With these two ways of writing the whole tone scale, we cover all the possible pitches from "C" to "C" and octave higher. (C, D flat, D, E flat, E, F, F sharp, G, G sharp, A, A sharp, and B)

You cannot construct any major or minor chords from the whole tone scale. The only chords that can be formed are augmented chords.

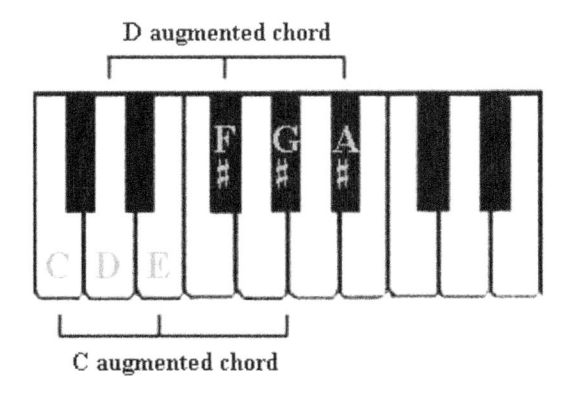

Because of this, music written using the pitches from the whole tone scale is very anxious and unsure (just like the augmented chord). Even more importantly, because there are no half steps in the whole tone scale, there is no leading tone. The absence of the leading tone means there is no tonic. No tonic means that we will never feel at rest. (There is no pitch that our ears will hear as the root, or "home key". The music will feel as if there is no beginning and no end. It will wander aimlessly.)

THE CHROMATIC SCALE

The **chromatic scale** is in a sense the opposite of the whole tone scale; it is made up entirely of half steps. It has 12 notes within an octave.

(Lesson 41 - Audio 2)

Since all of the pitches are equidistant from each other, there is no single pitch that sticks out as the tonal center. You can begin a chromatic scale on any pitch.

Here is the descending chromatic scale. Observe how it is notated using flats instead of sharps.

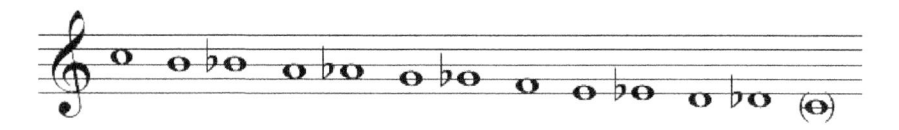

(Lesson 41 - Audio 3)

Although there is no one correct spelling of the scale, it is customary to use sharps when ascending and flats when descending. The spelling of the scale is also determined by the key signature of the song. For example, the key of D major has an "F sharp" and a "C sharp". We will continue to spell these pitches as such even when descending (i.e., we will not use their enharmonic equivalents "G flat" and "D flat".

It should be noted that when all 12 notes are used to write a song in which there is no tonal center, we call this "chromatic music" or "12 tone music". This is not to be confused with music written in major or minor keys (that do have tonal centers) in which "chromatic tones" are occasionally used. The word chromatic comes from the Greek "chroma", meaning "color". When speaking of music written in major and minor keys, chromatic notes are the notes that are not normally found in the diatonic major and minor scales. These extra notes are used by composers to "color" or embellish the music. For example, when Mozart composed a piece in C major, he was not limited to using the 7 pitches of the C major scale. He could give different expression to the music by adding any of the 5 chromatic tones not naturally present in the C major scale.

THE PENTATONIC SCALE

The pentatonic scale has a total of 5 pitches ("penta" = five) within an octave. It is widely used in the folk music of many countries around the world. The pentatonic scale has the pattern: whole step, whole step, minor 3rd, whole step. Here is a pentatonic scale beginning on C.

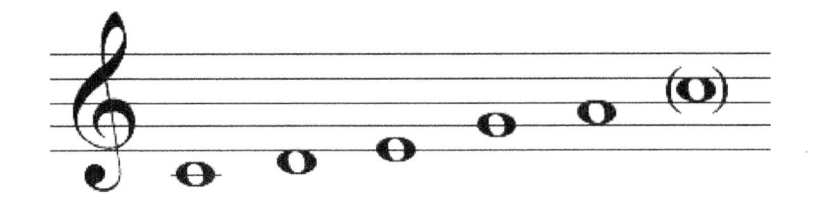

(Lesson 41 - Audio 4)

Since there are no greatly dissonant intervals in this scale (such as the major 7th, minor 2nd, or tritone), these 5 notes can be played in almost any order and combination and still sound relatively consonant. You can test this out for yourself by going to a piano and playing on just the black keys. That's right; the 5 black keys on the piano (starting from "F sharp") form a pentatonic scale!

Memory Questions

What is a hexatonic scale?
A hexatonic scale is a scale with 6 pitches within an octave.

What is a whole tone scale?
The whole tone scale is a type of hexatonic scale made up entirely of whole steps.

Which types of chords can be constructed from the pitches of the whole tone scale?
Only the augmented chord can be constructed from the pitches of the whole tone scale.

Does the whole tone scale have a tonic pitch?
The whole tone scale does not have a tonic pitch, since there are no half steps to create a leading tone.

What is a chromatic scale?
A chromatic scale is a scale made up entirely of half steps and has a total of 12 pitches within an octave.

Does the chromatic scale have a tonic pitch?
The chromatic scale does not have a tonic pitch, since the distance between all the pitches are the same, thus making impossible a single leading tone.

What is a pentatonic scale?
A pentatonic scale has a total of 5 pitches within an octave and consists of the pattern: whole step, whole step, minor 3rd, whole step.

Lesson 41 Quiz

Log in to your course at www.udemy.com and take the quiz for this lesson.

42. POLYTONAL & ATONAL

POLYTONAL MUSIC

Tonal music is music that is "key" centered. Key centered means that the music is written in a particular key and has a tonic pitch (root). For example, Mozart's sonata in C major is called tonal because it is key centered; it is written in the key of "C major" and has a tonic pitch "C".

In this lesson we are going to learn about two other forms of tonality: **polytonal** and **atonal** music. Music that is polytonal is not centered in "one" key (and thus does not have "one" tonic pitch); it is in multiple different keys at the same time! (*Polytonal* = many tones)

The most basic way for this to happen is to have multiple instruments each playing in a different key. Or in the case of piano music, the right hand would be in one key and the left hand would be in a completely different key. Let's take a look at an example.

(Lesson 42 - Audio 1)

The preceding music is the right hand of a piano piece. As you can see from the 4 sharps in the key signature, it is written in the key of "E major". (It uses the pitches of the "E major" scale and has "E" as its tonic.) Now let's look at the left hand of the same piece.

(Lesson 42 - Audio 2)

As you can see from the 3 flats in the key signature, the preceding music is written in the key of "E flat" major. (It uses the pitches of the "E flat" major scale and has "E flat" as its tonic.)

Here is what the right and left hands sound like together.

(Lesson 42 - Audio 3)

Not very pleasant sounding is it? Polytonality was not really used until around the 20th century. Before that, it was used very infrequently and only as a "comical effect". A famous example of this is the 4th movement of Mozart's "Musical Joke". The whole piece is very tonal except for the very end which is written in 4 different keys at once!

ATONAL MUSIC

Music that is **atonal** is not centered in any key and does not have a tonic pitch. Atonality disregards everything regarding the nature of music which was discovered by composers and music theorists throughout thousands of years of music history and instead says, "There are no rules". In atonality, no one pitch is more important than another; no one interval is more important than another; and no one chord is more important than another.

There are two types of atonal music. One type is called "free" atonality which began in the early 20th century. Basically, in free atonality, anything goes (as long as any sense of a key center is avoided). The other type of atonal music is called "strict" atonality. The most well-known method of composing strict atonal music was developed by an Austrian composer by the name of Arnold Schoenberg (1874 – 1951). Schoenberg's system of composing music without a tonal center is called the "twelve-tone" technique. In the twelve-tone technique, a composer chooses the order in which to arrange the 12 pitches of the chromatic scale. The order of pitches is called a "tone row". The basic rule is: once a particular pitch is played, it may not occur again until all of the other notes in the tone row have been played. By giving equal attention to all 12 pitches, any sense of a key center is avoided. This form of atonal music occurred during the mid-20th century. A good example of strict atonal music is the beginning of Schoenberg's *Wind Quintet*.

Memory Questions

What is tonal music?
Tonal music is music which is in a specific key.

What is polytonal music?
Polytonal music is music which is in multiple keys at once.

What is atonal music?
Atonal music is music which is not in any key.

What is free atonal music?
Free atonal music is music that has no key and no rules.

What is strict atonal music?
Strict atonal music is music that has no key, but follows a set of rules set out by the composer.

What is the most well-known type of strict atonal music?
The most well-known type of strict atonal music is "twelve-tone".

What is the twelve-tone technique?
Twelve-tone technique is a system of writing strict atonal music developed by Arnold Schoenberg, in which music is composed by tone rows.

What is a tone row?
A tone row is the order in which the 12 pitches of the chromatic scale must occur in the music, and is determined solely by the composer.

Lesson 42 Quiz

Log in to your course at www.udemy.com and take the quiz for this lesson.

43. MODES

THE ANCIENT GREEK MODES

In this lesson we are going to learn about **modes**. Modes have their origin in the scales of the ancient Greeks (although the actual term "mode" was not used by the ancient Greeks). As you may recall from previous lessons, the Greek scales were built from tetrachords. A tetrachord was a series of 4 pitches within the space of a perfect 4th consisting of 2 whole tones and 1 semi tone (the ancient Greek equivalent of 2 whole steps and 1 half step). The following example is an example of the ancient Greek "Dorian" mode.

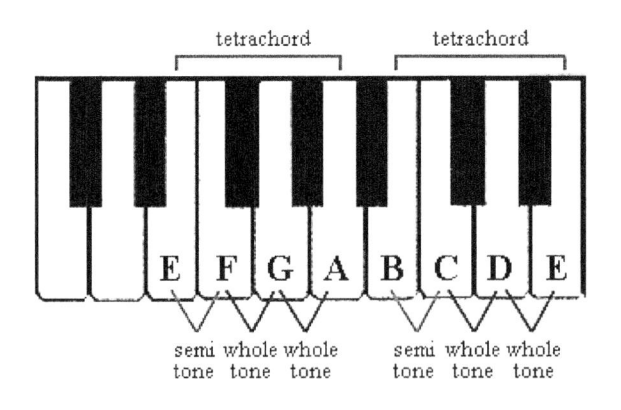

The highest and lowest pitches in a tetrachord always made up a perfect 4th ("E" to "A" or "B" to "E" in the preceding diagram). By changing the tunings of the two inner pitches of a tetrachord, a variety of modes could be formed each consisting of a different sequence of whole tones and semi tones. Here is an example of the ancient Greek "Phrygian" mode. Note the different sequence of whole tones and semi tones.

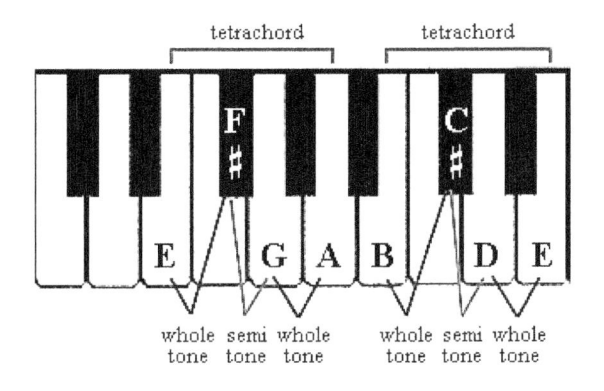

Because each mode had a different sequence of whole tones and semi tones, music written using the different modes sounded very unique. Here is a list of the seven ancient Greek modes. Each was named after different Greek peoples and their neighbors in Asia Minor.

Dorian

Hypodorian

Phrygian

Hypophrygian

Lydian

Hypolydian

Mixolydian

THE CHURCH MODES

The music of the Roman Catholic Church that we call "Gregorian chant" actually stems from the ancient Greek modes. In the 5th century the Catholic Church adopted four modes. These four modes were called the "authentic" modes. During the time of Pope Gregory the Great (c.540-604 A.D.), four additional modes were adopted called "plagal" modes.

Each mode had a "finalis" and a "dominant". The finalis was the closing note used to end a passage of music. It was the tonal center of the music, equivalent to our modern day "tonic" pitch. The dominant was also called the "reciting-tone". It was the note that was most often used for long recitations on the same pitch. It is sometimes referred to as the "secondary tonal center".

Like the ancient Greek modes, each church mode has a different sequence of half steps and whole steps. Here is a diagram showing the eight original church modes. It will be explained in detail below.

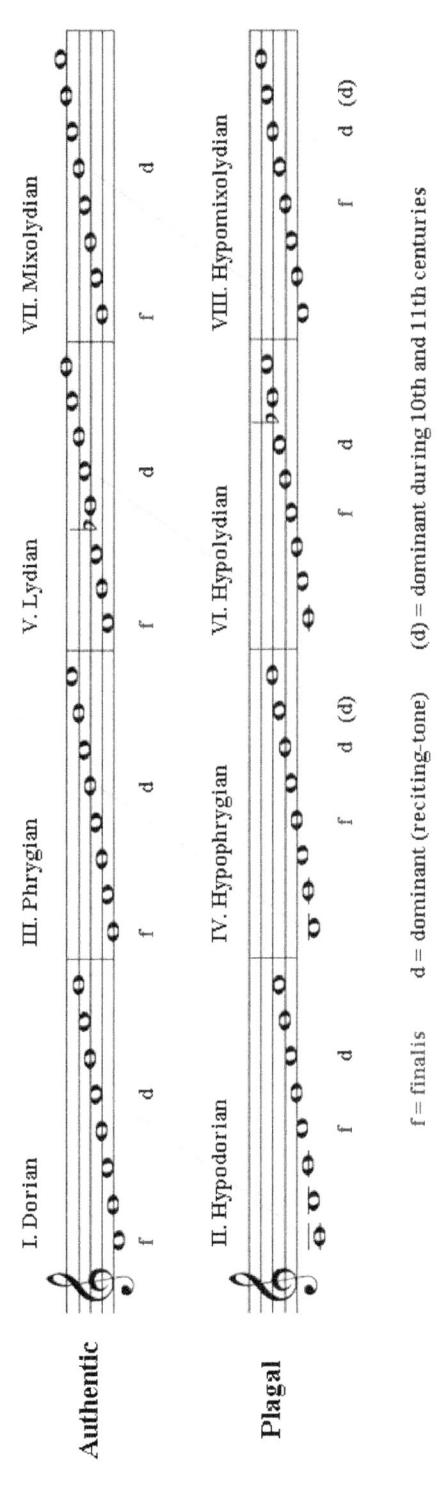

MODES

Authentic

I. Dorian   III. Phrygian   V. Lydian   VII. Mixolydian

Plagal

II. Hypodorian   IV. Hypophrygian   VI. Hypolydian   VIII. Hypomixolydian

f = finalis   d = dominant (reciting-tone)   (d) = dominant during 10th and 11th centuries

The authentic church modes begin on "D", "E", "F", and "G". The finalis is the first note, while the dominant is the 5th. Each authentic mode has a corresponding plagal mode which is indicated by the prefix "hypo". The dominant note in each authentic mode is the same as the first note in each corresponding plagal mode (see the diagonal line). To avoid the "reciting-tone" always being the highest or lowest pitch, a new dominant was chosen for each plagal mode.

Note how there were no church modes starting on "A", "B", or "C". Our modern system of tuning allows for any note to be played sharp or flat, but in the medieval modal system only "B" was allowed to be flat. (We'll learn more about tuning systems later in the course) With the addition of "B flat", the modes starting on "D", "E", and "F" would have the same sequence of whole steps and half steps as the modes starting on "A", "B", and "C" and therefore they were not included. In 1547 (about 1,000 years after Pope Gregory the Great) a Swiss monk by the name of Henricus Glareanus made the case for four additional modes (the authentic modes beginning on "A" and "C" and their plagal counterparts), thus bringing the total number of modes to 12.

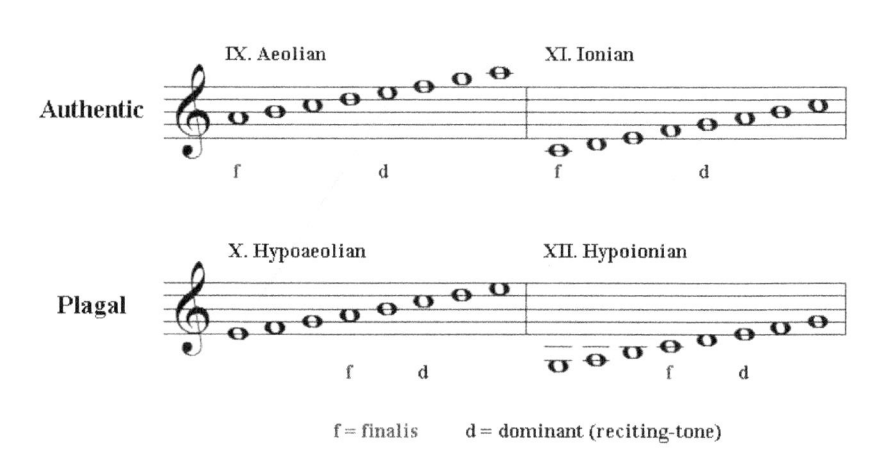

Authentic

IX. Aeolian   XI. Ionian

f   d   f   d

Plagal

X. Hypoaeolian   XII. Hypoionian

f   d   f   d

f = finalis   d = dominant (reciting-tone)

In the 19th century chant reformers added the mode beginning on "B" (even though they rejected its use in chant). It is a very dissonant sounding mode because of the diminished 5th between "B" and "F" (or an augmented 4th between "F" and "B" in the plagal).

MODES

Authentic — Locrian

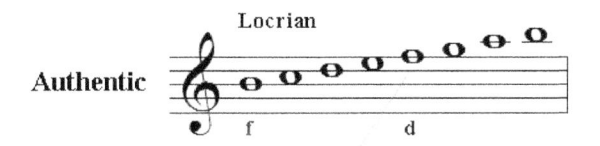

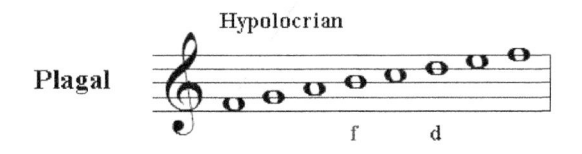

f   *d*

Plagal — Hypolocrian

f   *d*

f = finalis   d = dominant (reciting-tone)

Note: Although the Catholic Church borrowed the names of the modes from the ancient Greeks, their order got mixed up. (Different theories exist on how this actually occurred) Therefore the ancient Greek Dorian is not the same as the medieval church Dorian; the ancient Greek Phrygian is not the same as the medieval church Phrygian, etc.

It is important to draw the distinction between modes and scales. Modes are not scales. Here are a few differences. 1) A mode implies a specific range, whereas music composed from the pitches of a particular scale is not restricted to the pitches within an octave. 2) There were different melodic formulas for each of the modes that specified how melodies were to be constructed and sung according to which mode was used. Scales on the other hand give much more freedom to melodic creation. 3) There was also a specific emotional affect or character that each mode was considered to have. For example, music in the Hypolydian mode was considered pious. Hypodorian was considered sad or serious. Phrygian incited anger, while Hypophrygian tempered anger. Compare this with music composed from different major scales. A song in "C major" will sound very similar to the same song played in "E major", "F major" or any other major key. Changing the scale does not change the emotional affect, since all major scales have the same sequence of whole steps and half steps.

THE MODERN MODES

Modes dominated European music up until about 1500 A.D. For another hundred years or so they continued to have a strong influence on composers. As music became less melodically structured and more and more harmonically structured, the use of the modes started to fall by the wayside. Only two of the church modes endured. These were the Ionian and Aeolian modes. The authentic Ionian mode is equivalent to the modern day major scale; it has the same sequence of whole steps and half steps as the major scale. The authentic Aeolian mode is the equivalent to the modern day natural minor scale; it has the same sequence of whole steps and half steps as the natural minor scale. In fact we sometimes refer to these two scales as the major and minor "modes". Locate the authentic Ionian and Aeolian modes in the preceding diagrams and compare them to the major and natural minor scale.

Modes are still used today in chant and some folk music. In the 20th century, modes also started making a comeback in the works of certain classical composers and film composers.

The modern day modes come from the authentic modes of the church and have retained the same names. An easy way to remember the different sequences of whole steps and half steps is to play them using only the white keys on the piano.

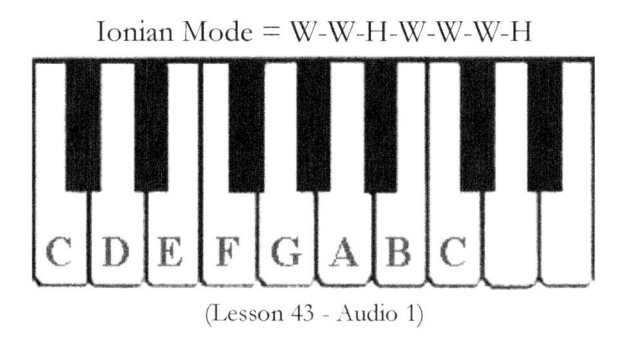

Ionian Mode = W-W-H-W-W-W-H

(Lesson 43 - Audio 1)

MODES

Dorian Mode = W-H-W-W-W-H-W

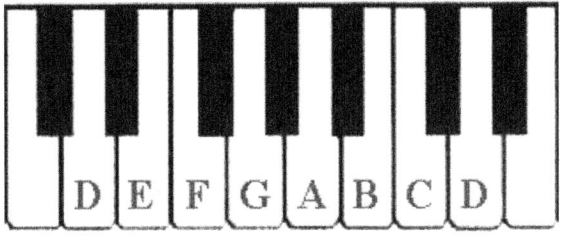

D E F G A B C D

(Lesson 43 - Audio 2)

Phrygian Mode = H-W-W-W-H-W-W

E F G A B C D E

(Lesson 43 - Audio 3)

Lydian Mode = W-W-W-H-W-W-H

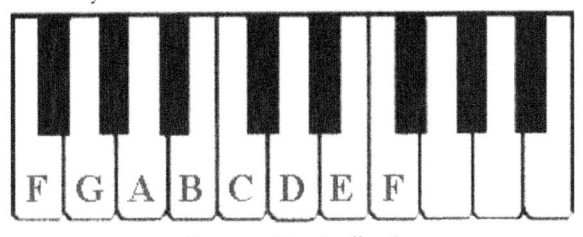

F G A B C D E F

(Lesson 43 - Audio 4)

Mixolydian Mode = W-W-H-W-W-H-W

G A B C D E F G

(Lesson 43 - Audio 5)

MUSIC THEORY

Aeolian Mode = W-H-W-W-H-W-W

| A | B | C | D | E | F | G | A |

(Lesson 43 - Audio 6)

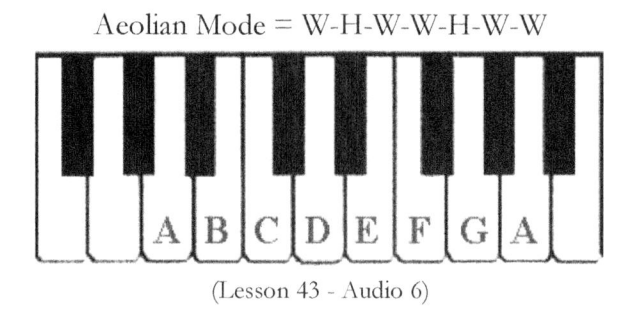

Locrian Mode = H-W-W-H-W-W-W

| B | C | D | E | F | G | A | B |

(Lesson 43 - Audio 7)

Here is a helpful mnemonic for remembering the modern modes.

I Don't **P**articularly **L**ike **M**odes **A L**ot.

Using the white keys of the piano and the above mnemonic, memorize the both the name and the whole step/half step sequence of each of the modern modes. You will need this information for your lesson quiz.

<u>Important:</u> these modes are not limited to the white keys. Arranging them using the white keys is just an easy way to remember the sequence of whole steps and half steps. Any mode may begin on any note. Here is an example of Dorian starting on two different notes.

"D" Dorian

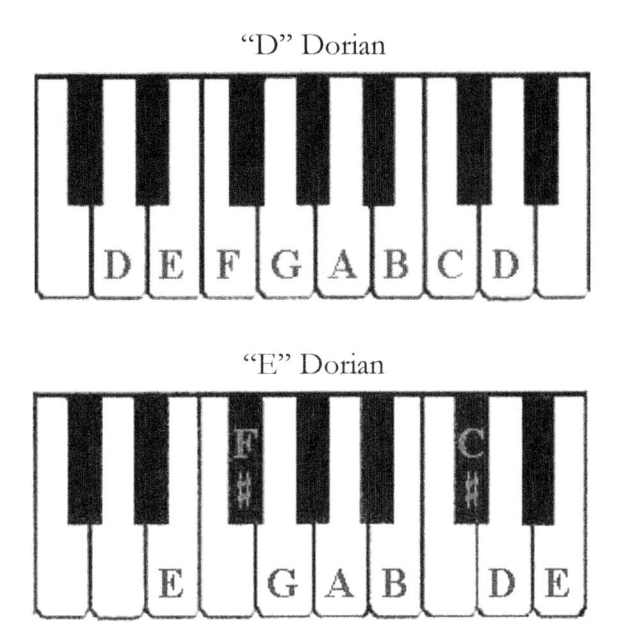

D E F G A B C D

"E" Dorian

E F# G A B C# D E

In the first diagram Dorian began on "D". In the second diagram Dorian began on "E". Both modes are called "Dorian" because the sequence of half steps and whole steps remains the same in each. (W-H-W-W-W-H-W)

Memory Questions

What is a mode?
A mode is a specific set of pitches used in a song; these pitches indicate a finalis and dominant, a range, an emotional affect, and melodic formula.

Where did modes originate?
Modes originated in ancient Greece.

Where does the Gregorian chant of the Roman Catholic Church stem from?
Gregorian chant stems from the ancient Greek modes.

Which are the original four "authentic" church modes?
The original four "authentic" church modes are Dorian, Phrygian, Lydian and Mixolydian.

Which are the original four "plagal" church modes?
The original four "plagal" church modes are Hypodorian, Hypophrygian, Hypolydian and Hypomixolydian.

Which four modes were added in the 1500's?
The four modes that were added in the 1500's were Aeolian, Hypoaeolian, Ionian, and Hypoionian.

Which modes were added by chant reformers in the 1900's?
The modes added by chant reformers in the 1900's were Locrian and Hypolocrian.

Which church mode is the equivalent of the modern day major scale?
The authentic Ionian church mode is the equivalent of the modern day major scale.

Which church mode is the equivalent of the modern day natural minor scale?
The authentic Aeolian church mode is the equivalent of the modern day natural minor scale.

What are the seven modern day modes?
The seven modern day modes are Ionian, Dorian, Phrygian, Lydian, Mixolydian, Aeolian, and Locrian.

What are the seven modern day modes based upon?
The seven modern day modes are based upon the authentic church modes.

Lesson 43 Quiz

Log in to your course at www.udemy.com and take the quiz for this lesson.

44. THE HARMONIC SERIES - PART 1

OVERTONES

In previous lessons we learned about Pythagoras and his very important discovery regarding the mathematical divisions of a vibrating string. Over the course of the next two lessons we are going to see how a discovery closer to our own time confirmed and also expanded upon Pythagoras' discovery about ratios.

This may come as a surprise to you, but when you hear a specific pitch you are not just hearing a single tone. You are actually hearing many tones all sounding together. This is because a vibrating string is not only vibrating as a whole…it is also simultaneously vibrating in fractional parts (halves, thirds, fourths, fifths, etc.)! These parts create their own sounds that blend together to form the sound of the whole. These other sounds are called **overtones**.

To access the following videos demonstrating overtones please log in to your course at www.udemy.com. In this first video you will see the string vibrating as a whole. The sound produced gives us what we call the **fundamental**. The fundamental is the main pitch that our ear perceives.

THE HARMONIC SERIES - PART 1

Harmonic 1 - The Fundamental (Lesson 44 - Video 1)

Next we will look at the string vibrating in halves. The vibration in halves gives us the first overtone of the fundamental. (They are called overtones because they are "over" or "above" the fundamental.) The first overtone is an octave above the fundamental. Note: In each of the videos the sound has been filtered so that you can hear the overtones if you listen carefully. The smaller waves near the bottom of the screen shows the entire string vibrating and each of the vibrating parts. The large string at the top of the screen shows the combination of these.

Harmonics 1 through 2 (Lesson 44 - Video 2)

The string vibrating in thirds gives us the second overtone of the fundamental. The second overtone is an octave plus a 5th above the fundamental.

Harmonics 1 through 3 (Lesson 44 - Video 3)

The string vibrating in fourths gives us the third overtone of the fundamental. The third overtone is two octaves above the fundamental.

Harmonics 1 through 4 (Lesson 44 - Video 4)

The string vibrating in fifths gives us the fourth overtone of the fundamental. The fourth overtone is two octaves plus a major 3rd above the fundamental.

Harmonics 1 through 5 (Lesson 44 - Video 5)

We call the fundamental and its overtones the **harmonic series**. The French Mathematician and Physicist, Joseph Sauveur (1653-1716) was the first to give a scientific account of this phenomenon.

Here is a diagram of what the harmonic series would look like on the grand staff. Although we can choose any note as our fundamental, we have chosen the low "C" as our fundamental for simplicity of demonstration. (On the piano, this is the "C" two octaves below middle "C".) When we hear this low "C", the sound we are hearing is made up of the fundamental (the entire string vibrating) and its overtones (the parts of the string that are vibrating simultaneously within the whole).

THE HARMOIC SERIES

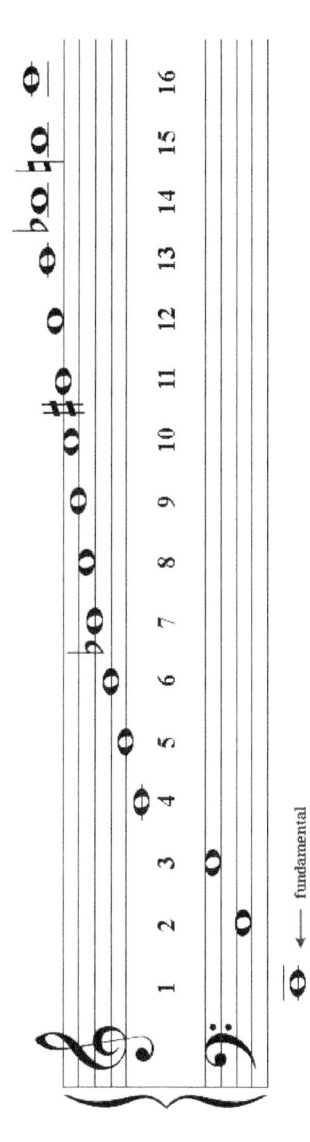

As you can see, each note in the series is numbered. The first note (the fundamental) is called the 1st harmonic. The second note (the first overtone) is called the 2nd harmonic. The third note (the second overtone) is called the 3rd harmonic, and so forth and so on.

These numbers also represent the frequencies of the harmonics. Harmonic 2 is vibrating twice as fast as the fundamental. Harmonic 3 is vibrating three times as fast as the fundamental, etc. (The numbers can also refer to the ratios of the string lengths as you will see in the next lesson.)

Since the harmonic series continues on indefinitely, only the first 16 notes in the series are listed here. Notice that as the series progresses the pitches get closer and closer in sound. Harmonics 1 and 2 give us the 8th. 2 and 3 give us the perfect 5th. Next come the perfect 4th, major 3rd, minor 3rd, major 2nd, minor 2nd, etc. If you kept going higher in the harmonic series you would end up with intervals smaller than half steps!

HEARING OVERTONES

Can we hear overtones with our ears? The answer is yes. Overtones are the reason that one instrument sounds different than another. For example, if a person plays middle "C" on a flute and another person plays middle "C" on an oboe, each will have a distinct quality or "color". This difference in color is called **timbre** (pronounced "TAM-ber") and is determined by the number and intensity of overtones for that particular instrument. Without overtones we would not be able to differentiate a flute from an oboe. (The quality of sound can even differ between two flutes!)

A pitch from an instrument capable of producing many overtones will have a richer sound than an instrument capable of producing fewer overtones. Certain playing styles and techniques can also determine which overtones are more prominently heard.

Here is a video that demonstrates how overtones affect the timbre of an instrument: http://www.youtube.com/watch?v=EfAzg59lKMQ

Would you like to hear some overtones isolated? If you have access to an acoustic piano (not a digital piano) you can do a very simple experiment yourself that will demonstrate overtones.

Step 1:
With your left hand press and <u>hold</u> down the "C" two octaves below middle "C". Do so without letting the hammer hit the string (without producing any sounds). By doing this you are removing the damper from the string so that it is free to vibrate. This note will be our fundamental.

Step 2:
With your right hand, press and release middle "C"; then press and release the "E" a 3rd above; then the "G" a 3rd above that. Make sure that you play the "C", "E", and "G" nice and loud!

Step 3:
Continue holding down the low "C" with your left hand while you listen. If your piano is in decent condition and properly tuned, you

will be able to hear the "C", "E", and "G" still sounding. The sound cannot be coming from the "C", "E", and "G" because once you release your fingers from the keys the dampers return to the strings and stop the vibrations. The sound must therefore be coming from the low "C" string! Instead of hearing the fundamental (low "C"), you are hearing overtones 3, 4, and 5 (harmonics 4, 5, and 6 in the preceding harmonic series diagram).

Important: In this lesson we spoke of overtones as sounds produced from the vibrating parts of a string. It should be noted here that overtones are also present in vocal music, wind instruments, and brass instruments, and are produced by vibrating parts of a column of air.

Memory Questions

What are overtones?
Overtones are the tones produced from the vibrating parts of a string (or column of air), which contribute to the overall sound of a pitch.

What is the fundamental?
The fundamental is the pitch that is produced from the vibration of the entire string (or column of air). It is the main pitch that our ear perceives.

What is the harmonic series?
The harmonic series is any fundamental pitch and its overtones.

What interval is produced from harmonics 1 and 2?
Harmonics 1 and 2 produce the 8th.

What interval is produced from harmonics 2 and 3?
Harmonics 2 and 3 produce the 5th.

What interval is produced from harmonics 3 and 4?
Harmonics 3 and 4 produce the 4th.

What interval is produced from harmonics 4 and 5?
Harmonics 4 and 5 produce the major 3rd.

What interval is produced from harmonics 5 and 6?
Harmonics 5 and 6 produce the minor 3rd.

Can you hear overtones with your ears?
Yes, you can hear overtones with your ears.

What is timbre? (pronounced "TAM-ber")
Timbre is the distinct quality or "color" of a tone, and is determined by the number and intensity of overtones.

Lesson 44 Quiz

Log in to your course at www.udemy.com and take the quiz for this lesson.

45. THE HARMONIC SERIES - PART 2

NATURE'S HIERARCHY OF HARMONIC SOUNDS

In the last lesson we learned about overtones and the harmonics series. In this lesson we are going to illustrate the most important characteristic of the harmonic series: **the order of the series is always the same, no matter which pitch is chosen as the fundamental**. In other words, harmonics 1 and 2 always create an 8th; harmonics 2 and 3 always create a 5th; harmonics 3 and 4 always create a 4th; etc. For example, if we chose "G" as our fundamental" the series would be "G", then "G" an 8th above, then "D" a 5th above that, then "G" a 4th above that, then "B" a major 3rd above that, etc. This is an astounding thing. Hidden within any pitch is this very same hierarchy of intervals. It is natures' inherent order of harmonic sounds!

For Pythagoras and the Greeks, pitches were considered consonant because of the ratio of the string lengths; the simpler the whole number ratio, the more consonant the sound. We see this confirmed by physics thousands of years later in the harmonic series! The lower you go in the harmonics series the more consonant the pitches.

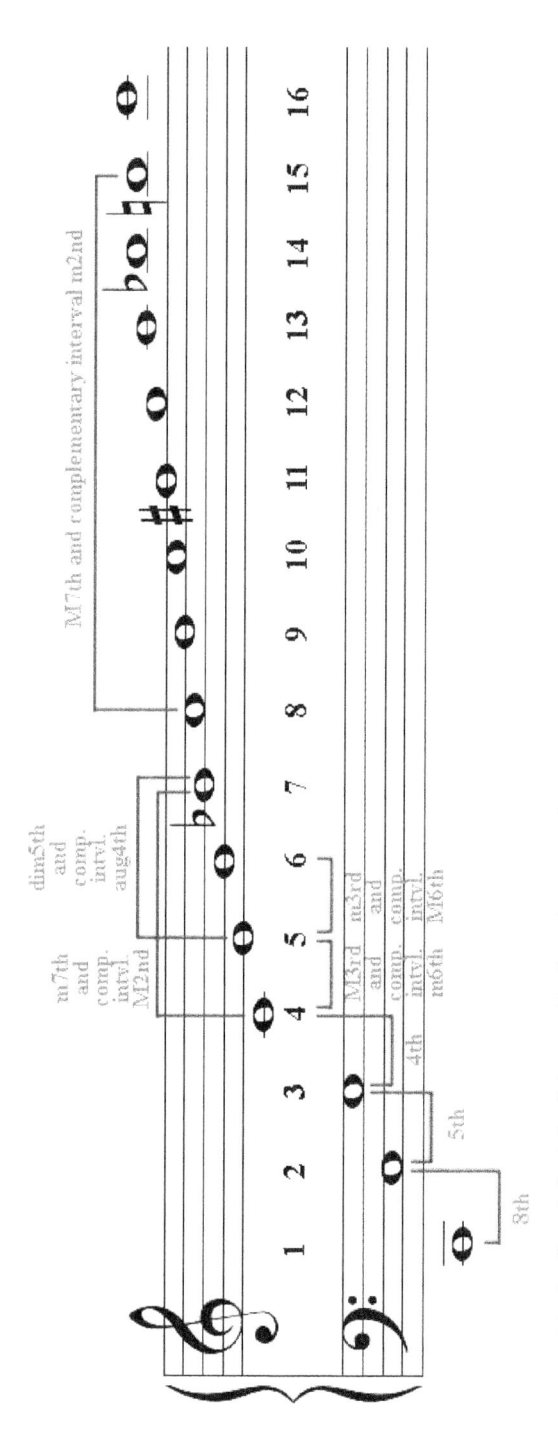

Harmonics 1 and 2 give us the 8th. This is the ratio of 2:1. (Remember, the ratio of the frequencies is the inverse of the ratio of the string lengths.) It is the most consonant sounding interval because it is the sound most similar to the fundamental. (Take a look at harmonics 1, 2, 4, 8, and 16. Did you notice that they are all "C's"? This is because they all have the ratio of 2:1; the ratio of the octave.) Harmonics 2 and 3 give us the 5th. This is the ratio of 3:2. It is the next most consonant interval because it is the sound after the octave that is most similar to the fundamental. Harmonics 3 and 4 gives us the 4th. This is the ratio of 4:3. It is the next most consonant interval because it is the sound after the 5th that is most similar to the fundamental.

Taking nature's hierarchy of harmonic sounds found in the harmonic series we get the following order:

Perfect 8th
Perfect 5th
Perfect 4th
Major 3rd and Minor 6th
Minor 3rd and Major 6th
Minor 7th and Major 2nd
Diminished 5th and Augmented 4th
Major 7th and Minor 2nd

Physics and the harmonic series give us an objective way of measuring the consonance or dissonance of harmonic sound!

If we take all the intervals found in the first 15 harmonics of the harmonic series and place them within one octave starting on "C" we would get the following:

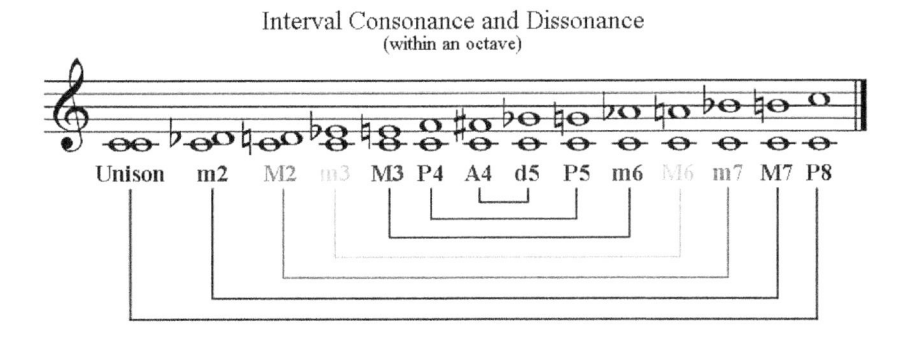

Interval Consonance and Dissonance
(within an octave)

| Unison | m2 | M2 | m3 | M3 | P4 | A4 | d5 | P5 | m6 | M6 | m7 | M7 | P8 |

Notice the pattern as we move from unison (on the left) to the octave (on the right). The sound becomes very dissonant the moment we leave unison but then slowly starts to become more and more consonant until we reach the perfect 4th. At the mid-point we have the harsh sounding "tritone". The reverse occurs as we travel from the mid-point (tritone) to the octave.

THE HISTORY OF CONSONANCE

It is important to realize that from the time of the Ancient Greeks until today, what people have considered as "consonant" and "dissonant" has often changed. For example, the Greeks did not consider the major 3rd to be a consonance, but today it is considered very consonant. Without the major 3rd we would not have most of Western music! (You will learn why the Greeks did not consider the major 3rd to be a consonance when we study tuning systems.)

Using the harmonic series as our standard for measuring consonance we will now briefly follow the history of Western music. You will see that over time, more and more dissonant harmonies began to be used in music. That which used to be considered "dissonant" was slowly re-defined and began to be considered consonant.

Most music of the ancient Greeks was "monophonic". Music that is monophonic consists of melody (pitches heard sequentially) rather than harmony (pitches heard simultaneously). If two notes were sung at the same time it was usually done in unison (the exact same pitch) or in octaves. (As you already know, 5ths and 4ths were also considered consonant by the Greeks but they were not sung together in harmony. They were used primarily as a basis for tuning their instruments.)

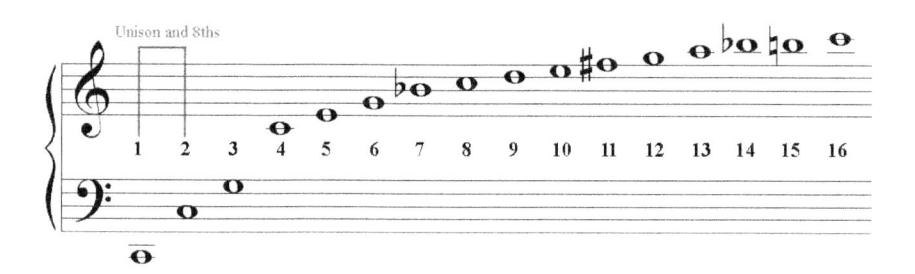

Around 900 A.D. (the Middle Ages) we begin to see 5ths and 4ths used as harmonies in "organum". Organum was a type of chant in which one person sang the melody and another person sang the same melody (at the same time) only a 5th or 4th higher or lower.

THE HARMONIC SERIES - PART 2

Around 1400 (the Renaissance), we see the first appearance of the triad. If we look at the harmonic series we can see that the major triad is one of the most natural elements of harmonic sound! If we take a look at the first 5 notes in the series we get "C", "C", "G", "C", and "E". If we remove the duplicate pitches (octave "C's") we get three distinct pitches "C", "G", and "E". These are the three pitches that form the major chord.

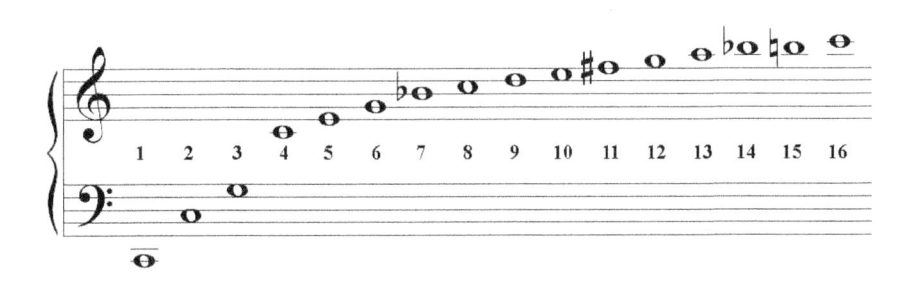

You can also see a major chord very clearly formed by harmonics 4, 5 and 6.

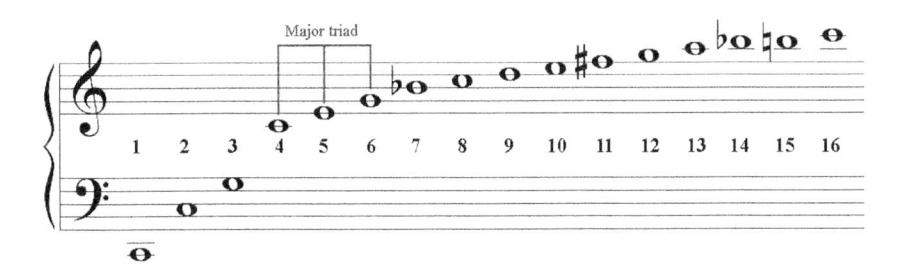

MUSIC THEORY

Other forms of the triad can also be found in the harmonic series. For example, the diminished chord can be found on harmonics 5, 6, and 7; a minor chord can be found on harmonics 6, 7, and 9; an augmented chord can be found on harmonics 7, 9, and 11. Also during the Renaissance, major and minor 3rds and their inversions began to be frequently used.

Around 1600 (the Baroque period), the dominant 7th chord (which involves the use of the minor 7th) began to be used.

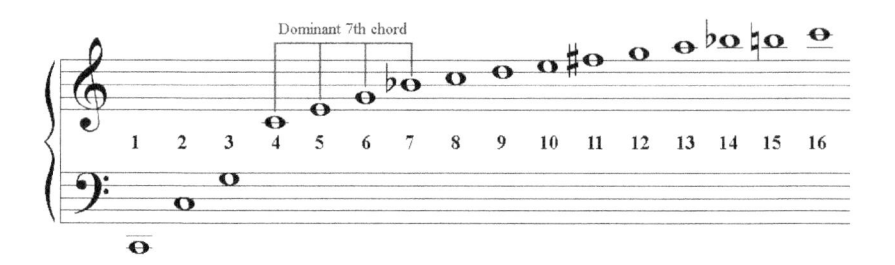

If we move higher up in the harmonic series, we find that the intervals are closer together. Instead of finding major and minor 3rds we begin to see 2nds (whole steps). In fact, harmonics 7 through 11 give us the first 5 notes of the whole tone scale. Around 1880 (the Romantic period), we begin to see music created using the whole tone scale.

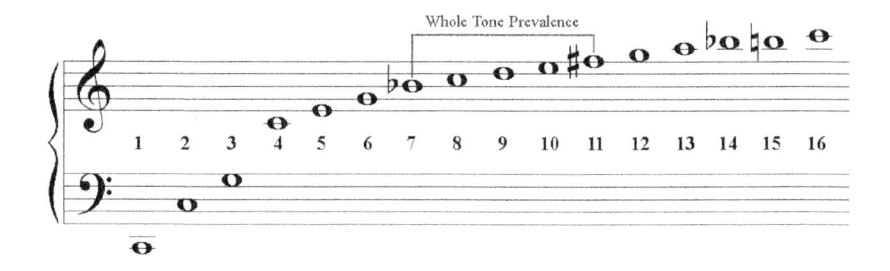

Even higher up in the harmonic series we begin to see a prevalence of semi tones (half steps). Around 1900 (the Modern/Contemporary period), we begin to see the use of "twelve-tone" atonal writing and total chromaticism.

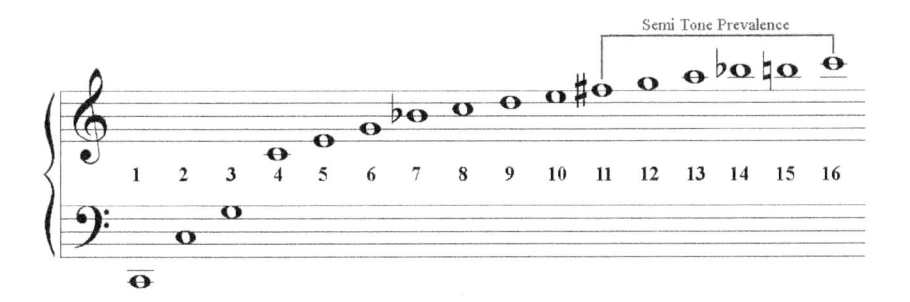

As you can see from the preceding seven diagrams, man's idea of consonance has broadened over the centuries to include more and more dissonant sounding intervals. This historical development of musical consonance can be traced through the harmonic series.

Memory Questions

What was the result of the discovery of the harmonic series on Pythagoras' earlier findings pertaining to musical ratios?
The discovery of the harmonic series confirmed and also expanded upon Pythagoras' findings pertaining to musical ratios.

What is the most important characteristic of the harmonic series?
The most important characteristic of the harmonic series is that the order of the series is always the same, no matter which pitch is chosen as the fundamental.

What does the harmonic series tell us about consonance and dissonance?
The harmonic series gives us an objective way of measuring the consonance or dissonance of harmonic sound.

What can we see outlined in the harmonic series?
Outlined in the harmonic series, we can see the historical development of musical consonance.

Lesson 45 Quiz

Log in to your course at www.udemy.com and take the quiz for this lesson.

46. TUNING SYSTEMS

TUNING PITCHES

When you tune an instrument you are adjusting the pitch of different notes so that specific intervals are created between the notes when played. Whether it is adjusting the tension of the strings on a stringed instrument, or changing the length of the tube of a wind or brass instrument, all instruments must be tuned. How to precisely tune intervals has been a debate for thousands of years. This lesson briefly covers a few of the different tuning systems that have been adopted over the centuries.

Believe it or not, there are many different ways to tune the same interval. For example, let's say we had two strings and tuned them so that when we play them an octave is created. Now, if we were to ever so slightly decrease or increase the tension of one of the strings, our ears would still perceive the resulting sound as an octave. Of course, if we decrease or increase the tension too much, we are going to end up with a totally different interval (a 7th or 9th). The point here is to show that tunings can differ very slightly and our ears will continue to hear an 8th as an 8th or a 5th as a 5th. So if our ears perceive slightly different tunings of intervals as the same sound, how should we tune our musical intervals? Let's look at the history.

PYTHAGOREAN TUNING

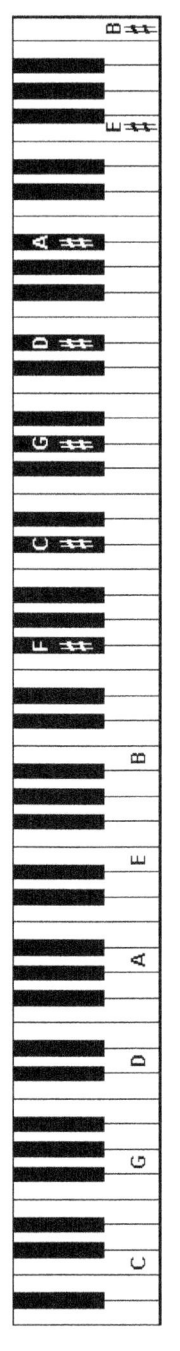

Pythagorean tuning was a system of tuning used by medieval music theorists. It was based on Pythagoras' own mathematical discoveries about the ratios of intervals. In Pythagorean tuning all pitches are derived from the ratio of a 5th - the ratio of 3:2. If we start on "C" and build successive 5ths we should end up at the "C" which is 7 octaves above. (The enharmonic "B sharp" is used in the diagram to maintain the correct spelling of an interval of a 5th between "E sharp" and "B sharp".)

This is basically the entire circle of 5ths that you studied in this course. The problem is, this "C" ("B sharp") is not really a true seven octaves higher than the "C" we started on. Let's do some math to prove this. First we will start on the low "C" and add twelve consecutive 5ths. Next we will start on the same low "C" and add seven consecutive octaves. Last we will compare the two results mathematically.

If we want to add intervals together we can simply treat their ratios as fractions and multiply them. Therefore, if we multiply the ratio of 3:2 by itself twelve times (twelve times because there are twelve 5ths in the circle of 5ths) we will get the following:

$$(3/2)^{12} = \frac{531441}{4096}$$

Try to remember that we are looking at ratios here. This fraction represents the ratio between the frequency of the highest and lowest octave. In other words, for every 531,441 times the string producing the highest pitch ("B sharp") vibrates (make one complete cycle), the string producing the lowest pitch ("C") will vibrate (make one complete cycle)

TUNING SYSTEMS

4,096 times. The inverse of this fraction represents the ratio between the string lengths needed to produce these two pitches.

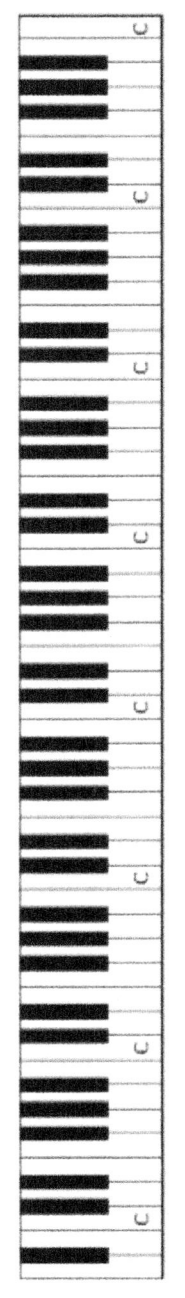

Now let's take the same low "C" and add seven consecutive octaves.

To add these intervals we multiply the ratio of the octave (2:1) by itself seven times. We can write this as:

$$(2/1)^7 = \frac{128}{1}$$

In other words, the string producing the highest pitch will vibrate 128 times for every 1 time the string producing the lowest pitch vibrates.

As you can see, the results should be the same but they are not. Twelve consecutive 5ths = **531441/4096**, whereas seven consecutive octaves = **128/1**. To find the difference between the twelve consecutive 5ths and the seven consecutive octaves we need to divide. (To add fractions we multiply; to subtract fractions we divide.)

$$\frac{531{,}441}{4{,}096} \div \frac{128}{1} = \frac{531{,}441}{524{,}288}$$

This resulting number (531,411/524,288) is called the "Pythagorean Comma". Twelve consecutive 5ths is actually slightly larger (sharper sounding) than seven consecutive octaves by this amount. In other words, the "B sharp" in the first diagram will vibrate 531,441 times for every 524,288 times the highest "C" in the second diagram vibrates.

Therefore the circle of 5ths does not complete a full circle since the circle does not truly "close" or come back around on itself. In other words, we don't end up back at "C"; instead we end up at a slightly sharper version of "C".

What does all this mean? It means we cannot generate a perfect tuning system based on the 3:2 ratio of the 5th. If we took all of the pitches in the circle of 5ths and placed them within one octave, some of the intervals would sound wrong, or "off", and so would some of the chords and scales.

With Pythagorean tuning we may get "pure" 5ths, 4ths and octaves, but in doing so we sacrifice the "pure" 3rds found in the harmonic series. Look at the Pythagorean tuning of a major scale below.

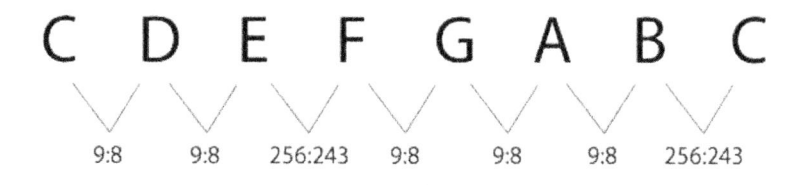

```
C     D     E     F     G     A     B     C
 \ /   \ /   \ /   \ /   \ /   \ /   \ /
  V     V     V     V     V     V     V
 9:8   9:8  256:243 9:8   9:8   9:8  256:243
```

If we add the ratio of two whole steps ("C" to "D" and "D" to "E") we should get the ratio of a 3rd. 9/8 times 9/8 = 81/64. This is the ratio of the Pythagorean 3rd. It is not however the same as the ratio found in the harmonic series or Pythagoras' mathematical division of a string (as seen earlier in the course). The pure 3rd is the small whole number ratio of 5:4. Let's compare the impure 3rd (81/64) to the pure 3rd (5/4). If we multiple 5/4 by a constant we will get a number which is close to the ratio of the impure 3rd. $5/4 \times 16/16 = 80/64$.

The difference between 81/64 and 80/64 is found by dividing (or cross multiplying) these two numbers. The 64's will cancel each other out and we end up with **81/80**. 81/80 is the difference between a Pythagorean 3rd and a pure 3rd and is called the "Syntonic Comma". At this time in music history (Medieval) 3rds were considered to be a dissonance and so it did not matter that the ratio was not a pure one. But when 3rds became more prevalent in music (with the development of polyphony during the Renaissance), a new tuning system had to be invented.

JUST INTONATION

The answer to pure 3rds was found in **just intonation**. In the last lesson, we observed how the intervals within the harmonic series were made up of small whole number ratios.

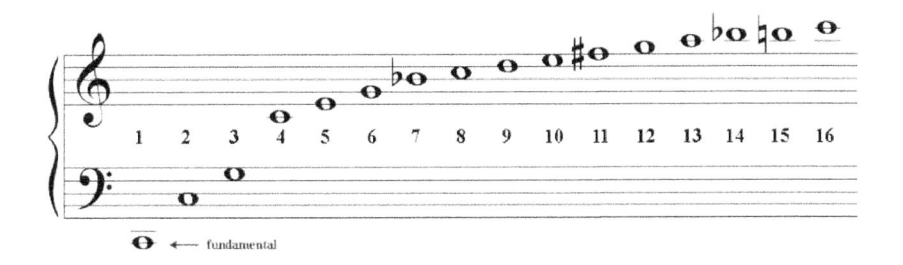

Whenever an interval is tuned according to the small whole number ratios found in the harmonic series, we refer to it as a "pure", "natural", or "just" interval. (Did you know that when people sing they tend to tune their intervals to these "just" intervals?)

So why can't we simply tune all of our intervals according to how they are found in nature and leave it at that? As you will see below, even nature's own tuning system has its problems. Here is a major scale tuned using just intonation.

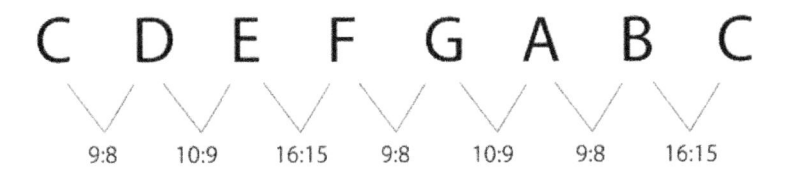

C	D	E	F	G	A	B	C
9:8	10:9	16:15	9:8	10:9	9:8	16:15	

All of the major 3rds in the preceding diagram are now pure because of just intonation. For example, "C" to "E" is made up of the ratios 9:8 and 10:9 (These ratios come from the two different sized 2nds found in the harmonic series; harmonics 8, 9, and 10. 9/8 times 10/9 = 90/72, which reduces to 5/4; the ratio of the pure major 3rd. The major 3rds "F" to "A" and "G" to "B" have this same pure ratio as well (each is made up of one 9:8 ratio and one 10:9 ratio).

But now that the 3rds are pure, not all of the 5ths are pure! If we look at the preceding diagram we can see why.

The 5th from "C" to "G" contains two 9:8 2nds, and one 10:9 2nd.

The 5th from "E" to "B" contains two 9:8 2nds, and one 10:9 2nd.

The 5th from "F" to the higher "C" contains two 9:8 2nds, and one 10:9 2nd.

But the 5th from "D" to "A" contains two 10:9 2nds, and one 9:8 2nd

This means, the 5th from "D" to "A" is a different size and thus has a different sound. It also means that one cannot change keys in just intonation. For example, if a song was in the key of "C major" and the first two notes of the melody were the tonic "C" followed by the supertonic "D", we would be hearing the ratio of 9:8. If the same song were in the key of "G major" and the first two notes of the melody were the tonic "G" followed by the supertonic "A", we would be hearing the ratio of 10:9. To be able to play songs in both keys we would need two different "A's"; one "A" for the sixth degree of the "C major" scale, and a different "A" for the second degree of the "G major" scale. The number of notes needed to play music in different keys would increase exponentially as we moved further away from the key of "C" to other keys with sharps and flats. Also, instruments would need many more strings, keys, pipes, etc. to accommodate all these new notes. Thus playing an instrument would be extremely difficult, if not impossible in most cases.

EQUAL TEMPERAMENT

As of today, no perfect tuning system has been discovered. The closest that we have come to a perfect system is something called **equal temperament**. Equal temperament was first attempted in the late 1500s and had become fairly widely used by the 1800s. In equal temperament the octave is divided into 12 equal half steps (or semitones). Each half step is equal to 100 cents. A cent is a logarithmic unit of measurement where 1 cent = 1/1200 of an octave. In the chart below you can see that every half step is equal to 100 cents, and that every whole step is therefore equal to 200 cents.

Pitch	Cents
C	0
C#	100
D	200
D#	300
E	400
F	500
F#	600
G	700
G#	800
A	900
A#	1000
B	1100
C	1200

In equal temperament, the impurities found in all of the previous tuning systems are spread out and distributed over all twelve tones within an octave. Now all of our 5ths are slightly smaller (flat) than the pure 5th, but they will all sound the same. For example, "C" to "G" = 700 cents; "D" to "A" = 700 cents. All of our 3rds are slightly larger (sharp) than the pure 3rd, but they will all sound the same. For example, "C" to "E" = 400 cents; "D" to "F sharp" = 400 cents. None of the intervals will have the pure ratios found in nature, but "like" intervals will sound "alike". This makes modulation (transition from one key to another) and transposition (playing a song in a different key) possible. The one exception to this is the all-important octave. The octave (2:1) is the only interval in equal temperament that maintains the pure ratio found in nature.

With equal temperament, we are in fact sacrificing the purity of sound for utility. The good news is, since the "out-of-tuneness" is distributed among the twelve pitches, it is not noticeable to the average person.

Note: Did you know that the piano is tuned using equal temperament? That's right. When you pay money to get your piano tuned you are actually paying the piano tuner to make the intervals out of tune but equal!

In this lesson we learned a little bit about tuning systems. Although Equal Temperament sacrifices the pureness of the intervals it allows musicians to play in any key. Because few people have the opportunity to hear the difference between Just Intonation and Equal Temperament, a link to an application that demonstrates the differences between these two tuning systems has been included with this lesson. In part one you will compare intervals in both Just Intonation and Equal Temperament. In part two you will compare chord qualities in both tuning systems. In part three you will listen to a short Bach chorale excerpt and compare the tuning systems in two different keys. Don't skip this last part! If your ear wasn't able to hear any difference between the intervals and chords, you will definitely be able to hear the difference when playing a song in different keys using Just Intonation.

Just Intonation app
http://briankshepard.com/learning_objects/JustIntonation.zip

To run this app you will also need to download **Max Runtime**. It is a free download for Windows or Mac. Due to an audio issue between the Just Intonation app and the newest version of Max Runtime, please download the older 5.1.9 version of Max Runtime: http://cycling74.com/downloads/older/

Once you have downloaded both of the above files, click on the Just Intonation app to open and then follow all of the instructions that appear on the screen. Make sure you listen to everything in order (intervals, chords, and then the song).

There is no quiz for this lesson.

47. THE PERIODS OF CLASSICAL MUSIC

A BRIEF HISTORY

No music theory course would be complete without taking a look at the different periods in the history of classical music. The four main periods of classical music are the **Baroque**, **Classical**, **Romantic**, and **Contemporary** periods. Note: the word "classical" refers to the specific period of years from 1750-1820, but it also refers to western art music as a whole. (There is no quiz for this lesson.)

BAROQUE (1600-1750)

Characteristics:
- Rhythms used lots of 16th and 32nd notes and usually had a consistent driving beat.
- Melody was decorated with many different kinds of ornamental frills and flourishes. (Performers were expected to improvise and add to the melody written on the page.)

- Texture was mainly polyphonic (many melodic lines happening at once rather than one melody with a chord accompaniment)
- Harmony was created through the polyphonic texture of multiple melodic lines.
- The use of 3rds and 6ths started to become more prevalent.
- Major and minor keys were used instead of the ancient church modes.
- Equal temperament was just beginning to be used more frequently.
- There were no dynamics (indications when to play loud or quiet) written on the music. There were also no gradual dynamics such as crescendos and decrescendos (gradual increases and decreases in the volume of the music). Instead dynamics were sudden shifts.
- There was usually one consistent mood per piece and one consistent tempo per piece.
- Simple 7th chords began to be used.
- Composers focused on writing instrumental music more than vocal music.
- Secular music became as common as church music had been in the past.

Instruments included:
Strings, Flute, Recorder, Oboe, Harpsichord (a keyboard instrument in which the strings are plucked rather than struck with a hammer as with the piano), Trumpet, and Horn

Major Composers:
Johann Sebastian Bach
George Frederic Handel
Antonio Vivaldi
Henry Purcell
Georg Philipp Telemann

Musical Example:
Brandenburg Concerto No. 3 - by J. S. Bach

CLASSICAL (1750-1820)

Characteristics:
- Rhythms were simple.
- Melody was clearer and had fewer decorative flourishes than in the Baroque period.
- Melodic phrases (musical sentences) tended to be 4 to 8 measures in length.
- Texture was much simpler than in the Baroque period. It was homophonic (one melody with a chord accompaniment) rather than polyphonic (simultaneous melodies).
- The form (structure or order) of the piece was very important. It was important for form to be symmetrical.
- Chords had particular functions and there were clearly marked cadences.
- Key changes and tempo changes began to be more common.
- Public concerts became common and composers could now earn a living writing for concerts rather than being supported by a single rich benefactor. With public concerts came the growth of the orchestra.

Instruments included:
Strings, Guitar, Harp, Flute, Oboe, Clarinet, Bassoon, Trumpet, Horn, early Trombone, Tuba and the pianoforte (an early version of the piano) which replaced the Harpsichord.

Major Composers:
Wolfgang Amadeus Mozart
Franz Joseph Haydn

Ludwig van Beethoven (early compositions)

<u>Musical Example:</u>
Piano Sonata No. 16 (K. 545) - by Wolfgang Amadeus Mozart

1. Allegro
2. Andante
3. Rondo

ROMANTIC (1820-1900)

<u>Characteristics:</u>
- Rhythms were more complex than in the Classical period.
- Melodies were very tuneful. They were easy to remember and sing.
- Harmonies were more complex and composers began to use more dissonant chords. Chromatic notes (notes not found in the particular key of the piece) were very common and colored the pieces of the Romantic period.
- Texture was mainly homophonic as in the Classical period, but there were more notes and so the sound was thicker.
- Form (structure or order) was not as important as freedom of expression and imagination.
- Emotion was supreme.
- Much emphasis was placed on individualism. Each composer looked for his own style.
- Music tended to be more virtuosic in nature (technically demanding or requiring much skill). Many of the performers and composers were virtuosos on their instruments. (This was the beginning of the modern day glorification of the artist.)
- There were extremes in dynamics, tempos and lengths of the pieces.

- Music was not written to exist simply as music. Instead music told a story. Many pieces told the story of people, places, things, and events.

Instruments included:
All of the instruments found in the modern day orchestra

Major Composers:
Ludwig van Beethoven (later compositions)
Felix Mendelssohn
Frédéric Chopin
Franz Liszt
Camille Saint-Saëns
Pyotr Ilyich Tchaikovsky
Antonín Dvořák
Sergei Rachmaninoff

Musical Example:
Symphony No.4 - by Pyotr Ilyich Tchaikovsky

1st Movement
2nd Movement
3rd Movement
4th Movement

CONTEMPORARY (1900-present)

Characteristics:
- Rhythms are very complex.
- There is a lack of meter or bar-lines in some music.
- Melodies have very large intervals and do not sound like traditional melodies.

- Harmonies are based upon nonconventional scales or sometimes no scale at all.
- Dissonances are now seen as consonances.
- Polytonal and Atonal music is more common place.
- The use of twelve-tone technique developed.
- Music is very experimental and every piece has its own set of rules.
- Nationalism is huge and many songs are inspired by folk songs.
- With technology came the advent of electronic music.

Instruments included:
Any and all types: including common everyday objects and electronic instruments.

Major Composers:
Arnold Schoenberg
Béla Bartók
Igor Stravinsky
Sergei Prokofiev
Paul Hindemith

Musical Example:
String Quartet No.4 – by Béla Bartók

1. Allegro
2. Prestissimo, con sordino
3. Non troppo lento
4. Allegretto pizzicato
5. Allegro molto

INDEX

A

Accidentals, 140
Arithmetic Mean, 199–200
Atonal, 284

B

Bar Lines, 24–26
Baroque Period, 322–24
Beat, 16–19

C

Cadence
  authentic, 270–72
  deceptive, 273–74
  definition, 269
  half, 272
  imperfect authentic, 271
  perfect authentic, 270
  plagal, 273
Chords
  augmented, 190–92, 200–201, 277, 310
  block, 184
  broken, 184
  diminished, 192–94, 201–3, 310
  diminished 7th, 266–67
  dominant 7th, 258–61
  extended, 258–59, 264–67
  inversions of, 240–45, 248–50, 260
  major, 183–84, 187, 196–98, 309
  major 7th, 264–65
  mathematical proportions of, 196–203
  minor, 184–85, 184–85, 199–200, 310
  minor 7th, 265–66
  of the harmonic minor scale, 228–29
  of the major scale, 206–7
  of the natural minor scale, 227–28
  primary, 235–38
  progressions, 247–50, 269–74
  voice leading in, 247–50
  voices of, 247–50
Chromatic, 279
Circle of 5ths, 142–49, 220–21, 223
Classical Period, 324–25
Clefs, 86–88
Common Time, 27
Consonance, 126–27, 307–8, 311
Contemporary Period, 326–27
Cut Time, 51–54

D

Dissonance, 126–27, 307
Dominant Degree, 253
Dotted Notes, 36–39
Duplets, 71–74

E

Enharmonic Equivalent, 108–11
  enharmonic intervals, 162
  enharmonic keys, 148–49, 223
  enharmonic scales, 149
Equal Temperament, 319–20

F

Flats
  double flats, 166–67, 194
  on the keyboard, 109–11
  on the staff, 114–16
  order of, 141–42
Frequency, 78, 124–26, 314

Functions, 252–55
Fundamental, 298–303, 305–6

G

Geometric Mean, 200–203
Grand Staff, 94–95

H

Half Steps, 103–4
Harmonic Mean, 196–98
Harmonic Series, 298–303, 305–11
Harmony
    definition, 8
    open & closed, 178–79

I

Intervals
    augmented, 160–64
    complementary, 172–75
    compound, 176–78, 179–80
    definition, 119
    determining quality of, 155–58, 170
    diminished, 164–67
    harmonic, 122
    inversions of, 172–75
    major, 152–54
    measuring on keyboard, 119
    measuring on staff, 120
    melodic, 122
    minor, 152–54
    number, 152
    of the major scale, 155–58
    perfect, 154
    quality, 152
    ratios of, 123–26, 185–86
    simple, 176
    tritone, 168–69
Inversion
    1st inversion, 240–41
    2nd inversion, 241
    3rd inversion, 260
    of chords, 240–45, 248–50, 260
    of intervals, 172–75

J

Just Intonation, 317–18

K

Key Signatures, 140–41
    with flats, 145–48, 223
    with sharps, 142–45, 221
Keyboard
    half steps & whole steps, 103–5
    intervals on the, 119
    letter names of the, 99–101
    relation to the staff, 101–3
    sharps & flats on the, 107–11
Keys
    definition, 139
    major, 139–49
    minor, 220–25
    parallel, 224–25
    relative, 220–23
    roots of, 208

L

Leading Tone, 255
Ledger Lines, 83–85
Limma, 135–36

M

Measures, 25–26
Mediant Degree, 253–54
Melody, 8
Meter, 24–29
    2/2, 51–54

2/4, 3/4, & 4/4, 26–29
3/8 & 6/8, 45–48
classifying, 56–62
complex, 61–62
compound, 58–60
definition, 24
duple, 56
quadruple, 56
simple, 56–58
strong beats, 27–29, 47–48, 54
time signatures, 26–27
triple, 56
Metronome Marking, 20–21
Modes
ancient Greek modes, 286–87
church modes, 288–91
modern modes, 292–95
Monochord, 123–27, 185–87
Multiples, 19
Music
definition, 5
elements of, 7
unique to mankind, 4
uses of, 3–4

N

Natural Sign, 116–17
Notes
assigning values, 16–19
beams, 12
eighth, 11–12
flags, 12
half, 10
parts of, 9
quarter, 10
relative durations, 9–13
sixteenth, 11–12
stem direction, 96–97
thirty-second, 12
whole, 9

O

Octave, 133
Overtones, 298–303, 305–11

P

Periods of Classical Music, 322–27
Pitch, 7–9, 76–80
definite, 77
indefinite, 77
Polytonal, 282–83
Pythagoras, 123, 126, 133–34, 136–37, 314
Pythagorean Tuning, 314–17

R

Ratio
definition, 123
in harmonic series, 306
in tuning systems, 314–20
of chords, 196–203
of intervals, 124–26, 133, 185–86
Rests, 32–34
Rhythm, 7–9
Roman Numerals, 231–33
Romantic Period, 325–26
Roots
of chord inversions, 242, 260
of chords, 205
of keys, 208
of scales, 207–8

S

Sauveur, Joseph, 300
Scales
chords of harmonic minor, 228–29
chords of major, 206–7

chords of natural minor, 227–28
chromatic, 278–79
degrees of the scale, 231–33, 252–55
enharmonic, 149
harmonic minor, 214–15
major, 130–32
melodic minor, 216–17
natural minor, 210–12
origin of, 132–37
pentatonic, 279–80
relation to keys, 139
roots of, 207
whole tone, 276–78
Semi Tone, 135
Sharps
double sharps, 163–64, 192
on the keyboard, 107–8
on the staff, 112–14
order of, 141–42
Sound Waves, 76–78
Staff
clefs, 86–88
grand staff, 94–95
ledger lines, 83–85
letter names of the, 92–94
lines & spaces, 82–83
movement on, 88–90
relation to keyboard, 101–3
sharps & flats on the, 112–16
stem direction on the, 96–97
Subdivisions, 19
Subdominant Degree, 254
Submediant Degree, 254
Subtonic Degree, 255
Supertonic Degree, 255

T

Tempo, 19–21
Tertrachords, 210
Tetrachords, 132–37, 286–87
Ties, 41–43
Timbre, 302
Time Signatures, 26–27
Tonic Degree, 252–53
Triad, 183
Triplets, 65–69, 73–74
Tritone, 168–69, 267
Tuning Systems
equal temperament, 319–20
just intonation, 317–18
pythagorean tuning, 314–17
Tuplets, 67, 71

U

Unit
multiples of the, 19
of measurement, 16–17
subdivision of the, 19

V

Vibrating String, 123–26, 299
Voice Leading, 247–50

W

Whole Steps, 104–5
Whole Tone, 134

Z

Zalino, Gioseffo, 196

ABOUT THE AUTHOR

Jonathan Peters is an award-winning composer currently residing in the beautiful state of Colorado. He has worked in the music business for 24 years as teacher, director, composer, and recording artist. Mr. Peters holds a B.A. in liberal arts from Thomas Aquinas College and continued his graduate work at California State University Northridge where he studied advanced composition, theory, orchestration, and film scoring.

Composer and Recording Artist
Mr. Peters has completed over 40 works including 2 full length operas, a symphony, orchestral works, chamber music, choral pieces, and works for solo piano. His pieces have won many awards and recognitions including 1st place in the 1996 Composers Today Contest. He has professionally recorded and produced 6 CDs. His music has been performed both in the United States and Europe, is heard on the radio, and sells in over 50 stores world-wide. He is also the author of the *Scholastic Music Series*, a collection of educational CDs that use music as a tool to teach various academic subjects. The series has received starred reviews from *School Library Journal* and is carried in libraries throughout the country.

Teacher and Director
Over the past 24 years Mr. Peters has given lessons in piano, composition, orchestration and music theory. He has worked with various orchestras, has been a guest conductor with the Cypress Pops Orchestra and has also directed various choirs in southern California.

www.ComposerJonathanPeters.com

Printed in Great Britain
by Amazon